The Taliban Misrule in Afghanistan

Suicide Brigades, the IS-K Military Strength and its Suicide Vehicle Industry

The Taliban Misrule in Afghanistan

Suicide Brigades, the IS-K Military Strength and its Suicide Vehicle Industry

Musa Khan Jalalzai

Dr. Sanchita Bhattacharya

Vij Books India Pvt Ltd

New Delhi (India)

Published by

Vij Books India Pvt Ltd
(Publishers, Distributors & Importers)
2/19, Ansari Road
Delhi – 110 002
Phones: 91-11-43596460, 91-11-47340674
Mobile: 98110 94883
e-mail: contact@vijpublishing.com
www.vijbooks.in

Copyright © 2022, *Musa Khan Jalalzai*

ISBN: 978-93-93499-92-9 (Hardback)

Contents

Introduction   1

Chapter 1   The Taliban, ISIS-K, Al Qaeda, the Haqqani Network,
             their Atrocities, Torture and the Degradation of
             Afghan Nation   10

Chapter 2   Military and Political Confrontations between
             Taliban and the IS-K in Afghanistan   26

Chapter 3   Suicide Brigades, IS-K Military Strength and
             Taliban's Misrule in Afghanistan   44

Chapter 4   The Taliban, IS-K, TTP and their War against
             Women, Children and Hazara Muslims in
             Afghanistan and Pakistan   56

Chapter 5   Al Qaeda, the Haqqani Terrorist Network,
             Lashkar-e-Taiba, Taliban and the Islamic State of
             Khorasan's Plundering of Mineral Resources in
             Afghanistan and their Expedition Towards
             Central Asia   74

Chapter 6   The IS-K, Central Asian Terrorist Groups, Taliban
             and Prospect of Nuclear Terrorism   91

Chapter 7   The Taliban Financial Resources: Drug Trafficking,
             Hawala, Illegal Mining, and Military Strength   104

             Dr. Sanchita Bhattacharya

Chapter 8   Under the Hood–Learning and Innovation in the
             Islamic State's Suicide Vehicle Industry   113

             Ellen Tveteraas

Chapter 9   Armed Governance: The Case of the CIA-Supported
Afghan Militias   135

Antonio De Lauri and Astri Suhrke

Postscript   152

Notes to Chapters   166

Index   197

Introduction

All interconnections between people of different colors and societies are interactions and interrelationships that bring to a close all segments of society, promote harmony and concordance. A country knows its citizens' demands, necessities and aspirations. An Intelligence agency also knows demands of the state and policy makers and a certain quality and quantity of information. In every society, an individual knows approximately what measure of culture he has to presuppose in each other individually. Intelligence relationships among states need interoperability and cooperation to share intelligence and protect their national security. The customary reciprocal presentation in the case of any national security issue, revolves around mutual cooperation and interconnection. All Western and South Asia Intelligence Agencies lack interconnection and interaction on security and law enforcement levels. Their agencies and decision-makers are male dominated, deciding their plans and strategies behind closed doors but view women as a commodity and a useless thing. In Pakistan, for example, there is no woman on an executive post within ISI, police and Intelligence Bureau (IB). These male dominated intelligence agencies are dancing all to male dominated tangos and view women as a half of the body of society and sex-toys. Since 2001, women have occupied secondary, superficial, or negative positions in all intelligence decision making processes in Pakistan. We are living in a global village where everyone is dependent on his companion and workmate. We need to know about our environment and threats to our existence. As we live under the umbrella of the state that protects us from physical harm, consternation and threats, we need to respect each other. After the cold war, national security threats exacerbated, the culture of civil war emerged, geographical challenges, political and economic competitions changed the shape of military alliances and the state became vulnerable. Intelligence war between states prompted many challenges, while cyber terrorism became the strongest military and economic weapon of states.

On 07 September 2021, Taliban announced an Interim Government in the presence of Pakistan's Inter-Services Intelligence (ISI) Chief, General Faiz

Hameed. The Interim Government was composed of over 30 Ministries. The miltablishment and the ISI view the Afghan Taliban as the 'Good Taliban', and support the latter's fight in Afghanistan as a welcome development. With reference to the issue of Good and Bad Taliban, Pakistan Army views all such Afghan groups, including the Quetta Shura in Baluchistan, and the Haqqani Network in agencies of North and South Waziristan as strategic assets. The Afghan Taliban is supported by the ISI to maintain its influence over Afghanistan, particularly in a scenario after the American drawdown of forces from the area, as many in Pakistan's military establishment continued to think of the Afghan landmass as Pakistan's backyard, and an area which will offer them 'strategic depth' in the event of hostilities with India. Pakistan has also encouraged and promoted terrorist organizations such as the Lashkar-e-Taiba (LeT), Jaish-e-Muhammad (JeM), and HuM, which it views as strategic assets as well. These terrorist groups have been waging a proxy war against India over the past three decades in Kashmir at very little cost to Pakistan–a policy of bleeding India with a thousand cuts, but keeping the conflict below perceived levels of India's threshold of response. Terrorist organizations including al Qaeda, LeT, Taliban, a range of Arab extremists and Takfiri jihadists in Central Asia pose a threat to regional security. They train suicide bombers across Asia and the Middle East, control business of fear in Waziristan, Kashmir, Kabul and Quetta. Pakistan has all the signs and symptoms of an ailing state that may not be able to sustain itself at the current rate of deterioration.

The ISI and the Army lost public confidence due to their political role, corruption and war crimes. People, an important constituent of the elements that define a State, are fast losing faith in their institutions. The point is, ISI lacks an adequate intelligence information from remote areas of Baluchistan, Sindh and Waziristan, lacks trained manpower, failure to understand modern technology, lacks proper intelligence sharing with policymakers, and lacks actionable intelligence. In the aftermath of the terrorist attacks in Punjab and Sindh, the ISI became subject to hot-blooded assessment. The IB (Pakistan) and ISI suffered from lack of check and balance, and the influence of government and private stakeholders. Scientific collaboration and interoperability between the ISI and civilian agencies, and intelligence agencies of neighbouring states can bring all Neighbours to a close. Democratically elected governments have been accused of shameless inability and inefficiency in handling the tottering state, particularly over the past four decades. Pakistan is, moreover, at war with itself. This partial civil war has been caused by the misadventures of many state agencies, as well as of many internal and external forces. All these forces are working on divergent agendas, with little care about the future of Pakistani citizens and the implications of these deadly agendas for South Asia and the rest of the world. The war in neighbouring Afghanistan is weakening Pakistan as a modern state. The longer the war in Afghanistan continues, the more it will complicate the situation in Pakistan. In view of this illegal business, the ISI lost its professional capabilities and hung in the air as a militant agency.

The rivalry between the IB and ISI boiled over in June 2017 when a Joint Investigation Team (JIT) probing alleged money laundering by the Sharif family made a written complaint to the Supreme Court that the IB was wiretapping JIT members, including ISI and military intelligence personnel. The JIT further reported that the IB was hampering its inquiries, adding that military-led intelligence agencies were not on "good terms" with the IB. It said that IB had collected intelligence on members of the JIT from the National Database and Registration Authority (NADRA) and presented it to Prime Minister Nawaz Sharif for use against them. In the present situation, it is not clear what roles are being allocated to the three major agencies. The crucial question that still needs to be addressed is whether these agencies function under the watchful eyes of an elected government or are they still so sturdy that they are themselves instrumental in installing or toppling such governments. All civilian and military agencies have a specific mind set, and their sectarian affiliation and dearth of electronically trained manpower, lack of professional surveillance approach, and the absence of a proper intelligence sharing culture raised serious questions about their credibility. Pakistan's miltablishment and its secret agencies have been using jihadists in Afghanistan to achieve their strategic goal. Pakistan backed Taliban are fighting to control natural resources and sites in different provinces of Afghanistan. It was reported in May 2019 that illegal mining of gold and other precious minerals dramatically increased in Taliban-controlled regions close to the border with Pakistan.

Intelligence community of Pakistan faces numerous challenges, including a widespread lack of political support, public confidence, corruption, sectarian affiliations, political and ethnic associations, war crimes in Waziristan, and Baluchistan and political loyalties. The ISI and civilian intelligence agencies have ultimately failed to bring Gallus-Gallus from the remote regions of Sindh, Khyber Pakhtunkhwa and Baluchistan provinces due to their inability to balloon their networks to these regions and make a friendly relationship with the local population. There are numerous stories of the IB and ISI successes and failures in these regions as agencies faced condemnation from politicians and civil society due to their sarcastic behaviour, enforced disappearances and political involvement. The intelligence cycle is a structured process, to gather information, convert it into relevant intelligence, and pass it to those who require it–the decision-makers, but the ISI and civilian intelligence agencies of Pakistan have painted a new picture of intelligence cycle by sharing state secrets with political, sectarian and religious stakeholders in order to justify their loyalties. There is an impression in Pakistani media that the ISI has become a state within a state, where no real check and balance existed to oversee its enforced disappearance and illegal harassment business. The failure of Inter-Services Intelligence to intercept consecutive terror attacks on Pakistan, and its intransigence to maintain professional intelligence cooperation with civilian intelligence agencies raised many questions.

The list of problems faced by the Pakistani intelligence machine is long. This unreformed and unchecked secret machine has suffered numerous diseases and forced it to demonstrate like a schizophrenic and batty man. The Inter-Services Intelligence and Military Intelligence lack of trust has been a longstanding concern in civilian circles. Writers and intellectuals in their forums have also raised the question of public confidence. These unreformed civilian and military intelligence agencies and their members retrieve massive and large amounts of money from kidnapping for ransom and enforced disappearances, and now they ballooned their business of killing and torture to Afghanistan. Majority of the members of intelligence agencies of the country belong to different sectarian, ethnic, political and jihadist groups. They leak important security and intelligence information to these entities and sects. This illegal affiliation also directed intelligence operations on sectarian and ethnic bases. Poor data collection with regard to the activities of militant sectarian organizations and their networks across the country is a challenging problem. Many criminals who joined terrorist groups were not tracked and profiled effectively. Intelligence agencies of the country protect professional criminals and sectarian elements in safe houses, and used them against politicians and those who criticized corruption and war crimes of the Armed Forces in Waziristan and Baluchistan. In Afghanistan, trained intelligence units of ISI, MI and civilian intelligence agencies are making things worse by harassing and kidnapping men and women opponents of the Taliban government. Pakistani intelligence agencies now need to change their way of operations in countering extremism and militancy across the country. The Inter-Services Intelligence was a professional intelligence agency 50 years ago that gathered, processed and analyzed information to make policy makers competent in designing military and security strategies, but at present, they are running behind political workers, politicians, Ghaddars, and sectarian mafia groups. The ISI provided intelligence to Pakistani policy makers and performed several operations but extremely failed to achieve a single objective.

The shrewdness and perception that ISI is a number one intelligence agency in South Asia is not accurate; the agency is weak, corrupt, politicized, militarized and its national security approach is controversial. It collects intelligence in uncustomary manner, which leads policymakers in the wrong direction. Its intelligence officers are not so greatly educated and unable to use modern intelligence technology properly. There are thousands of volunteer informers who work for the agency in different environments, but don't even know the basic knowledge of intelligence information techniques and settling political vendettas through illegal means. Their purveyed low-quality intelligence information led policy makers in the wrong direction. The agency views Afghanistan with hostile military glasses. Well-known British Journalist, Declan Walsh in his book (The Nine Lives of Pakistan) noted some controversial aspects of the ISI demonstrations and manifestations: "While it is effective on street level. The ISI is not a professional service in the Mould of the CIA or Britain's MI6. The organization is afflicted by the same bungling and corruption as the rest of the Pakistani state. It has frequently lost control of its most dangerous assets-Puppet masters who can't control their puppets," as Robert Grenier, a former CIA station chief in Islamabad, put it. "And when it comes to analysis, the ISI has a poor record. 'They saw everything through pre-determined ideological prisms, rather like the KBG during the Cold War, a senior British official who worked with the ISI for decades told me; 'Frankly,' he added. 'None of their analysis was worth the paper it was written on'. Journalist Declan Walsh noted.

The tug of war between ISI and the IB and their operational interests in Afghanistan is being discussed in intellectual circles in Pakistan and Europe. Their so-called sympathy with Afghans fully exposed when they started investigating Afghan men and women in their secret investigation and torture cells in all provinces of Afghanistan. Their rivalry and secret war intensified when a Joint Investigation Team (JIT) probing alleged money laundering by the Sharif family made a written complaint to the Supreme Court that the IB was wiretapping JIT members, including ISI and Military Intelligence (MI) personnel. General Faiz Hameed, former DG of ISI visited Kabul in 2021 to finalize the Taliban cabinet. Inter-Services

Intelligence (ISI), forced the Taliban to announce an interim government that was guaranteed to preserve ISI's control over the crankshaft of power in Kabul. The ISI also secretly announced a coalition of small jihadist groups (The Islamic Invitation Alliance) in Afghanistan, which was separate from the Taliban and the ISKP. The purpose of the formation of this alliance was to crush Taliban leadership if they refused to follow the ISI's instructions.

Foreign Policy Magazine reported that the Islamic Invitation Alliance (IIA) was founded in 2020 with funding from the ISI and has been on the radar of US intelligence for more than a year. General Faiz Hameed's interference in Afghanistan and the constitution of a controversial cabinet there caused his removal by the Army Chief General Bajwa. War of words between the Baloch Regiment Group with the unwanted groups of sarcastic generals and formation commanders intensified. Faiz was replaced by Lt Gen Nadeem Ahmed Anjum as the Director-General of the ISI. Faiz Hamid was deeply criticized by the leadership of Pakistan Muslim League-N in its meetings and protests for his controversial role in politics. These appointments come at a crucial time for the country's politics. Expert and journalist, Mr. Abbas Nasir has documented (14 September 2017) Pakistan's intelligence infrastructure weaknesses, lack of confidence and its growth in the size and scope of intelligence activities that might be linked to their role, but some analysts understand that Pakistan never changed the old British culture of intelligence and never tried to adopt modern intelligence and technological culture to make intelligence fit to the fight against radicalization and terrorism.

Pakistan's own experience in intelligence failure is not confined to Inter-Services Intelligence (ISI), failure of civilian intelligence agencies to counter-terrorism, radicalization and political turmoil are prime examples. The number of reports and recommendations to improve performance and operational mechanism have remained only on papers, while agencies didn't allow to change their manner of operation. On matters of foreign affairs and intelligence, the ISI and civilian intelligence failed to create a friendly environment with neighbouring states while intelligence related to national security is marked more by failures than successes is a sad reality. Intelligence war and short-term remedies all combine to lead up to flawed outcomes. Centre-provincial relationships have never been improved due to strained civil-military relations. Since the fight against insurgency in Waziristan and Baluchistan started, civilians have been wrongfully harmed in both crossfire and air force bombardments. Many of these mistakes are said to result from conflicting commands due to rivalries among security agencies. Since the rise in violent attacks perpetrated across the country, the army failed to differentiate between terrorists and insurgents. Countless security lapses, including incidents such as attacks on the army amplified the importance of resolving intelligence failures. According to Dr. Nadeem Malik, 'Imran Khan's recent ousting as Pakistan's Prime Minister was just the latest manifestation of the failure of hybrid regimes in Pakistan–hybrid in the sense that behind the scenes of every civilian government, the military elite continues to manage things. But this time the influence of the military is now being called out like it hasn't before'.

Expert and Senior Lecturer, School of Social and Political Sciences, Faculty of Arts, University of Melbourne, Dr Nadeem Malik in his analysis (Imran Khan's failure exposed Pakistan's military problem: Since its establishment, Pakistan's governments have been dominated by the military, but there is hope for change- 21 April 2022) has documented some aspects of hybrid nature of Pakistani governments, political turmoil and involvement of military establishment in politics: "This hybrid nature of Pakistani governments has led to frequent conflict between civil governments and the military, culminating in the eventual collapse of civilian administrations. Imran Khan's regime was an ideal type in this context in that the military was able to use Imran Khan's fame to win power, with the aim of governing through him. In a recent television interview, the speaker of the Provincial Assembly of Punjab, Chaudhry Pervez Elahi, one of Khan's own allies, openly blamed the military for the government's collapse. He said in an interview in Urdu on HUM television Pakistan, "... they (the military) kept changing Khan's nappies all the time instead of providing him opportunities to learn politics and the art of governance". Dr Nadeem Malik Noted. However, he also noted failure of the hybrid Khan-military regime miserably, worsening the instability in the country and leaving a legacy of high inflation, especially food inflation, dwindling foreign reserves and increasing deficits. In addition to the economic crisis, Pakistan faces ongoing challenges, including balancing global pressure to prod the Taliban in neighbouring Afghanistan to meet human rights commitments while trying to limit instability and terrorism within the country. Previously, the onus for the failure of Pakistan's hybrid regimes has fallen on civilian governments". Dr Nadeem Malik Noted.

Furthermore, the military-madrasa-mullah nexus has deliberately manipulated and encouraged jihadism by favouring a tactical deployment of jihadi groups in Kashmir and Afghanistan to expand Pakistan's regional influence. The internal conditions within Pakistan have also deteriorated over the past decades because of the focus on building up militancy and grooming Islamist extremist groups as weapons, in Rawalpindi's eternal and obsessive struggle against India. The military-militant cabal is the core problem of Pakistan today. The Abbottabad raid and the Mehran Naval Base attack were strong enough pointers in this direction. These two incidents were symptomatic of a larger malaise that has been eroding the Army's professionalism for quite some time. The Army has failed to develop a true ethnic representation process or to motivate Baloch and Sindhis to join the ranks of the armed forces. However, a great deal of experience in the killing of innocent civilians has been amassed. In Baluchistan, thousands of Baloch men and women disappeared in so-called military operations over the last 15 years, while the tortured and mutilated bodies of thousands of missing persons turn up on roadsides. Despite the Pakistani state's denial, there have been clear pointers to the existence of sympathizers and collaborators of Islamist radical organizations within all three-armed forces. Every major attack on a military installation in the country bears clear marks of collusion by elements from within. Many of Pakistan Air Force (PAF) and army personnel, including six officers, were convicted for attempts on the life of General Pervez Musharraf in December 2003, when he was the country's President.

Recent events in Kazakhstan and Tajikistan have raised the prospect of extremist and jihadist groups using biological, radiological and chemical weapons against military installations and critical national infrastructure in both states. Russia is vulnerable to such attacks by these terrorist groups who received military training from the US Army in Afghanistan and Pakistan. The greatest threat to the national security of Russia stems from the business of nuclear smuggling of state-sponsored terror groups operating in Central Asia. Increasingly sophisticated chemical and biological weapons are accessible to these organizations and ISIS and their allies, which is a matter of great concern. These groups can use more sophisticated conventional weapons as well as chemical and biological agents in near future. Before the rise of ISIS, the Islamic Movement of Uzbekistan (IMU) was the main Central Asian extremist organization in the field. Its base of operations is in Afghanistan and Pakistan. Central Asian fighters linked to ISIS headquarter in Syria also participated in acts of terrorism in other countries. The ISIS has previously restrained itself from getting involved in attacks in Central Asia as the group's leadership emphasized that attacking this region was not the highest priority. In July 2018, five Tajik men killed four foreign cyclists in a car-ramming attack, accompanied by an on-foot gun and knife assault in the Khatlon province of Tajikistan.

The presence of Daesh in Iraq and Afghanistan, and participation of Central Asian jihadists in it prompted consternation in the region. In Syria, the radical Islamic militants from Central Asia established terrorist organizations of their own. These terrorists have Salafi-Wahhabi inclinations and are among the backers of al-Qaeda, al-Nusra Front, and Daesh group. The ISIS and Central Asian terrorist groups seek biological and nuclear weapons to use against security forces in Russia and Central Asia. The modus operandi of ISIS or ISIS inspired individuals are diverse and show no moral restraints–as recent attacks in Brussels and Berlin demonstrated. The use of biological and chemical weapons by terrorists has prompted huge fatalities in Iraq and Syria. However, preventing dangerous materials from falling into the hands of ISIS, Pakistani terrorist groups, and Central Asia extremists is a complex challenge. Since 2013, there has been extensive use of chemical weapons in armed conflicts in Syria by US backed terrorist groups. The deadliest attacks were carried out with chemical agents by the ISIS terrorist group in Syria that needed significant knowledge and the specialized resources. This book has been edited and proofed by writer and analyst, Dr. Sanchita Bhattacharya editor Faultlines and research fellow in the New Delhi bases Institute for Conflict Management India. I am highly indebted to Dr. Sanchita Bhattacharya for her vigorous efforts and recapitulation of my book.

Musa Khan Jalalzai, London
Telepathic and Geospatial
Intelligence Expert-10 June 2022

Chapter 1

The Taliban, ISIS-K, Al Qaeda, the Haqqani Network, their Atrocities, Torture and the Degradation of Afghan Nation

We live in an era of fear market where only ignorance drives our thoughts and responses every day. We observe many incidents of auctions in terror markets across the globe, in which innocent children are being sold for suicide terrorism. These are spreading successfully because we do not do our homework and we have no specific counterterrorism strategy. In India, Pakistan and Afghanistan, the terror market is viewed in different perspectives. If we deeply study the news stories of suicide terror-related incidents, we will find that terrorists use different techniques in their attacks. The method of destruction and killing is the same but techniques and strategies are different. Terrorist organisations suchlike ISIS, and the Taliban through Facebook, YouTube and Twitter invite young people to join their networks by using various marketing techniques. These terror groups are marketers as well as consumers to a degree; their recruiters 'market' boys and use them as human bombs against civil society and military infrastructure. They supply suicide bombers across Asia and the Middle East in a cheap rate. Religious and political vendettas are being settled by using suicide bombers against rival groups or families. This generation of fear and panic is controlled by extremist elements and non-state actors. Fear and terror marketing systems are updated every year and new techniques of destruction are being introduced. The way the Afghan Taliban design their strategies for training and brainwashing suicide bombers is not quite different from the suicide techniques of the ISIS-K. They market fear and terror according to their demand. If we deeply consider the terrorism marketing techniques of both the Afghan Taliban and the IS-K, we will clearly observe approximation in their way of killing.

The concept of suicide attacks, or dying in order to kill in the name of religion become a supreme ideal of Taliban and IS-K groups that have been carrying out suicide attacks against the innocent civilians of Afghanistan and Pakistan. After the US invasion of Afghanistan, Taliban resorted to suicide terrorism to force the United States and its NATO allies to withdraw their forces from the country and restore Emirate Islami of Taliban. Taliban and the IS-K became dominant forces in suicide terrorism to internationalise and justify it. Modern suicide terrorism emerged in Afghanistan after 9/11, but it was introduced in different shapes. Over the past two decades, the tactic of suicide terrorism in Afghanistan and Pakistan were modified and justified by religious clerics. According to expert, Assaf Moghadam (Suicide Terrorism, Occupation, and the Globalization of Martyrdom: A Critique of Dying to Win, published in 2006), "the growing interest in suicide terrorism in recent years has generated a steep rise in the number of books that address a topic that is inherently fascinating—a mode of operations that requires the death of its perpetrator to ensure its success". In Dying, in order to kill Strategic Logic of Suicide Terrorism is possible to assemble statistical data about terrorist incidents. Experts and analysts, Yoram Schweitzer and Sari Goldstein Ferber, in their research paper (Al-Qaeda and the Internationalization of Suicide Terrorism. Jaffee Center for Strategic Studies, Tel Aviv University. Memorandum No. 78 November 2005) have highlighted some aspects of Istishhad or suicide terrorism:

"The concept of istishhad as a means of warfare is part of an overall philosophy that sees active jihad against the perceived enemies of Islam as a central ideological pillar and organizational ideal. According to al-Qaeda's worldview, one's willingness to sacrifice his or her life for Allah and 'in the path of Allah' (fi sabil allah) is an expression of the Muslim fighter's advantage over the opponent. In al-Qaeda, the sacrifice of life is of supreme value, the symbolic importance of which is equal to if not greater than its tactical importance. The organization adopted suicide as the supreme embodiment of global jihad and raised Islamic martyrdom (al-shehada) to the status of a principle of faith. Al-Qaeda leaders cultivated the spirit of the organization, constructing its ethos around a commitment to self-sacrifice and the implementation of this idea through suicide attacks. Readiness for self-sacrifice was one of the most important characteristics to imbue in veteran members and new recruits. The principal aim of a jihad warrior: sacrifice of life in the name of Allah, is presented in terms of enjoyment: "We are asking you to undertake the pleasure of looking at your face and we long to meet you, not in a time of distress...take us to you." The idealization of istishhad, repeated regularly in official organizational statements, is contained in its motto: "we love death more than our opponents' love life. This motto encapsulates the lack of fear among al-Qaeda fighters of losing temporary life in this world, since it is exchanged for an eternal life of purity in heaven".[1]

Taliban and the IS-K emerged as terrorist organizations with their dynamic structures. The ISIS reshaped jihadist landscape with its bloody strategy more than that of the Taliban. In Afghanistan, US and NATO forces ousted the Taliban and in a way paved the road for establishment of the IS-K terrorist group. In 2006, when NATO deployed its forces across in the south, insurgents shifted to asymmetric tactics. On 19 October 2021, Taliban's acting Interior Minister hosted a ceremony in Kabul to honour suicide bombers responsible for the killings of innocent Afghans, and deployed suicide brigades to take on Pakistani forces on Durand Line. He praised the families of 1,500 suicide bombers in Afghanistan and fixed monthly salary for them. In October 2021, ISIS suicide bombers attacked the Fatemiyyeh Brigade's mosque in Kandahar, killing at least 33 people and injuring 74 others. Another attack in 2022, in which an IS-K suicide bomber hit a mosque in Kunduz, killing at least 100 people. However, BBC in its news story (Iraq bombing: IS says it was behind deadly suicide attacks in Baghdad, published on 22 January 2021) reported attacks of IS-K in Afghanistan. Suicide tactics of ISIS and IS-K in Iraq and Afghanistan are identical but recent development in using Armoured Suicide Vehicles (ASV) in Iraq made a huge difference. Expert, Ellen Tveteraas (Under the Hood–Learning and Innovation in the Islamic State's Suicide Vehicle Industry, Studies in Conflict & Terrorism, 2022) has documented operations of the ISIS armoured Suicide Vehicles in Iraq that emerged around Baghdad in October 2014:

"The first reports of up-armoured suicide vehicles in Iraq emerged around Baghdad in October 2014, with the Islamic State employing Humvees left behind by the Iraqi army following the fall of Mosul in June that same year. Because they were a limited resource and had utility in other aspects of battle, these cars proved impractical to use for suicide bombings in high numbers. Combining the benefits of the Humvee with the requirement for mass production, the group gradually developed a reproducible and bulletproof design based on civilian vehicles. Personnel would cover all or parts of cars with thick iron plates, slanting it in front to increase the effective thickness of the metal and heightening the odds of small arms and heavy munitions ricocheting off. They also added metal grids to increase the distance between exploding munitions and the car. In rural operations, the group would paint the armour beige to blend in with desert terrain and make the discovery by reconnaissance units more difficult. In urban operation the armour would be painted in more radiant colours to mimic civilian vehicles. The added armour initially caught the Iraqi military off-guard, and to effectively stop some of these new contraptions they had to procure Kornet missiles at around $250 000 apiece. Suicide operatives were the purview of the special skills bureau, with prospective bombers organized in a section called the Martyrdom Operatives Battalion (Katibat al-Istishadiin). Members of the suicide battalion would normally arrive at the area of operation shortly before the execution of an attack and spend the preparation period in isolation with clerics to build the mental fortitude required to execute this type of mission. The battalion had no shortage of volunteers and, following the group's acquisition of territory, its size far outgrew the tactical demand for suicide operations."[2]

After the American Army took to one's heels at midnight, Afghanistan faced numerous political, economic and health care challenges. Causes of the failure of Central Intelligence Agency (CIA) and NATO's intelligence machine to stabilize Afghanistan, or defeat Taliban were multitudinous. First, Afghan Army officers and commanders sold their weapons and check posts to Taliban to address their financial hardship because they were denied their salaries in war zones. Second, they started transporting terrorists in Army vehicles and helped the Islamic State in carrying out suicide attacks against civilians and government installations. Third, they protected foreign intelligence networks, plundered military funds and resources due to their personal and anti-state attitude. Fourth, the Afghan Army and the National Directorate of Security (NDS) were on the payroll of CIA and NATO member states to implement their agendas. Fifth, Generals of Afghan National Army (ANA), directors of foreign office and national security office maintained secret accounts abroad to easily receive funds from foreign intelligence agencies. Some of them were involved in money laundering, and some were tasked to humiliate Afghans in print and electronic media. Sixth, the issue of landmines was also not addressed properly by the US and NATO member states which prompted the death of thousand civilians. Seventh, the Afghan army was personally involved in planting landmines in Pashtun provinces to intercept the Taliban incursions. On 15 March, 2021, Daily Siasat reported the killing of more than 120 Afghans by landmines every month. Directorate of Mine Action Coordination of Afghanistan (DMAC) said in a statement: "An average of 120 people, including children were being killed or maimed by unexploded ordnance and landmines, every month". Expert and analyst, Michael A. Peters in his research paper (Declinism' and discourses of decline-the end of the war in Afghanistan and the limits of American power, Educational

Philosophy and Theory) has documented the real failure of US Army in Afghanistan and the abrupt announcement of the Biden administration to leave Afghanistan surprised everyone and caused a rift with NATO allies who wanted to stay in Afghanistan:

"The ignominious end of the Afghan War after twenty long years, often referred to as the 'forever war', was brought to an abrupt end by Joe Biden in such haste that it surprised everyone and caused a rift with NATO allies who wanted to stay a presence in Afghanistan. Whatever spin can be placed on the end of US involvement, the withdrawal was messy and unplanned, air lifting US troops and well over 120,000 Afghan US supporters from Kabul airport. Many more Afghans who were part of the US war effort remain trapped in the country. Even with American support, the Afghan army was routed in a week and the Afghan government also collapsed. The embattled president Ashraf Ghani fled the country reportedly with a 'helicopter full of cash'. His swift departure left the best possible opening for the Taliban, who are talking of forming an 'open, inclusive Islamic government' and have established an interim government yet without the representation of women. President Biden first went on record as saying that nation-building was never part of the original mission yet the official justification for the Americans being in Afghanistan after the killing of Bin Laden had evaporated. Mission-creep set in with the downscaling US forces from 20,000 a couple of years ago to less than 2,000 in the final years".[3]

With the establishment of Taliban government in Afghanistan in 2021, mentally and physically tortured civilians experienced every mischance and stroke of bad luck. The proxy militia inflicted deep pain and torment on minorities by attacking mosques and religious places, and protecting Pakistani and Central Asian terrorist organizations. Women were tortured, humiliated and incarcerated, girls were deprived from education and their schools were shamelessly closed. After taking control of Ghazni province on 21 August 2021, they used inhuman and illegal strategies and policies that resulted in huge barriers to women's health and girls' education. Afghan women experienced collapsed human rights and risk of basic rights, and were treated like goats and dogs. Human Rights Watch (HRW) and SJSU interviewed women in Ghazni province and documented their spiralling prices for food, transportation, and schoolbooks. The poorer and hungry parents sold their girls and sons for a piece of bread. Taliban kidnapped women, sexually abused and tortured transgender then killed them. Some women felt heightened risk because of gender, ethnicity and religious sect.

14

Human Rights Watch in its recent report (Afghanistan: Taliban Deprive Women of Livelihoods, Identity: Severe Restrictions, Harassment, Fear in Ghazni Province-18 January, 2022), noted intimidation of villagers by Taliban fighters: "Taliban authorities have also used intimidation to extract money, food, and services. 'When the Taliban visit a village, they force the households to feed them and collect food items from people,' a woman from a village said. 'The Taliban and their fighters call us in the middle of the night to cure and give special treatment to their patients and families,' a health worker said. They enter the hospital with their guns, it's difficult for the doctors and nurses to manage."[4] HRW noted.

Following the US and NATO withdrawal from Afghanistan, more than 3,000 Hazara Muslims were tortured and forcibly evicted from their homes by Taliban terrorist militia. As mentioned earlier, Taliban and the IS-K terrorist organizations have been killing Hazara Muslims in all provinces of Afghanistan since 1990s, destroying their houses and kidnaping their women and girls for sexual exploitation. After the 9/11 terrorist attacks in the United States, the Hazara Muslims experienced further harassment and intimidation. Successive Afghan governments failed to protect their agricultural land, houses and children. In her recent research paper, analyst and expert, Kate Clark (Afghanistan's conflict in 2021 (2): Republic collapse and Taliban victory in the long-view of history. Afghanistan Analysts Network, published in 30 December, 2021) documented civilian's pain, killings, and destruction after the US withdrawal from Afghanistan:

"The high number of civilians killed and injured in the conflict in 2021 was striking because the war in Afghanistan was then being fought mainly between Afghans. After the US-Taliban February 2020 agreement, which bound the two parties not to attack each other, but allowed the Taliban to attack the Afghan National Security Forces (ANSF), the US largely removed itself from the battlefield. This spared the Taliban their most dangerous enemy, while denying the Afghan National Security Forces US support except in extremes. It translated into the US taking a much reduced and sporadic part in the war after February 2020. According to the US's own published statistics, the number of 'weapons' dropped by the US Air Force in 2020 was 1,631 (almost half of the yearly total came in the two months before the Doha agreement was signed), compared to 7,362 in 2018 and 7,423 in 2019, and 801 in 2021 (first eight months only). In the chart below, it can be seen that the number of air munitions fell after February 2020 and rose somewhat in autumn 2020 as the US used airstrikes, for example, to drive back Taliban offensives in the south (see a call by Amnesty

International for safe passage for civilians out of Lashkargah in October and Washington Post reporting on Kandahar in November). The number of munitions that the US Air Force dropped again after Biden's decision to withdraw, rising only in August 2021 as the US Air Force made last-ditch efforts to shore up the ANSF..... The campaign of targeted killings, which were often unclaimed but largely believed to be carried out by the Taleban, that had begun in late 2020, did not let up, but represented the third most likely way for civilians to be injured or killed: UNAMA said the campaign targeted an "ever-widening breadth of types of civilians… human rights defenders, media workers, religious elders, civilian government workers, and humanitarian workers." The campaign also targeted members of the ANSF. According to one security source in Kabul, twice as many ANSF were targeted and killed or injured as civilians."[5]

The Taliban militia killed more than 5000 members of former Afghan security forces. The HRW accused leadership of "condoning" the "deliberate" killings. Taliban were held responsible for a bloody campaign of murder and torture against journalists and rights activists. Taliban with the assistance of Pakistani ISI located addresses of Afghan soldiers and government officials who helped the US and NATO in the illegal war against Afghanistan. HRW in its report (Afghanistan: Taliban Kill, 'Disappear' Ex-Officials: Raids Target Former Police, Intelligence Officers, published on November 30, 2021) noted, "Taliban forces in Afghanistan have summarily executed or forcibly disappeared more than 100 former police and intelligence officers in just four provinces since taking over the country on August 15, 2021. The 25-page report, "'No Forgiveness for People Like You,' Executions and Enforced Disappearances in Afghanistan under the Taliban," documents the killing or disappearance of 47 former members of the Afghan National Security Forces (ANSF) – military personnel, police, intelligence service members, and militia – who had surrendered to or were apprehended by Taliban forces between August 15 and October 31."[6]

The IS-K group was also in contact with Lashkar-e-Jhangvi (LeJ) and Lashkar-e-Taiba (LeT) in Jalalabad to target the Taliban forces, but failed to gain control of Jalalabad province. On December 11, 2014, former Interior Minister of Pakistan, Rehman Malik told a local news channel that IS-K had established recruitment centres in Gujranwala and Bahawalpur districts of Punjab province. The wall-chalking campaign and leaflets prompted fears about the terrorist group making inroads in the country. According to the leaked government circular in Balochistan and Khyber

Pakhtunkhwa provinces, ISIS recruited more than 10,000 to 15,000 fighters in 2015 for the next sectarian war in Pakistan. In Kabul, on 08 December, 2014, Reuters reported a 25-year-old student from Kabul University vowed to join the mujahideen of IS-K. "When hundreds of foreigners, both men and women, leave their comfortable lives and embrace Daesh, then why not us?" he asked. The influx of terrorist groups like the Islamic State of Khorasan in Jalalabad province challenged the writ of the Taliban local administration. Former Afghan President Ghani also warned that 30 terrorist groups were operating across the country posed serious threat to the national security of Afghanistan. The UN experts also believed that more than 45,000 terrorists were fighting against the Afghan National army and between 20 to 25 percent were foreigners. Pakistan military establishment secured peace agreements with certain Taliban factions by legitimising the Talibanization of the region. Experts and analysts, Qasim Jan, Yi Xie, Muhammad Habib Qazi, Zahid Javid Choudhary and Baha ul Haq in their research paper (Examining the role of Pakistan's national curriculum textbook discourses on normalising the Taliban's violence in the USA's Post 9/11 war on terror in South Waziristan, Pakistan. British Journal of Religious Education, 2022) have documented Talibanization process of Waziristan:

"After 9/11, South Waziristan attracted global attention as an epicentre of terrorism. In the wake of the US invasion of Afghanistan, the Taliban and al-Qaida escaped from Afghanistan through the North-western border to the tribal areas including South Waziristan, Pakistan. Pakistan, as the US ally, launched several military operations against these religious militants, mainly the Taliban, in this hideout. However, Pakistan's military establishment has been accused of playing a 'secret double game', named 'tournament of shadows', clandestinely supporting militants including the Taliban as their 'strategic asset'. At a later stage, the Pakistani establishment secured peace agreements with certain Taliban factions, legitimising the Talibanization of the region. The legitimisation of the Talibanization, in this context, refers to the state of Pakistan's approval of the Taliban's styled Sharia law in South Waziristan. Its practices included public flogging, hand amputation, beheading and stoning to death, proportionate to minor/major offences of the accused/guilty. Besides eroding the writ of the state (Pakistan), these peace agreements resulted in the creation of new binary i.e. 'Good Taliban' who pointed their guns on Afghanistan and fulfilled the objectives of Pakistan's security establishment, while those who didn't fall in line were called 'Bad Taliban'. The peace deal helped the Taliban and their affiliates in finding safe heavens in South Waziristan. Their commanders visited schools and colleges and delivered speeches about the glorification of Jihad and sacrifices for the cause of Allah/Muslim God. Hence, the Talibanization of the border region of tribal areas seems to be linked to Pakistan's strategic interests in Afghanistan and the South Asian region".[7]

Terrorism, violence and civil war in Afghanistan prompted catastrophe, displacement and financial destruction. With the establishment of the IS-K terrorist group in 2015, and its war against Taliban and the Afghan government further added to the pain of civilian population. The IS-K killed women, children and kidnapped young girls, looted houses and beheaded senior citizens in all provinces of Afghanistan. Both Pakistan and former Afghan government facilitated and financially supported Daesh and transported their terrorist fighters to their destination. The IS-K carried out dozens of terrorist attacks in Pakistan and Afghanistan with the help of ANA. The group has trained its fighters to carry out biological and nuclear terrorist attacks. Expert and analysts, Eric Schmitt (in "ISIS Branch Poses Biggest Immediate Terrorist Threat to Evacuation in Kabul", published on 03 November, 2021, The New York Times) has highlighted rivalries between Taliban and the IS-K terrorist group in Afghanistan:

"The rivalry between the Taliban and its partners and ISIS-K will continue after the last American troops leave, analysts say. And the fragile cooperation between American and Taliban commanders is already fraying, and the two could easily revert to their adversarial stances. The American military is treating the Taliban's red line about Aug. 31 seriously. The recent evacuations have been possible because of Taliban cooperation—in allowing most people to reach the airport unscathed, and in working against the threat of ISIS attacks, commanders say. After Aug. 31, military officials say, there is a real concern that at best, the cooperation with the Taliban will end. At worst, that could lead to attacks on U.S. forces, foreign citizens and Afghan allies, either by Taliban elements or by their turning a blind eye to Islamic State threats. Mr. Biden has pledged to prevent Afghanistan from again becoming a sanctuary for Al Qaeda and other terrorist groups that want to attack the American homeland. Military commanders say that will be a difficult task, with no troops and few spies on the ground, and armed Reaper drones thousands of miles away at bases in the Persian Gulf. In the February 2020 agreement with the Trump administration, the Taliban vowed not to allow Al Qaeda to use Afghan territory to attack the United States. But analysts fear that is not happening and that Al Qaeda remains the longer-term terrorism threat."[8]

In 2015, the IS-K was established to fight and tackle Pakistan based extremist groups who were trying to hijack the US war according to their agenda. Pakistanis from Southern Punjab rushed to join the terrorist infrastructure to sustain their poor families. In 2020, according to former Interior Minister of Pakistan, Rahman Malik, more than 80,000 poor madrasa students from Southern Punjab had joined the IS-K and participated in the civil war in Syria, Iraq and Afghanistan. These revelations generated panic in both Pakistan and Afghanistan that these fighters will further add to the pain of the Pakistan military establishment in the near future. The IS-K's intent is clear, and the Wilayat Khorasan is the ISIS most viable and lethal regional affiliate based on an expansionist military strategy. This is designed to enable the group's encirclement of Jalalabad city and is foundational to its expanded operational reach. Despite their Wahhabi backgrounds, the IS-K and Taliban groups follow a common agenda to destabilise Central Asia. The relationship between the Taliban and ISIS in Afghanistan is friendly. Taliban and ISIS are parts of a broader Deobandi and Wahhabi movements in Afghanistan who want to create misunderstanding between Islam and the west. Clayton Sharb, Danika Newlee and the CSIS iDeas Lab in their joint work (Islamic State Khorasan (IS-K), Center for Strategic and International Studies, 2018) have highlighted the IS-K global agenda and its intentions in Kashmir and Pakistan:

"IS-K carries out its global strategy in different operating environments by curating it to local conditions. Consider, for example, the divided region of Kashmir. It sits at the top of the Indian subcontinent and serves as a flashpoint for conflict between historically feuding nuclear powers, Pakistan and India. With nationalistic leaders dominating politics in both Islamabad and New Delhi, perpetual unrest in the disputed territories, and precedent of state-sponsored terrorism, Kashmir is fertile ground for future IS-K subversion. In Afghanistan and Pakistan, IS-K's strategy seeks to delegitimize the governments and degrade public trust in democratic processes, sowing instability in nation-states, which the group views as illegitimate. Recently, in the lead up to 2018 parliamentary elections in Afghanistan, IS-K warned citizens in Nangarhar province, "We caution the Muslims in the province from approaching election centres, and we recommend that they stay away from them so as to safeguard their blood, as these are legitimate targets for us." IS-K claimed multiple attacks on "elections centres" and security forces during the Afghan parliamentary elections, following through on their warning to "sabotage the polytheistic process and disrupt it."[9]

The IS-K is the strangest non-state actor in Afghanistan that poses a serious security threat to Taliban and Pakistan. The IS-K has deep roots in South Asia, with its branches in Pakistan, India, and some Southeast Asian states. Well-organized and well-established organization with over 250,000 trained fighters that can anytime challenge the authority of the failed state in Afghanistan. There are countless books and journals in markets and libraries that highlight infrastructure of the IS-K with different perspectives and view its operational mechanism and suicide technique with different glasses. My glasses are not as different from them as I have written books on the suicide operation of the ISIS and IS-K, and contributed article to the newspapers and journals. The IS-K threat to the existence of Taliban is intensified by the day as the group consecutively targeted government installations and public places. Expert and analyst, Mohamed Mokhtar Qandi in his paper (Challenges to Taliban Rule and Potential Impacts for the Region: Internal and external factors are weakening the Taliban, making the group's long term stability increasingly unlikely, Fikra Forum, The Washington Institute for Near East Policy, 09 February 2022) has noted the intensifying threat of ISIS and IS-K in Afghanistan, and asserted that the ISIS seeks to be an alternative to the Taliban movement:

"ISIS views the Taliban movement as a major strategic foe in South Asia. From the outset, members of Khorasan Province began questioning the Taliban's legitimacy in jihadi circles, which helped ISIS win new followers who splintered from the movement. Furthermore, ISIS may be attractive to those seeking revenge on the movement. In some cases, ISIS has attracted former Afghan intelligence members as well as younger middle-class youth who may become increasingly disaffected with the Taliban. There is also the dispute between the Taliban and the Salafist current inside Afghanistan that is not affiliated with Khorasan Province. The Taliban's harassment of these Salafists may push them to join the ranks of ISIS, or at least provide a haven for its members. Since the Taliban came to power by force, their lack of legitimacy can quickly lead to a decline in their popular support vis-à-vis ISIS, especially if they fail to meet the needs of the people and improve the economic situation. Despite the power that the Islamic State demonstrated in Khorasan, it is unlikely that the movement will be able to plan or launch attacks on distant targets. However, if ISIS-Khorasan succeeds in controlling more territories in Afghanistan and recruiting elements who resent Taliban, it will be tantamount to reviving the organization in the Middle East. On the one hand, the organization will intensify its propaganda and its claims that it is the sole carrier of the banner of jihad and hence, must be supported in establishing the Islamic caliphate as a global project. This will provide the organization with many opportunities to set up training camps for its elements and export them to the Middle East where they previously experienced a harsh defeat".[10]

Transnational extremist groups suchlike IS-K, Lashkar-e-Taiba, al Qaeda, and Taliban are relying on domestic extremist organizations that control thoughts and minds of citizens. The yesteryear analysis explored survival of groups in alliances. We can find these trends in Afghanistan where Taliban have entered into alliance with different Pakistani and Arab terrorist groups. Although ISIS also collaborated with different Afghan, Pakistani and Central Asian organizations, but it follows American agenda and wants to export jihad and suicide terrorism to Central Asia. In areas under its control, the IS-K terrorist group manage its own strategies of governance. The terrorist group killed hundreds in Afghanistan to justify its presence. In Afghanistan, if other groups leave the area under their control, the IS-K will either kill its members or force them to pledge allegiance and work with IS-K. Experts and analysts, Amira Jadoon, Abdul Sayed and Andrew Mines in their research paper ("The Islamic State Threat in Taliban Afghanistan: Tracing the Resurgence of Islamic State Khorasan", The Combating Terrorism Center at West Point, January 2022, Volum 15, Issue-1) have noted military confrontations between Taliban and the Islamic State of Khorasan:

"Since its inception, ISK has viewed the Afghan Taliban as its main strategic rival in the region.100 In a quest to outbid and outcompete its rival, ISK has not only attacked Afghan Taliban targets regularly since 2015, but also recruited heavily from the organization's ranks and leadership, which ISK has categorized into three general groups: first, the 'sincere Taliban jihadis' who defected to join ISK; second, those who kept a neutral stance toward ISK; and third, the ones who are the puppets of regional governments and motivated by personal interests. ISK has made delegitimizing the Afghan Taliban's purity as a jihadi movement one of its main messaging priorities. This is reflected in ISK's media campaigns for the last several years, which consistently highlight idolatrous Afghan Taliban-supported or tacitly approved religious and cultural practices, as well as relationships with foreign states that ISK views as heretical. Undermining the Afghan Taliban's legitimacy as a jihadi movement is a key pillar to ISK's organizational identity that is unlikely to change. Since the former took power, ISK's strategy has evolved not only to challenge the Afghan Taliban's legitimacy as the predominant jihadi force in the region (given their negotiations with the United States, and links to Pakistan, China, and Iran), but also their competency as a governing actor. ISK's two-pronged attack on the Afghan Taliban's legitimacy is likely to persist as long as the Taliban remain in power."[11]

On 19 April 2022, Radio Free Europe/Radio Liberty reported Uzbek Presidential Spokesman Sherzod Asadov denial of the IS-K claim that it had fired missiles towards Uzbekistan, and called on Uzbek citizens to disregard what he called provocations. According to the Defense Ministry and Uzbekistan's border guard troops, there were no active military developments along the Uzbek-Afghan border, the situation was stable, Asadov said in a statement placed on Telegram. Moreover, Salam Times reported the IS-K claim that a rocket attack against Uzbekistan from neighbouring Afghanistan was fired and it was the first such bombardment of the Central Asian nation by the group. "The group fired 10 Katyusha rockets at Uzbek forces stationed in the border city of Termez in southern Uzbekistan, IS-K said, adding that the attack followed an audio message from an IS-K spokesperson. On April 17, IS-K called on all fighters around the world to carry out "big and painful" attacks targeting officials and soldiers". Salam Times noted.[12] These rocket attacks generated fear in Central Asia amid prevailing political and economic uncertainty in Afghanistan and raised concerns that the group was expanding its recruitment campaign in the country and posed a serious threat to the region. "ISIS is seizing the current power vacuum in Afghanistan as an opportunity to rapidly increase the number of its militants across the country, said Mohammad Naim Ghayur, a military analyst in Herat. The increasing number of attacks carried out by ISIS in recent months indicated that this terrorist group had not only solidified its footprint but also had built its capacity to challenge Afghanistan's security," Salam Times noted. Expert and analyst, Roshni Kapur in his paper (The Persistent ISKP Threat to Afghanistan: On China's Doorstep. Middle East Institute, January 6, 2022), has noted recent attacks of the IS-K in Afghanistan:

Two separate bombs were detonated in Dasht-e-Barchi in Kabul on December 10, killing two and injuring three others. Although no group has claimed responsibility for the attack, the Islamic State of Khorasan Province (ISKP) is likely behind the latest bout of violence. IS-K's fingerprints have been on other attacks. One of the worst, which killed over 180 people and injured hundreds, took place outside the Kabul airport in August 2021 during the final days of evacuations....The Taliban and ISKP will try to project themselves as the authentic representative of Islam and use that as a recruitment and expansion strategy. Nevertheless, experts have said that rivalry between the two is likely to be confined to a protracted guerrilla-style conflict with direct battles and clashes instead of descending into a civil war. While the Taliban has given amnesty to former security members, the same concessions have not been extended to ISKP. The Taliban is likely to carry out raids against ISKP hideouts, similar to the operation in Nangarhar and detainment of 80 ISKP fighters, as the latter seeks to pose a formidable challenge to the Taliban's rule. ISKP is also likely to regroup, change its modus operandi, become more resilient, and recruit more hardliner fighters to enhance its position in Afghanistan and the surrounding region. Although the US launched a drone strike against ISKP in late August 2021, it has not implemented a long-term counter-terrorism strategy against ISKP. The intelligence-gathering and surveillance systems used by the US and its allies have been dismantled. The chief of US Central Command, Gen. Frank McKenzie, also confessed that Washington is providing only limited security assistance to the Taliban to counter the threat from ISKP. Regional countries may step into the security void to prevent the threat of ISKP spilling into their territories".[13]

Concerns of India are genuine that the Taliban and the IS-K terrorist groups can anytime transport their fighters with sophisticated weapons into Kashmir and Punjab. In March 2022, Indian Army seized US made weapons in Kashmir. Now, there were speculations that if the Taliban guaranteed security, South and Central Asian states would recognize the Taliban government. Beijing is also at the spike due the Taliban attitude towards neighbouring states. China is in hot water that if the East Turkestan Islamic Movement (ETIM) collaborated with the IS-K terrorist group, they might possibly orchestrate terrorist attacks in Xinjiang province. Editor of Terrorism Monitor, Jacob Zenn in his article (Islamic State in Khorasan Province's One-Off Attack in Uzbekistan, Volume XX, Issue 9, 06 May 2022), has highlighted issue of the IS-K missile attack and response of Uzbekistan:

"On April 18, 2022, the Islamic State (IS) released a short video of Islamic State in Khorasan Province (ISKP) fighters firing rockets from the outskirts of Mazar e Sharif, Afghanistan into Termiz, Uzbekistan. Uzbekistan denied that any ISKP attack took place on its soil. This was in lieu of the fact that IS provinces tend to be accurate about their claims, albeit inflating the severity and casualties of their attacks. According to the Uzbek presidency's spokesperson, the reports of the ISKP attack were not "reality" and there were no military operations on Uzbekistan's territory nor any instability along its borderlands…..A more plausible explanation came from the Taliban's deputy spokesperson, however, who asserted that ISKP did launch rockets toward Uzbekistan from Afghan territory, but the rockets failed to reach the Uzbekistan border. As is typical of Taliban foreign policy, the deputy spokesperson affirmed that Afghan soil would not be allowed to be used by any militant group to attack any external country. Video footage also emerged of the Taliban uncovering the ramshackle hideout that ISKP had used to fire the rockets, including the empty rocket launchers".[14] Taliban are in deep water due the attitude of international community and domestic sectarian and terrorist organizations that have put their government at spike. Their recognition and social problems are associated with their domestic policies, torture, humiliation, arrest and closure of girl's schools. Islamic State of Khorasan Province has retrieved military and financial strength and now challenge their authority and carrying out suicide attacks to target religious places. Expert and analyst, Amy Kazmin in her article (Isis-K insurgency jeopardises Taliban's grip on Afghanistan: New rulers accused of betraying Islam by jihadis intent on creating ideologically pure caliphate, October, 26, 2021) has highlighted military and political rivalries between Taliban and the Islami State of Khorasan in Afghanistan:

"After the Taliban Two months after the Taliban seized power, violence, death and fear still stalk Afghanistan. US troops might have departed but the new Islamist rulers in Kabul are now threatened by an insurgency launched by Islamic State-Khorasan Province, an Isis-inspired jihadi movement that has deep ideological differences with the Taliban. Since the Taliban takeover in August, Isis-K has mounted a series of suicide bomb attacks, including at the Kabul airport and at two Shia mosques, as well as assaults on Taliban convoys, which have killed hundreds. Analysts have warned of further violence as Isis-K tries to prevent the Taliban from consolidating their grip on Afghanistan. Isis-K's more hard-line stance has proved attractive to disgruntled Taliban fighters. Dismayed at the new regime's reluctance to impose tougher restrictions on women and its diplomatic overtures to countries such as the US, China and Russia, former Taliban members have switched allegiance to Isis-K. "The American war is over, but the Afghan wars are not," said Avinash Paliwal, deputy director of the SOAS South Asia Institute and author of "My Enemy's Enemy", a book about Afghanistan. The Taliban's long time goal has been to establish an Islamic government in Afghanistan. But Isis-K, which has been active in Afghanistan since 2015, wants to establish an Islamic caliphate across Afghanistan, Pakistan and parts of India and Iran. Isis-K militants consider the Taliban, who have held talks with regional powers and the US in a quest for diplomatic recognition, as "filthy nationalists" who have betrayed the greater Islamic cause, according to an analyst. "Isis-K sees the Taliban as just another kind of political outfit- cutting a deal with the Americans- that is ideologically not pure," Paliwal said. "Their aim is to destabilise an already struggling regime."[15]

Taliban's controversial policies and their resentment towards minorities in Afghanistan divided communities on sectarian bases. As there is no state and legitimate government in the country, they arrest, torture and sexually abuse women with impunity. They have arrested dozens of intellectuals, doctors, former military officers, journalists and social media activists. Some were tortured to death and some were hanged publicly. Analyst and expert, Salman Rafi Sheikh in his article (Eight months on, Taliban's rule is far from stable: Resistance groups are mounting an increasingly potent challenge to the Taliban and may have Pakistan's clandestine support, Asia Times, May 2, 2022) has noted internal policies of Taliban of divided and rule. He also painted a picture of their violence and incompetency to stabilise Afghanistan and maintain friendly relations with neighbouring states: "On April 29, a blast in Kabul in a mosque belonging to a Sunni minority group–the Zikris–killed at least 50 people. On Thursday, a bomb blast in a van carrying Shiite Muslims in the northern city of Mazar-e-Sharif killed at least nine people. The attack on the Shiite van came after Taliban leaders claimed to have captured an ISIS-K mastermind of the previous attack in Mazar-e-Sharif on a Shiite mosque that killed at least 31 people. These attacks challenge the Taliban leadership's claims to have eliminated opposed terror groups like ISIS-K, offered full protection to minorities and claimed groups like ISIS-K do not pose a serious threat. While their claims have by now clearly been proven wrong, there is little denying that the continuing success of ISIS-K is directly tied to the Taliban regime for several reasons. First, some hardliner groups within the Taliban–including the Haqqanis, who control the Ministry of Interior responsible for tackling such threats and whose ties with the ISIS-K go back to their joint attacks on the US-NATO-Afghan forces–are reluctant to take effective tough action against the terror group. It was the same internal division with ISIS-K that led the Taliban, despite their apparent ideological rivalry with the group, to release several hundred ISIS-K fighters after their August takeover, allowing the organization to increase its numbers to 4,000, according to a February 2022 estimate by the UN, from 2,000 previously. This has allowed the ISIS-K to operate freely inside Afghanistan, giving it the leeway to establish cells in almost all of Afghanistan's provinces".[16]

Chapter 2

Military and Political Confrontations between Taliban and the IS-K in Afghanistan

There is a general perception that as extremist and sectarian groups have already used some dangerous gases in Iraq, Afghanistan and Syria, on that account, they could use biological weapons against civilian populations in Europe. If control over these weapons is weak, or if their components are available in open market, terrorists can inflict huge fatalities on the region. Experts recently warned that the availability of such materials in open markets of some European states can fall into the hands of local terrorist organisations, which may further jeopardise the security of the region. Two Brussels based nuclear power plant workers had joined ISIS, leading to fears that jihadists had the intelligence to cause a meltdown disaster. The gravest danger arised from the access of extremist and terror groups to the state-owned nuclear, biological and chemical weapons of Iraq and Syria. Counterterrorism expert Olivier Guitta told The Times that the threat of improvised chemical bombs was also increasing. Extremist infrastructure, widespread networks of militant groups and poor governance have put the national security of the country in danger. A Taliban victory in Afghanistan in August 2021 diverted attention of young Afghans from various colleges and schools to the business of dying in order to kill. The Urdu-medium public schools of Pakistan that serve more than 70 percent of the poorer students played a vital role in their radicalisation. In Southern Punjab, majority of students in these schools come from poor families. The madrasa culture in Pakistan has created tensions between Muslims and the followers of other religions. Experts and analysts, Niamatullah Ibrahimi and Shahram Akbarzadeh in their research paper (Intra-Jihadist Conflict and Cooperation: Islamic State–Khorasan Province and the Taliban in Afghanistan, Studies in Conflict and Terrorism) has raised the question of Taliban and the IS-K relationship and their operational mechanism:

"Since it formally announced its establishment in January 2015, the Islamic State–Khorasan Province (IS-K) has maintained a contradictory relationship with the Taliban in Afghanistan. As an off-shoot of the Islamic State of Iraq and Syria (ISIS), IS-K has been competing with the Taliban in mobilizing and claiming ownership of material and symbolic resources of jihad, encouraging Taliban fighters to defect and challenging the Taliban's nationally focused strategy of jihad and cooperation with regional powers such as Pakistan. It has also attempted to buttress its position by attracting resources from ISIS and its global supporters. On 4 March 2018, ISIS released a video calling on its supporters to travel to Khorasan if they could not go to Syria and Iraq. As it emerged, IS-K relied on ideological affinity and group solidarity to establish good relations with the Taliban in Afghanistan and the Tehrik-e Taliban Pakistan (TTP). Furthermore, IS-K's transnationalist rhetoric and more explicit sectarian agenda has indirectly benefited the Taliban by posing a threat that is seen as more urgent than the Taliban insurgency by the Afghan government, the United States, and North Atlantic Treaty Organization (NATO) forces and other countries in the region. It has also intensified sectarian dimensions of the conflict by escalating attacks on civilian targets, especially Shi'a Hazara mosques, protests, and cultural and educational centres. Nonetheless, the two groups have also engaged in fierce violent conflicts. The relationship between the Taliban and the IS-K is at the heart of a broader debate on the dynamics of conflict and cooperation between various jihadist groups. What drives conflict and cooperation among jihadist groups? A growing literature has focused on the mechanisms and drivers of intra-jihadist competition and rivalries".[1]

Taliban have failed to control, or defeat the IS-K due to their foreign designed policies. IS-K now controls parts of Nuristan, Kunar and Jalalabad districts. The presence of the terrorist group has increased because majority of its fighters and commanders have shifted from Iraq to Afghanistan. With the Taliban takeover of Afghanistan in August 2021, the IS-K changed its strategy to restart military operations across the country. Some Central Asian terrorist groups have been critical of Taliban's return to power in Afghanistan but they cannot fight against Taliban. While the Taliban are now in power, IS-K argued that its ideology was not being realised, highlighting its failure to enforce the Shariah as soon as it seized power. Their abrupt capture of power raised important questions, including their divide and rule policies and the exponentially growing instability. Moreover, the Indian government was deeply concerned about the militant activities in Kashmir. Lashkar-e-Taiba and Jaish-e-Muhammad were operating there with full power. Expert and analyst, Seth G. Jones in his paper (Center for Preventive Action: Countering a Resurgent Terrorist Threat in Afghanistan, Published on 14 April 2022) viewed the ISIS and its Khorasan ally's future attacks against the United States positions in Afghanistan:

"ISIS-K's size has now doubled in less than a year, increasing from two thousand to roughly four thousand operatives following the release of several thousand prisoners from Bagram Air Base and Pul-e-Charkhi prison outside of Kabul. Up to half of ISIS-K's operatives are foreign fighters. The group is led by Sanaullah Ghafari (also known as Shahab al-Muhajir), an Afghan national. Other ISIS-K leaders include Sultan Aziz Azam, Maulawi Rajab Salahudin, and Aslam Farooqi. In addition, some former members of the Afghan military and Afghanistan's intelligence agency, the National Directorate for Security, have joined ISIS-K because it is the most active opposition group to the Taliban in Afghanistan. Much like al-Qaeda, ISIS-K is unlikely to successfully orchestrate a centrally planned attack in the United States because of improved US homeland security measures, though ISIS-K has been more successful than al-Qaeda in inspiring attacks in the United States. In addition, ISIS-K could conduct attacks against US targets in other countries. In Afghanistan, ISIS-K has already demonstrated an ability to conduct high-profile and complex attacks—including an attack at the Kabul airport on August 27, 2021, which killed more than 180 people. According to one estimate, ISIS-K carried out seventy-six attacks on Taliban forces between September 18 and November 30, 2021, a significant jump from 2020, when it conducted only eight attacks during the entire year".[2]

With the establishment of the IS-K in Jalalabad province of Afghanistan in 2015, six commanders of the Tahrik-e-Taliban Pakistan immediately joined the group. Hafiz Saeed Khan became the top commander of the group, and started terrorist attacks against the Afghan government forces and civilian population in Kunar and Jalalabad provinces. The scoffing is that Afghan parliamentarians, Ministers and military commanders purchased weapons for the IS-K group, lurked its fighters and suicide bombers in their houses and offices, and transported them to the centre-stage. The role of Afghan police was under whelming as well. They all received millions of dollars and appreciation certificates from the US government. The Jalalabad governor, and war criminal Muhammad Gulab Mengal was dancing to the CIA and MI6 tangos by protecting the IS-K fighters in governor house. He financed and armed its leadership. Former spy and Foreign Minister Hanif Atmar purveyed millions of dollars in helicopters to the IS centres in Paktika province to expand the network of the terrorist group. Reporting on the group's early expansion efforts indicated that IS-K, at its height, had controlled eight districts across southern Nangarhar province with the military and financial assistance of war criminals Muhammad Gulab Mengal and Hanif Atmar. Muhammad Gulab Mengal committed war crimes by supporting the IS-K to kill and behead innocent Afghans. Experts and analysts, Amira Jadoon, Abdul Sayed and Andrew Mines in their recent research paper (The Islamic State Threat in Taliban Afghanistan: Tracing the Resurgence of Islamic State Khorasan. The Combating Terrorism Centre at West Point, published in January 2022, Vol 15, ISSUE-1) have reviewed suicide attacks of Islamic State-K and its strength:

"The suicide bombing that struck the Kabul airport in August 2021 not only shocked the world due to the hundreds it left dead or wounded, it also refocused attention on the threat of the Islamic State Khorasan Province (often abbreviated to ISIS-K or ISK). The attack ushered in urgent questions about the implications of the ISK threat on the remainder of U.S. withdrawal efforts, the stability of a Taliban-controlled Afghanistan, and the security of the country's neighbours. While the spectacular nature of the Kabul airport attack led many to view ISK as a renewed threat in the country, warning signs of a resurgent ISK had actually started to permeate in the preceding year. The Taliban's swift takeover of Afghanistan, along with an abysmal collapse of the Afghan government, created new opportunities for ISK to undermine the legitimacy and control of an internationally isolated Taliban. ISK is now present in almost every province of Afghanistan, according to the United Nations, as Taliban forces engage in a deadly counterinsurgency campaign against their jihadi rivals with limited measurable success reported thus far. Understanding the future trajectory of ISK, its rivalry with the Taliban, and the regional security risks it poses requires tracing the adaptation of the group's violent strategies in various periods of its existence: the early period of its emergence, years of intense U.S. and Afghan forces-led military operations, and finally, the period of its intensified battle with the Taliban after the U.S. withdrawal".[3]

As mentioned earlier, the relationship between the Taliban and the IS-K has been both friendly and hostile and there have been clashes between the two groups in major Afghan provinces. Taliban were inculcated by both US army and unity-government not to attack the IS-K positions. They were equally receiving money and weapons from the US army through different stakeholders like war criminals Muhammad Gulab Mengal and former Foreign Minister Muhammad Hanif Atmar. On 30 November 2915, Alim Latifi and Mohammad Harun Arsalai reported accusations of Zahir Qadeer against Mohammad Hanif Atmar to Los Angeles Times: "Qadir said Ghani's National Security Advisor, Mohammad Hanif Atmar was responsible for the increased Islamic State profile in Afghanistan. "This is all Atmar's game," he noted the foreign presence in Afghanistan. Though Qadir's accusations against Atmar were likely to ruffle feathers in Kabul, he was not the first high-profile Afghan official to accuse the National Security Council, headed by Hanif Atmar, of aiding and abetting the enemy. However, Abdul Karim Matin, then governor of the Eastern Province of Paktika, accused former Foreign Minister Mohammad Hanif Atmar and his office of providing $200,000 in monetary assistance to families in Barmal district who he said were allied with Islamic State. The Newspaper noted. The relationship between the two terrorist groups have been living under different phases, but the IS-K group didn't want to accept the terms of the Taliban to stop war against Afghan civilians and keep its forces to a specific region, but the IS-K never agreed with that proposals. Experts and analysts, Niamatullah Ibrahimi and Shahram Akbarzadeh in their research paper (Intra-Jihadist Conflict and Cooperation: Islamic State–Khorasan Province and the Taliban in Afghanistan, Studies in Conflict and Terrorism) have reviewed fighting and peace negotiation between the IS-K and Taliban. They also argued that the IS-K experienced major setbacks as a result of fighting with the Taliban and air and ground offensives by Afghan and U.S. military forces:

"Many underestimated ISIS's capacity to establish roots in the already crowded jihadi scene of Afghanistan and Pakistan. A central reason for why ISIS was underestimated was its perceived foreign origin, which many presumed restricted its access to local jihadist resources. Because of ISIS's perceived lack of local connections, McNally et al. argued that Afghanistan was "not a natural expansion for IS." Furthermore, the IS-K faced the Taliban, the dominant ideological and military actor in the jihadist landscape of the region. As a new player in the jihadi landscape of Pakistan and Afghanistan region, the IS-K sought to challenge the Taliban ownership of the symbolic and material resources of jihad. As the RMT approach would suggest, IS-K appealed to the broader supporters of the jihadist movement by seeking to distinguish itself as an authentic, transnational, and ideologically non-compromising group and criticizing the TTP, the Taliban in Afghanistan, and Al Qaeda for colluding with the incumbent governments. For example, in an interview with the organization's Dabiq magazine, Hafiz Saeed Khan, the first governor of IS-K, criticized the Taliban, the TTP, and Al Qaeda for working with the Pakistani intelligence agency, mixing religion with tribal traditions, and allowing and even participating in the opium and heroin economy. Attacking the Taliban as a "nationalist movement" he said, "Rather, they rule by tribal customs and judge affairs in accordance with the desires and traditions of the people, traditions opposing the Islamic Shari'ah."[4]

In 2014, Russian Television (RT) aired an interview of Wikileaks founder, Julian Assange with a UK based Australian journalist, John Pilger. Assange uncovered important facts about the wealthy officials from Saudi Arabia and Qatar donating money to the Hillary Clinton's Foundation and Islamic State (IS) respectively. On 17 August 2014, Assange made public an email in which Hillary Clinton had urged the then advisor to US President Barak Obama, Mr. John Podesta, to pressure Qatar and Saudi Arabia for funding Islamic State (IS). These revelations sparked wide-ranging debates in print and electronic media across the globe, which affected relations of the Qatar and Saudi governments with the Gulf and South Asian states. It is alleged that Saudi financial assistance to extremist organisations prompted unprecedented civil wars, devastation, torture and displacement of millions Muslims in Middle East, South Asia, and Gulf regions. Similar rumours were at spin regarding the militant Islamic group Daesh. There were different opinions about the strength and area of Daesh's influence, but recent events proved that Daesh was more powerful than the Taliban terrorist groups. In January 2015, Islamic State (IS) announced the formation of another terrorist group named Islamic State of Khorasan (ISKP), which represented a Salafi school of thought and allegedly received financial assistance from US, NATO allies. Expert Salman Rafi Sheikh in his article (Why the Taliban won't tackle ISIS-K: Afghanistan's new rulers know if they seriously crack down on the terror group their new government could collapse overnight-Asia Times, published on October 21, 2021) has raised the question of Taliban failure to tackle the ISIS-K in Afghanistan:

"While the Taliban struggles to consolidate its power two months after toppling Kabul, the rival Islamic State-Khorasan (ISIS-K) militant group represents a rising and potentially existential threat to its rule. The militant group world-renowned for its own terror tactics is now on the receiving end of rising terror attacks. On October 16, ISIS-K took responsibility for an attack on a Shiite mosque in Kandahar that killed at least 60 people and injured scores more. The attack came just a week after ISIS-K claimed another attack on another Shiite mosque on October 8 in the northern city of Kunduz that killed more than 50 and injured over 140. During the first four months of 2021, the UN Assistance Mission in Afghanistan recorded 77 ISIS-K attacks, an assault record that shows the terror outfit is neither "weak" nor "defeated", as some analysts have claimed in recent weeks. The recent wave of ISIS-K attacks on Shiite targets, including lethal hits on the Hazara community, aims to exploit Afghanistan's delicate sectarian fault lines under a Taliban regime that is baldly ethnically exclusive and dominated by Sunni Pashtuns. The attacks also aim to weaken the Taliban's hold on power by casting doubts on the militant group's ability to govern and provide the economic and social security it has promised since seizing power in August. By pushing the Taliban into a new low-intensity fight, ISIS-K seeks to prevent the group from permanently consolidating its hold".[5]

A number of Afghan parliamentarians from the Kunduz province accused the government and its armed forces for supporting terrorist organisations like IS-K and Taliban. They alleged that military commanders were providing arms, financial assistance and sanctuaries to terrorists, and transported their suicide bombers to their destinations. These were some of the most disturbing accusations in Afghan history at the floor of parliament. The MPs also accused the Afghan National Army commanders for handing over dozens of check posts along with sophisticated arms to the Taliban. An MP from the Kunduz province, Miss Fatima Aziz said that Defence and Interior affairs Ministries failed to maintain security and law and order in the country. She also accused police commanders for facilitating Taliban against ANA positions. Expert and analyst, Scott Lucas in his article (ISIS-K violence could force the West into alliance with Taliban: The August 26 attack reconfigured the Afghan mosaic, pushing the US and other countries to recalculate their approach, published in Asia Times, on 01 September 2021) noted that the IS-K terrorist attacks might force the West into alliance with Taliban:

"Islamic State's lightning advance across Iraq and Syria in 2014, and its declaration of a "caliphate," spawned affiliates. These groups promoted the ideological line of, and received assistance from, the core of ISIS – but developed from local conditions. One was ISIS-K, established in January 2015 and naming itself after "Khorasan," part of an Islamic empire that stretched from Iran to the western Himalayas from the 6th century. The group consists of local militants and former Afghan and Pakistani Taliban, pushing an even more radical ideology and implementation, as well as some former al-Qaeda members. Spanning the Afghan-Pakistan border, ISIS-

K's centre is in eastern Afghanistan, in Nangarhar and Kunar provinces. While the Taliban sought to take control of Afghanistan, through military operations and then political talks, ISIS-K has sought to recruit members by generating publicity through deadly attacks on civilian targets. Their targets have included protest rallies, schools providing education for girls, and a Kabul maternity ward. Afghan security forces and US aerial operations including the "mother of all bombs" in April 2017, crippled ISIS-K. And beyond Afghanistan, the US killing of Islamic State leader Abu Bakr al-Baghdadi in northern Syria in October 2019 was a further blow. By 2020, ISIS-K's estimated membership was reduced to between 1,500 and 2,200. But a new commander, Shahab al-Muhajir, energized the group with operations such as an August 2020 attack on a prison in Jalalabad, some 100 kilometres west of Kabul, which freed hundreds of fighters. There was also as an assassination attempt on Vice-president Amrullah Saleh, which left 10 people dead".[6]

The Afghan opposition perceived persisting disagreement between the former government, and poor leadership for the reason that the Kunduz city fell to the Taliban. Moreover, prominent military analyst, Javed Kohistani, hammered the Afghan National Army for selling weapons to the Taliban. "We have evidence that proves there are people inside the security forces that sell weapons and checkpoints to the Taliban and let their fellow colleagues being arrested by insurgents. There is the type of betrayal that exists among the security forces, especially the local police," said Kohistani. Other MPs also levelled the same accusations against ANA commanders and local administration. "Lack of a coherent strategy in the Kunduz province and corruption are the bigger challenges [there]," said Mirdad Nijrabi, head of the internal security committee in parliament. The Governor of the Kunduz province, Assadullah Omar Khel, slammed Vice Chief of Army Staff, General Murad Ali for the collapse of the city. "I asked that first, we should clear the entire city, but General Murad did not accept my suggestions and acted according to his own plan… In these attacks the people of Kunduz suffered a lot," said the Governor. However, the chief of the Afghan intelligence agency, NDS, apologised for his failure to counter Taliban insurgents. Muhammad Masoom Stanekzai acknowledged that the government failed to intercept the Taliban outside the Kunduz city. In 2016, amid this dirty warfare, the Taliban introduced new strategies of war by controlling districts and provinces without fighting against the Afghan security forces. Expert and analyst David Fox in his article (Kabul Airport Islamic State bombers kill dozens: Taliban denounce jihadist rival group's attack; Biden vows vengeance; UN Security Council to meet) has documented attacks of the ISIS on Kabul airport:

"Islamic State suicide bombers, attacking crowds of people gathered Thursday outside Kabul airport hoping to flee Taliban-controlled Afghanistan, killed dozens including 13 US troops. US President Joe Biden vowed to hunt down those responsible. The Islamic State group claimed responsibility for the attack, which added more urgency and heartbreak to the frantic US-led campaign to airlift people out of Afghanistan now that the hard-line Islamist group has seized power. The airport blasts came as the August 31 deadline looms for the United States to withdraw its troops, and for it and other Western countries to end a massive airlift that has already evacuated nearly 100,000 people. With the crisis in Afghanistan rocking his presidency, a clearly shaken Biden went before TV cameras to address the American people after the worst single-day death toll for the US military in Afghanistan since 2011. He said the US soldiers who died in the airport blasts were heroes, and vowed to catch those behind the attack. "We will not forgive. We will not forget. We will hunt you down and make you pay," he said. Biden said the evacuation effort would proceed and end on schedule at the end of the month. Asked by a reporter if he bore any responsibility for the death of the US service members killed, Biden said: "I bear responsibility fundamentally for all that's happened of late."[7]

The Taliban militia failed to restore the confidence of the civilian population and manage law and order. The Attack on Mazar-e-Sharif Mosque sparked reactions. The Si-Dukan Mosque was rocked by a blast that left dozens of worshipers dead and wounded. Former President Hamid Karzai in a tweet condemned that attack in strongest terms. However, ABC News (Children among victims of blast at entrance of school in Kabul, Afghanistan: No one has immediately claimed responsibility for Tuesday's attack. Somayeh Malekian, published on 19 April 2022) reported the killing of schoolchildren in a series of deadly blasts in Afghan capital Kabul. The UN Mission condemned the "heinous" attack in a tweet that said, "Those responsible for the crime targeting schools and children must be brought to justice." Moreover, on 22 April 2022, Asharq Al Aausat in its report (Who Is Slaughtering the Hazaras of Afghanistan? Asharq Al Awsat, Camelia Entekhabifard. Editor-in-chief of the Independent Persian, published on 22 April, 2022) accused the Haqqani terrorist group behind suicide attacks in Afghanistan:

"When the United States gave up Afghanistan to Taliban, Haqqanis entered the government and Sirajuddin Haqqani, a terrorist fugitive wanted by the FBI, was put in charge of the interior ministry. This is a man for whom a 10 million dollar reward had been set...Those who worked for the previous Afghan government are being murdered and massacred. Targeted bombings come one after the other. The US-Taliban agreement has meant only death, hunger and displacement for the Afghan nation. Popular resistance continues in Panjshir, Andarab, Mazar Sharif, Khost and Kabul. But so does the repression by the Taliban. But massacring the Hazaras of Afghanistan in a targeted suicide operation can be part of the strategy by Taliban to gain the attention of the international community.... The only weapon it has is to victimize itself, exaggerate the presence of terrorist groups in Afghanistan and use the name of ISIS to create terror amongst the Westerners. Taliban has now created an imaginary group (which, in reality, consists of suicide bombers trained by themselves) which it introduces as ISIS so as to not take responsibility for murdering of innocent people. Meanwhile, during a trip to Turkey, Taliban's foreign minister claimed that ISIS's reach was exaggerated and the terrorist group had no base in Afghanistan. The suicide bombers are a death brigade for Sirajuddin Haqqani. This is why, last fall, he went to see the family of suicide bombers (martyrs, as Taliban calls them) in Kabul's Hotel Intercontinental. He praised the families of 1,500 suicide bombers in Afghanistan and dedicated a monthly salary for them. For the first time, Haqqani openly admitted to Taliban running suicide bombers and called them "heroes of the homeland."[8]

The Haqqani terrorist organization played a crucial role in the destabilization process of Afghanistan, killed thousands in its suicide attacks and kidnapped young boys to recruit for suicide terrorism. Now Haqqani terrorist group controls Afghanistan and directs Afghan security policy. Mullah Sirajuddin Haqqani has become Interior Minister of Afghanistan to transform the Taliban from an insurgency to a government and control the approximately 10,000 Jihadis linked to the Taliban and Al-Qaeda. European Foundation for South Asian Studies (EFSAS), Amsterdam in its article-No. 2. (The Haqqani Network: A brief profile, February 2022) noted: "While it is anticipated that the rise of the Haqqani's opens the gates for al-Qaeda to re-establish itself in Afghanistan (Raghavan, 2021), Taliban enemies will also be looking to develop their capabilities and reconstituting in war-ridden Afghanistan. The Afghan branch of the Islamic State (IS-K) has an interest in using the political turmoil in the country to add new members to their core group of 1,500 to 2,200 fighters (UNSC, 2021). While the IS-K is assessed to be the 'mortal enemy' of the Taliban by Pentagon Officials, the Afghan Ministry of Defense has claimed that at least one attack for which IS-K has asserted responsibility was in fact carried out by the Haqqani network (Doxsee et al., 2021; Ibrahimi & Akbarzadeh, 2020). Claims of collaboration between IS-K and the Haqqani network have been refuted by experts in the field (Clarke & Sayed, 2021). However, limited local coordination has allegedly taken place on some occasions (Ibrahimi & Akbarzadeh, 2020). Additionally, the appointment of Shahbab al-Muhajir, an alleged former mid-level commander in the Haqqani network, as ISK's new Emir in June 2020 has fueled suspicion about the extent of local intra-jihadist cooperation (Doxsee et al., 2021). Other experts have stressed that "the Haqqanis have the deepest links with IS-K of any faction within the Taliban" (Farrell et al., 2019)".[9]

The Taliban were treating Afghan citizens like animals. They tortured, killed and kidnapped women and girls, and looted their houses. They were mostly illiterate and didn't favour education, schools and universities. Their relationship with Al Qaeda, Islamic State of Khorasan, Al Nusra, Lashkar-e-Taiba, Jaish-e-Muhammad, Islamic Movement of Uzbekistan, Katibat Imam Bukhari and Tablighi Jamaat characterised and portrayed their organization as the most lethal terrorist group. As the state and government collapsed in Afghanistan, every terrorist organization was trying to establish its own network in the country. Taliban control of Afghanistan was weak and unable to establish basic services. Harold Brown Chair and Director, Transnational Threats Project, Centre for Strategic and International Studies, Seth G. Jones in his research paper (Countering a Resurgent Terrorist Threat in Afghanistan. Centre for Preventive Action, Council on Foreign Relations, published on 12 April 2022) highlighted activities of some terrorist organizations in Afghanistan:

"Afghanistan is different from any other country where al-Qaeda operates because the group enjoys a sympathetic regime with the Taliban. Al-Qaeda leaders have a particularly close historical relationship with some Taliban leaders—such as Sirajuddin Haqqani, the Taliban interior minister and a U.S.-designated terrorist. Haqqani's government position is roughly equivalent to the combined jobs of the director of the FBI and secretary of Homeland Security, giving him enormous power in Afghanistan and making him a serious threat to the United States. ISIS-K's size has now doubled in less than a year, increasing from two thousand to roughly four thousand operatives following the release of several thousand prisoners from Bagram Air Base and Pul-e-Charkhi prison outside of Kabul. Up to half of ISIS-K's operatives are foreign fighters. The group is led by Sanaullah Ghafari (also known as Shahab al-Muhajir), an Afghan national.

Other ISIS-K leaders include Sultan Aziz Azam, Maulawi Rajab Salahudin, and Aslam Farooqi. In addition, some former members of the Afghan military and Afghanistan's intelligence agency, the National Directorate for Security, have joined ISIS-K because it is the most active opposition group to the Taliban in Afghanistan….. In addition to al-Qaeda and ISIS-K, other regional and international terrorist groups now operate in Afghanistan. These include the Tehreek-e-Taliban Pakistan, Eastern Turkistan Islamic Movement, Islamic Jihad Group, Khatiba Imam al-Bukhari, and Islamic Movement of Uzbekistan."[10]

The IS-K conducted multiple attacks inside Kabul including the attack on the police academy and killed hundreds of ANA soldiers and officers, but the Taliban government did not dare to condemn these attacks. However, despite all the progress made during the 22 years of the war on terror, the country is still in turmoil. The Taliban artificial state was weak, corrupt and fragile, facing huge political, economic and security challenges. The country was being run by terror mafia groups that maintained criminal trade and economy, created problems for neighbours, trained terrorists and promoted the business of killings and kidnapping for ransom. Analyst, Joshua T. White in his article (Nonstate threats in the Taliban's Afghanistan, published on 01 February, 2022) has noted risks of terrorist attacks in Afghanistan: "The first risk is that the Islamic State Khorasan (ISK), which has had an openly adversarial relationship with the Taliban, takes advantage of the new government's weakness and preoccupations to bolster its own recruiting, fundraising, and territorial control within Afghanistan; and that its pressure on the government makes the Taliban leadership less likely to offer concessions to domestic or foreign critics. ISK, the Afghanistan affiliate of the larger Islamic State group, emerged in 2015 and established a main base of operations in the country's mountainous eastern regions. Salafi in outlook, it is militantly anti-Shia and rejected both the Pakistani government and the Western-backed Afghan government as apostate regimes that ought to be overthrown and replaced. The second risk is that a Haqqani-dominated Taliban government in Kabul, with few reputational incentives to constrain the activities of al-Qaida or Pakistan-aligned militant organizations such as Lashkar-e-Taiba (LeT) and Jaish-e-Mohammad (JeM), will allow these groups increased freedom to use Afghanistan for logistics, recruiting, and planning, and to reduce their dependencies on Pakistan".[11]

Taliban kidnapped, abused and tortured transgender, gay and lesbian and then killed them. Some women felt heightened risk because of both gender and ethnicity and religion. Human Rights Watch (HRW) in its recent report (Afghanistan: Taliban Deprive Women of Livelihoods, Identity: Severe Restrictions, Harassment, Fear in Ghazni Province, published on 18 January, 2022) noted intimidation of villagers by Taliban fighters: "Taliban authorities have also used intimidation to extract money, food, and services. "When the Taliban visit a village, they force the households to feed them and collect food items from people," a woman from a village said. "The Taliban and their fighters call us in the middle of the night to cure and give special treatment to their patients and families," a health worker said. "They enter the hospital with their guns, it's difficult for the doctors and nurses to manage." HRW noted. Following the US and NATO withdrawal from Afghanistan, more than 3,000 Hazara Muslims were tortured and forcibly evicted from their homes. As mentioned earlier, Taliban and the IS-K terrorist organizations have been killing Hazara Muslims in all provinces of Afghanistan since 1990s, are destroying their houses and kidnap their women and girls for sexual exploitation.

After the 9/11 terrorist attacks in the United States, the Hazara Muslim experienced further harassment and intimidation. Successive Afghan governments failed to protect their agricultural land, houses and children. Taliban have targeted women journalists-intimidating and harassing in their workplaces. Some women journalists were incarcerated, tortured and threatened of dire consequences. Their intelligence department intercepted their communication and spying on their homes. Writer Alice Speri has highlighted their challenges and difficulties in her article (Women and journalists are targeted of violence in Taliban-ruled Afghanistan, The Intercept, published on 14 April 2022): "Journalists and women, particularly those participating in or covering demonstrations in opposition to Taliban rule, have been increasingly targeted, as have members of the former government and security forces. But Taliban infighting, clashes between the Taliban and the Islamic State, and incidents involving half a dozen anti-Taliban armed groups that have emerged or regrouped in recent months are also increasing, raising the prospect of escalating political violence in the months ahead. The data was compiled by the Armed Conflict Location & Event Data Project, or ACLED, in partnership with Afghan Peace Watch, an Afghan-run violence monitoring group. The analysis underscores the growing challenge of monitoring reports of political violence at a time when more than 300 Afghan news outlets have shut down, and while many of those that continue to operate have been forced to adapt to Taliban censorship or face significant threats to their staff's safety".[12]

Taliban's way of governance has taken place under the conditions of civil war. They have adopted culture of violence, torture and jihad against education of Afghan girls. They haven't relinquished the culture of terrorising civilians. How the Taliban seized power in Kabul was a major question. Contexts of civil war and state weakness were often characterized by situations of governance by terror actors. The failure of Taliban intelligence to provide reliable information about ISIS's military strength has raised serious questions about the credibility of their misgovernment, but they know everything about the IS-K. Taliban have deployed suicide units to defend their government, but without a professionally trained army, suicide bombers cannot defend a state and a government. Broadcast journalist, Mrityunjoy Kumar Jha (Taliban deploy fresh unit of suicide bombers to take on Pakistani forces on Durand Line, published on 25 February 2022) has noted effectiveness and operational mechanism of Taliban suicide units in Afghanistan:

"According to the Taliban's Interior Ministry, these special units are also being deployed on the Central Asian Borders following the tension in the region because of the "fights" between Russia and Ukraine to "maintain" stability. Interestingly two days ago, the elusive Interior Minister of the Taliban regime and chief of the UN-designated terrorist organisation Haqqani Network had announced in a madrasa in Kandahar that another 1500 suicide bombers were being inducted in the Taliban army. "Our struggle for the last 20 years was for establishing the Islamic govt. There have not been as many martyrdom operations (suicide attacks) in history as we did," said Haqqani, the self-acclaimed expert who introduced "suicide bombers" in the Taliban's "war" strategy. As usual, the video clips of Haqqani addressing the gathering did not show the face of the elusive most wanted terrorist who is carrying a bounty of $10 million on his head. Addressing his squad of "suicide bombers" Haqqani said that so far his trained bombers had carried out 1,050 attacks alone and achieved martyrdom."[13] The father of suicide terrorism in Afghanistan, Sirajuddin Haqqani alias Khalifa, was born in December 1979. He has been the deputy leader of the Islamic Emirate of Afghanistan since 2016. Sirajuddin Haqqani is the son of Commander Jalaluddin Haqqani, associated with Maulvi Yunus Khalis Group during the Afghan war in 1980s. Taliban Interior Minister, Sirajudding Haqqani is presently wanted by American FBI, with the US State Department offering reward of $10 million for information about his location but US intelligence agencies, Pentagon and government are currently working with their designated terrorists shamelessly. Analyst and expert, Mahir Hazim in his article (An Urgent Need for Justice: Expediting the International Criminal Court's Afghanistan Investigation: Given the Taliban's atrocities, past and present, there's an urgent need for the ICC to move more quickly in the pursuit of justice. The Diplomat, published on 09 February 2022) argued that there is an urgent need for justice to punish Taliban for their atrocities:

"After retaking control of Afghanistan on 15 August, 2021, the Taliban, one of the main perpetrators of past major atrocities in Afghanistan, allegedly continue to commit war crimes and crimes against humanity. With the legitimate Afghan government gone, it is the time for the International Criminal Court (ICC), as the only available international body with jurisdiction over the alleged crimes, to act swiftly and responsibly and make a difference by expediting its intervention in Afghanistan. The Taliban and its affiliate terrorist groups such as the Haqqani Network have been accused of committing heinous war crimes and crimes against humanity over the last 20 years. They have indiscriminately targeted civilians, causing some of the most tragic events in Afghanistan. Besides international forces and the former government's national security forces, the Taliban has been accused of carrying out major war crimes and crimes against humanity prior to taking control of the country. According to a decision of the ICC"s Pre-Trial Chamber-II, some examples of the Taliban's alleged crimes against humanity include "the crimes of murder, imprisonment or other severe deprivation of physical liberty and persecution on political and gender grounds." The ICC also lists a number of war crimes that were committed by the Taliban, such as "intentionally directing attacks against the civilian population, humanitarian personnel and protected objects; conscripting or enlisting children under the age of 15 years or using them to participate actively in hostilities; and killing or wounding treacherously a combatant adversary."[14]

The war in Syria, Iraq and Afghanistan, humanitarian crisis in the region and the weakening of state structure have created many problems like the invasion of refugees and infiltration of extremist and terrorist forces into the region. The EU may further face a deteriorating security environment and an unprecedented level of threat, while Brexit has made the security of the project complex. The threat of nuclear terrorism and the use of dirty bomb by terrorist organisations in Britain and Europe cannot be ruled out as these groups have established close relationships with some disgruntled elements within government circles. They have established strong contacts with foreign embassies and terrorist organisations across the borders. The threat is very real, but some irresponsible states do not realise the sensitivity of the situation. The changing nature of the threat and the dramatic rise of ISIS is a matter of great concern for major nuclear powers in Europe. Terrorists could attack or sabotage nuclear facilities, such as commercial nuclear power plants or research reactors, to cause a release of radioactive elements. On April 1, 2016, The Telegraph reported that the British Prime Minister had warned that ISIS was planning to use drones to spray nuclear materials over Western cities. A British official told newspapers that world leaders already fear that ISIS was trying to get nuclear, chemical and biological weapons to use against civilians and nuclear installation in Europe. Expert and analyst, Marco Nilsson in his research paper (Motivations for Jihad and Cognitive Dissonance–A Qualitative Analysis of Former Swedish Jihadists, Studies in Conflict & Terrorism, Volume 45, 2022 - Issue 1, published on 18 June 2019) spotlighted how Muslims in the west become foreign fighters in the battlefield of jihad:

"Scholars have sought to understand why some Muslims in the West become foreign fighters in the battlefields of global jihad in, for example, Syria, or become terrorists in their homelands. So far, however, we know quite little about Islamic radicalization in the West. In an effort to avoid a static view, some scholars have described it as a long process rather than an incident limited in time. It has been labelled a staircase, a pyramid, and even a conveyor belt. However, the results of various studies have often been conflicting. For example, the impact of educational success, economic resources, prior criminality, and family responsibilities on radicalization is unclear. While research has failed to establish a typical profile of a violent radical, two approaches with quite opposite explanatory models have become the centre of the debate. Kepel looks for answers in the sociology of the socioeconomically disadvantaged suburbs and the spreading of fundamentalist Islam, especially Salafism. To him, the source of violence lies in the radicalization of Islam, that is, in an Islamic community where fundamentalist ideas abound. Roy argues instead that violent Islamic radicalization should be understood as the Islamization of radicalism. From this perspective, the problem is not Salafism itself, but rather young people who embrace jihadist ideas because they are violent nihilists. Many recruits have previously expressed this radical revolt against society with criminality, and Islam and ideology have become a mere cover to legitimize violence. Radicalization is often a social process affected by group dynamics such as kinship, friendship, and even the increased status that can be gained by joining a jihadist group. Moreover, second-generation Muslim immigrants may sometimes experience tensions between their western identity and inherited ethnic or religious identity".[15]

Why Muslims becoming radicalized in Europe and the United States, harbouring Wahhabist culture of terrorism and recruiting young generation for future war. In Europe and in the west they feel secure and understand that they are free to do everything-challenge authority of the state and government and declare jihad on local population. Over the past four decades, we have experienced growing trend in jihadism, radicalization and extremism in all but every EU member state where Christian covers and Muslim converts have established extremist groups in towns and cities. In February 2015, the EU council member states agreed on the fight against terrorism upon three pillars; security of the citizens, preventing radicalization and safeguarding value, and better cooperation among all member states. The issue of free movement across the EU has become a matter of great concern when terrorists availed this opportunity, reaching France and Germany and killed hundreds of innocent civilians. During the last four decades, there were some legal developments in the United Kingdom dealing with terrorism and radicalization. In October 2010, the government published the National Security Strategy, which identifies terrorism, and in July 2011, the contest strategy was also published due to the increase in terrorist incidents, and some developments in Asia and Africa. Expert and analyst, Marco Nilsson in his research paper (Motivations for Jihad and Cognitive Dissonance – A Qualitative Analysis of Former Swedish Jihadists, Studies in Conflict & Terrorism. Volume 45, 2022 - Issue 1, published on 18 June 2019) spotlighted how Muslims in the west become foreign fighters in the battlefield of jihad:

"Scholars have sought to understand why some Muslims in the West become foreign fighters in the battlefields of global jihad in, for example, Syria, or become terrorists in their homelands. So far, however, we know quite little about Islamic radicalization in the West. In an effort to avoid a static view, some scholars have described it as a long process rather than an incident limited in time. It has been labelled a staircase, a pyramid, and even a conveyor belt. However, the results of various studies have often been conflicting. For example, the impact of educational success, economic resources, prior criminality, and family responsibilities on radicalization is unclear. While research has failed to establish a typical profile of a violent radical, two approaches with quite opposite explanatory models have become the centre of the debate. Kepel looks for answers in the sociology of the socioeconomically disadvantaged suburbs and the spreading of fundamentalist Islam, especially Salafism. To him, the source of violence lies in the radicalization of Islam, that is, in an Islamic community where fundamentalist ideas abound. Roy argues instead that violent Islamic radicalization should be understood as the Islamization of radicalism. From this perspective, the problem is not Salafism itself, but rather young people who embrace jihadist ideas because they are violent nihilists. Many recruits have previously expressed this radical revolt against society with criminality, and Islam and ideology have become a mere cover to legitimize violence"[16]

Chapter 3

Suicide Brigades, IS-K Military Strength and Taliban's Misrule in Afghanistan

In January 2022, Taliban announced to put in place a Suicide-Brigade. Before this development, the Taliban acting Interior Minister, Sirajuddin Haqqani and acting Defence Minister Mullah Muhammad Yaqoob hosted a ceremony in Kabul to honour Afghan and Pakistani Suicide Bombers responsible for the killings of thousands of Afghan and Pakistani citizens. Sirajuddin Haqqani, is representing the Haqqani Network-affiliated with the Taliban and al Qaeda. The group has been behind some of the deadliest attacks in the country two-decade-long war, including a truck bomb explosion in Kabul in 2017 that killed more than 150 people. Unlike the wider Taliban, the Haqqani Network has been designated a Foreign Terrorist Organisation by the US. It also maintains close ties to al Qaeda. Haqqani who carries a US bounty of $10m met with the US Chief of counter-terrorism in February 2022 in Kabul to discuss the exponentially growing tension in Afghanistan. Haqqani has been killing Afghan civilians since 2003, and the group's fighters were trained by the Pakistan Army to serve the interests of US and NATO forces in Afghanistan. They used Improvised Explosive Device in suicide attacks, and destroyed critical national infrastructure in the country. The group was based in North Waziristan, Pakistan in yesteryears, while now is part of Taliban government. Adopting strategy of suicide bombing was not an easy task for Haqqanis, but with the support of Pakistan Army, the group recruited thousands of its fighters for suicide terrorism.

Some scholars have asserted that suicide attacks were legitimate and HALAL in Islam, while conversely, majority of Barelvis, Deobandis and Liberal scholars understand that suicide terrorism is strictly prohibited in Islam that cause deaths and catastrophe. Suicide terrorism in Pakistan and Afghanistan have been neglected by Middle Eastern scholars due to their limited information about the military tactics of terrorist groups.

Expert and analyst, Atal Ahmadzai in his paper (Dying to Live: The "Love to Death" Narrative Driving the Taliban's Suicide Bombings) highlighted the Istishhadi narrative of Taliban: "The Taliban in Afghanistan have embraced suicide bombings since 2003. Within a short period of time, the group developed an infamous industry of manufacturing 'human bombs.' They soon became the leading terrorist organization in the world, claiming responsibility for the greatest number of suicide bombings. Two narratives assist the Taliban in supplying their bombing campaigns with large numbers of bombers. First, an Istish-haadi narrative, which is based on authoritative reasoning derived from sacred texts. In addition, the group has resorted to logical fallacy/circular reasoning in producing the desired narrative. This narrative serves as the conceptual foundation for providing moral-legal legitimacy to suicide bombings. However, legitimization does not mean the practicality of these terminal missions, especially in a social and cultural milieu that is dismissive of suicide killing in warfare. To overcome this challenge, the group constructed yet another narrative; "love to death." It is based on an irrational and dystopian interpretation of the mundane existence. It promotes an alternative comprehension of reality that is beyond the premises of time and space, one which does not bear any relation to rationality. Two aspects of these narratives are prominent. First, martyrdom is the central tenet of the Taliban's suicide bombing industry. However, their understanding of martyrdom induced by suicide bombings is different. The decision to choose subjects for these bombings does not reside with the bombers, but rather is bestowed upon them by the divine."[1]

With the establishment of Islamic State (ISIS) in Syria and Iraq, and its secret networks and propaganda campaign in Pakistan and Afghanistan, the international community focused on the proliferation and smuggling of chemical and biological weapons in the region. Recent debate in Europe-based think tanks suggested that, as the group retrieved nuclear and biological material from the Mosul University in Iraq, it can possibly make nuclear explosive devices with less than eight kilograms of plutonium. The debate about bioterrorism and biodefense is not entirely new in the military circles of South Asia; the involvement of ISIS in using biological weapons against the Kurdish Army in Kobane is a lesson for Pakistan and Afghanistan to deeply concentrate on the proliferation of these weapons in the region. A document from Pakistan's Internal Security Policy (2014-2018) categorically stated that the country's security faced the threat of nuclear terrorism. The threat, according to the document's contents, is in addition to the possibility of chemical and biological terrorism. As the fatal war against terrorism has entered a crucial phase, another powerful extremist militant group (IS-K) has emerged with a strong and well-trained army in Afghanistan and parts of Pakistan to establish an Islamic state. The massacre of 100 innocent civilians, including an Afghan national army soldier in the Ajristan district of Ghazni province by IS-K forces, and the brutal killings of children in the Army School in Peshawar have raised serious questions about the future of security and stability in South Asia. The Tehreek-e-Taliban Pakistan (TTP) claimed responsibility and called it a revenge attack for the Pakistan Army's Operation Zarb-e-Azb in North Waziristan and erstwhile FATA regions. Research Scholars Amira Jadoon, Andrew Mines and Abdul Sayed in their research paper (The evolving Taliban-ISK rivalry, published on 07 September 2021, The Interpreter) have reviewed the IS-K attacks on Kabul airport:

"The attack on evacuation efforts at the Kabul airport by the Islamic State-Khorasan Province (ISK, ISKP, or ISIS-K) triggered much speculation about the Afghan Taliban's ability to constrain terrorism in the country. But it also served as a reminder of the intense rivalry between the Taliban and ISK; while the attack's lethality shocked many, the two organisations have engaged in intense clashes as militant organisations since ISK's emergence in 2015. However, as the Afghan Taliban now transition into a legitimate political entity, the nature of their clashes is likely to change as ISK will tackle the Afghan Taliban as more of a state actor–whose credibility can be undermined domestically and internationally. In order to understand this new phase of the Taliban-ISK rivalry, it's important to look forward but also to frame the recent attack by ISK within the context of the original clash between the two groups' ideologies and agendas; there are important lessons from the past that can help us assess how the two groups may compete for dominance in Afghanistan, and the associated security implications".[2]

The Looting and ransacking of Afghanistan's natural resources by NATO and the United States, and their criminal militias; suchlike the ISIS and Taliban terrorist groups, caused misunderstanding between the Afghans and International Coalition that they all were involved in looting of mineral resources of their country. The IS-K controls a large amount of territory in Afghanistan, and that includes parts of the country's rich mineral wealth, especially talc, chromite and marble. According to the Global Witness research report, several insurgents' groups, militias, Taliban and the ISIS are deeply involved in the plunder of these resources: "The Islamic State in Afghanistan (ISKP) controls major mining sites in eastern Afghanistan and has a strategic interest in the country's rich mineral resources, new

Global Witness research shows–a powerful example of the wider threat posed by armed groups and corrupt actors in Afghan mining. The Islamic State in Afghanistan (ISKP) controls large talc, marble and chromite mines in the Islamic State stronghold of Achin district in the Nangarhar province of eastern Afghanistan–the same area where in April 2017 the US military dropped the 'Mother of All Bombs' against ISKP-held caves. Nangarhar was the deadliest Afghan province for US troops in 2017. An estimated 380,000 tons of talc was imported into the United States in 2017. On average around 35% of US imports are from Pakistan, according to the US Geological Survey. From our research we also estimated that around 80% of Pakistan's 2016 exports of talc actually originated in Afghanistan. Of those exports, 42% went to the US, and another 36% went to EU countries, especially the Netherlands and Italy".[3]

However, in 2016, Global Witness report (War in the treasury of the people: Afghanistan, lapis lazuli and the battle for mineral wealth) noted the importance of mining, especially of lapis lazuli, for the Taliban in Afghanistan. The report warned that armed groups including the Taliban were earning tens of millions of dollars per year from Afghanistan's lapis mines, the world's main source of the brilliant blue lapis lazuli stone, which is used in jewellery around the world. Moreover, experts and analysts, William A. Byrd and Javed Noorani, in their report (Industrial-Scale Looting of Afghanistan's Mineral Resources, 2017, the United States Institute of Peace) warned that international community and different sectarian, militant and terrorist organization of Pakistan and Afghanistan are looting mineral resources of Afghanistan on an industrial scale: "Based on the evidence from fieldwork and case studies, a different explanation is far more compelling. The post-2001 Afghan government from the time of its formation has been politically penetrated by networks of power holders—actors with their own access to the means of organized armed violence—whose members are involved in, or at least benefiting from, ongoing mineral exploitation. These networks, which had formed and developed during the resistance against the interests of different power holders and funding their political and security expenditures; reductions in one kind of rent may well push the political system to increase rents in other spheres of activity. The high profits that can be relatively easily obtained from mineral looting constitute a strong pull factor attracting interest groups into the mining business. These profits have become progressively more accessible as experience is gained, markets are identified and exploited (for example, lapis in China, and talc in Europe), transport channels open, and business linkages are developed. Such dynamics can result in snowballing of extraction over time, as has occurred in the case of lapis, talc, and apparently chromite, among others".[4]

The presence of the ISIS terrorist group in South East Asian states suchlike Philippines and Indonesia, has generated fear and intimidation. The Philippines has so far controlled ISIS but its recruitment process hasn't halted. In Malaysia, the Eastern Sabah Security Command (ESSCOM) eliminated individuals attempting to create a safe haven in Sabah for Abu Sayyaf members fleeing from the AFP. In Indonesia, national counter terrorism force hasn't achieved their gaol, but trying to dismantle sleeping cells. However, more than 2,000 nationals of South Asian states have joined the ISIS terrorist group in Iraq, Syria and Afghanistan. Citizens of some states have joined Al Nusra terrorist group. These recruitments heighten concerns about the potential threat posed by returnees who may seek to relocate to the region with the fall of ISIL's so-called caliphate. The IS-K was founded in 2015 by the US army to counter Taliban in Afghanistan. Immediately after its establishment, the IS-K launched attacks against Shia communities, state and private institutions, and government targets in major cities across Afghanistan and Pakistan. The IS-K targeted minorities suchlike Hazara and Sikhs, journalists, aid workers, security personnel and government infrastructure.

BBC reported (11 October 2021) the establishment of the Khorasan-K, and its successful attacks in Iraq, Syria and Afghanistan: "Islamic State Khorasan Province - is the regional affiliate of the Islamic State group. It is the most extreme and violent of all the jihadist militant groups in Afghanistan. IS-K was set up in January 2015 at the height of IS's power in Iraq and Syria, before its self-declared caliphate was defeated and dismantled by a US-led coalition. It recruits both Afghan and Pakistani jihadists, especially defecting members of the Afghan Taliban who don't see their own organisation as extreme enough. "Khorasan" refers to a historical region covering parts of modern-day Afghanistan and Pakistan."[1] The power structures, social institutions and local authorities of the Central Asian states are unable to work with radical Islamic groups. The prospect of nuclear terrorism in Central Asia and possibly in Russia, is crystal clear. The risk of a complete nuclear device falling into the hands of terrorists will cause consternation in the region. Nuclear terrorism remains a constant threat to global peace".[5] BBC reported.

Despite initial scepticism about the group's existence from analysts and government officials alike, IS-K is responsible for attacks against civilians in Afghanistan and Pakistan. Wilayat Khorasan, or ISIS-K, intends to secure Afghanistan to legitimize the Islamic State's caliphate across the 'Khorasan Province' including portions of Central Asia, China, Iran, the Indian Subcontinent, and Southeast Asia. In 2014, a Pakistani terrorist Hafiz Saeed Khan became the first leader of the ISIS-K terrorist group, Hafiz Saeed Khan was commander of TTP in Pakistan. He brought Sheikh Maqbool and other individuals to the Khorasan leadership. Expert and analyst, Niels Terpstra (2020) Rebel governance, rebel legitimacy, and external intervention: assessing three phases of Taliban rule in Afghanistan, Small Wars & Insurgencies,31:6, published on 25 May 2020) in her research paper has documented dynamics of Taliban, Mujahideen and rebel governance and legitimacy:

"The dynamics of rebel governance and rebel legitimacy, however, do not exist in isolation from other powerful actors. The actions/responses of the state are relevant to the analysis of rebel legitimacy as well. Powerful external actors may also influence the relations between armed groups and civilians. Much research has been devoted to the effects of external support to rebel groups and the attempts of rebel groups to acquire international legitimacy and/or recognition. In this article I shift the perspective and demonstrate how powerful external actors that support the incumbent government shape (though less directly) the dynamics of rebel governance and rebel legitimacy. The presence of foreign enemy forces is an important source of legitimacy for rebel groups and has remained relatively under-studied in the literature on rebel governance. Rebel legitimacy is a function of present-day events but also of prior armed conflicts and societal tensions. As Schröder and Schmidt observe, 'the most important code of the legitimation of war is its historicity. 'In other words, the 'symbolic meaning of prior wars is re-enacted and reinterpreted in the present, and present violence generates symbolic value to be employed in future confrontations.' It is therefore necessary to study rebel governance and legitimacy from a longitudinal perspective. Whereas current sources of legitimacy, such as service provision and protection, are an important part of the analysis, the legitimizing effect of prior events, and external interventions in particular, require further scrutiny. Omitting historical sources of legitimacy may lead to an incomplete understanding of rebel groups' legitimacy."[6]

The perception that Taliban are ideological fighter is wrong, the reason for that they are acting like terrorist organizations, carrying out suicide attacks against civilians and destroy everything they don't like. They have committed war crimes, beheaded innocent Muslims, kidnapped women and children and used them for sexual exploitation. They are proxies of Pakistan's military establishment, barking for the American Army and ISI equally. They have established suicide brigades, and threatened Afghanistan's neighbours. They have looted natural resources and established units of the Pakistan Army in several provinces of the country. Later on, the Pakistan Air Force targeted Afghan civilians in Panjshir, Khost and Kunar provinces. The Taliban's relationship with al Qaeda and the IS-K further generated fear and consternation. As Afghanistan remained a top destination for foreign terrorist groups, Taliban entered into alliances with different groups. Expert and research scholar, Asfandyar Mir in his recent paper (The IS-K Resurgence, published on 08 October 2021) noted hostilities between Taliban and the IS-K group, and the enmity between the two groups:

"ISIS-K sees the Taliban as an irreconcilable enemy that needs to be militarily defeated. The enmity between the two groups has been aggravated by sustained military hostilities, but the main cause remains their sectarian difference. ISIS-K subscribes to the Jihadi-Salafism ideology—and plays up the 'purity' of its anti-idolatry credentials. The Taliban, on the other hand, subscribe to an alternative Sunni Islamic sectarian school, the Hanafi madhhab, which ISIS-K regards as deficient. The two groups also differ over the role of nationalism. ISIS-K fiercely rejects it, which runs counter to the Afghan Taliban's aims of ruling over Afghanistan. One recurring question is if the Taliban have used ISIS-K as a cover for violence, especially in the lead up to their August takeover. The former Afghan government, for instance, would argue that ISIS-K and the Afghan Taliban—specifically its sub-group the Haqqani Network—were collaborating on violent attacks in cities, but the U.S. government didn't support this assessment. On August 31, President Joe Biden observed that ISIS-K and the Taliban are "sworn enemies." The United Nations has also cast doubt on any major strategic alignment between ISIS-K and the Taliban but suggests the possibility of localized collaboration between elements of the two groups. Some analysts believe that ISIS-K's co-optation with Taliban defectors—specifically from the Haqqani Network—contributes to this conflation".[7]

The growing military and political influence of IS-K in Afghanistan means that the Taliban government and its allies have failed to bring stability to Afghanistan. Ethnic violence has created a hostile environment across the country. The Hazaras are being subjected to violence and torture. Afghans who returned from Pakistan face violence and harassment, and are struggling to survive in their own country, but regional Taliban warlords are not willing to allow them to return to their hometowns. There are more than three million internally displaced Afghans who also face the wrath of Taliban warlords and private militia commanders. At present, IS-K is trying to extend its tentacles to all parts of the Afghan state. The Taliban also do not have armed drones, which are needed for use against al Qaeda and IS-K targets. ISIS in 2014 declared a caliphate in Iraq and in 2015, IS-K was established in Afghanistan. The Asia Pacific Group on Money Laundering and Global Centre on Cooperative Security in its report (Financing and Facilitation of Foreign Terrorist Fighters and Returnees in Southeast Asia," Asia Pacific Group on Money Laundering and Global Centre on Cooperative Security, published in November 2021) has documented some aspects of Foreign Terrorist Finance and operational mechanism of terrorist groups across the globe:

"There is a long-standing desire of some groups in the Southeast Asia region to establish Islamic rule, which may be part of why ISIL targeted Southeast Asia for recruitment. A Bahasa-language video titled Joining the Ranks urged Southeast Asians to travel to Syria, and ISIL's propaganda and social media support networks influenced numerous regional groups and thousands of individuals to pledge support, most notably at a wave of public rallies in 2014. That same year, ISIL established the Katibah Nusantara, a military unit within ISIL for Malay-speaking individuals. The unit sought to address communication challenges between ISIL and its Southeast Asian FTF recruits, many of whom were not fluent in Arabic or English. Katibah Nusantara recruited, united, trained, and mobilized FTF recruits from Southeast Asia. The unit was first led by Indonesian national Bahrum Syah, who traveled to Syria at the age of 29. Bahrum Syah's leadership later faced competition from other prominent Indonesians, including Abu Jandal (also known as Salim Mubarok) and Bahrun Naim. According to some accounts, Katibah Nusantara had as many as 200 members, though other estimates are much lower, closer to 30–40.....Bahrum Syah worked with M. Fachry, together with the support of Omar Bakri Muhammad, to establish the Forum of Islamic Law Activists (FAKSI) in 2013, which became the "engine" of the pro-ISIL network in Indonesia".[8]

Afghan society had to collect its shattered pieces during the last four decades of war without the presence of a legitimate and functioning state, but internal migration, power games and foreign interference washed away its dreams. Civil War has destroyed the state, its institutions, and devastated the economy. The mujahideen in the 1990s did not discriminate between innocents and criminals in the course of fighting in Kabul. From 1992 to 1994, they killed over 60,000 men, women and children in Kabul alone. The rise of the Taliban in 1994 kept the war ignited and they started their business with a new strategy of killing, abduction and humiliation of the innocent citizens of the country. The criminal structure that fuelled the civil war is still in place. Jihadist groups in Afghanistan have played major role in Civil War. Their competition was known due to their mutual differences and power game. Afghan government and its international partners underestimated the power of the IS-K due to its foreign origin and the ISIS perceived lack of local connections. Experts and analysts, Niamatullah Ibrahimi and Shahram Akbarzadeh in their research paper (Intra-Jihadist Conflict and Cooperation: Islamic State–Khorasan Province and the Taliban in Afghanistan, Studies in Conflict & Terrorism) have noted the intra-jihadists conflict and cooperation:

"To the extent that a nationalist/transnationalist distinction holds, the Taliban and ISIS occupy the two different ends of the spectrum in the global jihadist movement. While ISIS is generally recognized for its ambition of dismantling borders and recruiting from across the world, the Taliban is often noted for their nationally focused strategy in Afghanistan. Specifically, IS-K was established to revive the historical region of Khorasan, which besides Afghanistan included parts of Iran, Pakistan, and Central Asia. ISIS and the Taliban are also two of the richest jihadist organizations. Although IS-K remains comparatively small in Afghanistan, ISIS quickly became a dominant actor in the global jihadist industry, accumulating an unprecedented share of material and symbolic resources. In 2016, with an annual budget of US$2 billion, ISIS was the richest jihadist group in the world. With an estimated $800 million annual budget, according to Forbes Magazine, the Taliban ranked one of the richest terrorist organizations in the world. Consequently, the IS-K represented an important shift in Afghanistan's jihadi industry by bringing two of the most resourceful jihadist organizations with two different strategies into a single theatre of conflict. In this section, we will discuss some of the key commonalities and differences of the two groups as members of the jihadist movement industry, before examining how those differences influences their relationship in Afghanistan."[9]

Private mercenaries and foreign funded militias once more reshaped the culture of Civil War in Afghanistan in a modern form, and contributed significantly to the Taliban disputed leadership and misgovernment. They received financial and military support from domestic and international stakeholders to consolidate the form of armed governance, and the collapsed infrastructure of the Afghan State. The past 42 years of conflict and transformation of social fabric have configured the political landscape of Afghanistan, and significantly empowered local war criminals. The collapse of the Afghan state in 1992 and 2021, left a huge political and military vacuum permeated by Mujahidin militias, Taliban, the ISIS and US militias. Afghan politicians and warlords also gained financial and political advantage from the building-up of these inexplicable militias while Interior and Defence Ministries sought to take them under their control. The Taliban return to power brought further destruction and poverty to the country, where Afghan citizens are selling their daughters for food. The US, Europe and Iran that could not defend the values of democracy are now finding themselves in a tight spot as their influence and rules-based world order continues to be questioned by the revisionist trio of China, Russia and Iran.

The fall of Afghanistan to the Taliban generated a news terror threat in South and Central Asia. The Taliban's close relationship with several Pakistani terror groups and its inability to govern the whole country may turn Afghanistan into a nest of terror militias. In Afghanistan, close cooperation between Daesh and some disgruntled Taliban groups added to the pain of the Taliban Government. The Khorasan terrorist group, which emerged with a strong military power in 2015, is in control of important districts in Jalalabad province. The group's military tactics include beheading, public prosecution, kidnapping, and torture, looting and raping, and also forcing families from their homes. Due to the weakness of Taliban and local administration, the IS-K expanded its networks to all districts of Jalalabad. In Kunar, Nuristan and Jalalabad provinces, more than 13 terrorist groups were operating with their strong networks. Some of the groups including Quetta Shura, Tora Bora Jihadi group, Gul Buddin Hekmatyar group, Salafi group, Fidayee Karwan, Sia Pushan groups (identified as black-clad and masked terrorists) were in clandestine collaboration with the Khorasan group, TTP, and Lashkar-e-Islam group. In Mohmand Agency, Jamaat Al Ahrar and TTP were operating in collaboration with ISKP. Expert and analysts, Sushant Sareen in his paper (The ISKP is Nothing but an Exaggerated Threat, Special Report. Of Observer Research Foundation: Afghanistan and the New Global (Dis)Order: Great Game and Uncertain Neighbours, published on December 2021) has documented suicide terrorism of the Islamic State-K in Afghanistan that targeted mosques and religious places of Hazara Muslims:

"After the horrific suicide bombing at the Kabul airport in August 2021, the international spotlight and scrutiny shifted from the Taliban and its close ally al-Qaeda to the shadowy terror group Islamic State Khorasan Province (ISKP). Suddenly, the real problem in Afghanistan was not the capture of that country by the Taliban, but the presence of the ISKP. The Taliban and Pakistan are being presented as the good guys who everyone should help and fund to fight against the ISKP, which is the real threat to global security. With US President Joe Biden calling the ISKP "an archenemy of the Taliban," it seems like a slam dunk for the new narrative that is being manufactured of 'good Taliban' vs 'bad ISKP'. The US military seems to have developed so much faith, trust, and confidence in the Taliban that they even share extremely sensitive information with them. There is now talk of intelligence sharing with the Taliban to target ISKP. Even as the ISKP is being built up as some kind of ISIS on steroids to justify possible cooperation, coordination and even collaboration with the Taliban regime, no one is asking some simple questions: just how dangerous is the ISKP really? Does it have a global or even regional footprint outside the Afghanistan-Pakistan (AfPak) region or is it a local terror group with a very tenuous international affiliation? Is it only using the label of an international terror brand to build its profile? What are its strength and capabilities to carry out big terror attacks outside of AfPak region and destabilise other countries? The data just does not bear out the hype surrounding ISKP".[10]

The full body of Islamic State machine is strong as its radio stations, photographic reports, and bulletins are being circulated in different languages. The Internet is also the source of propaganda of the IS-K groups where experts of the group disseminate controversial information through videos and articles. Moreover, the group challenged the presence of US and NATO forces in Afghanistan. Some members of the Afghan parliament severely criticised the United States and its NATO allies for their support to the Islamic State. They also raised the question of foreign financial support to the terrorist group, and asked the Unity Government to positively respond to the brutalities and atrocities of the IS-K commanders. However, Daesh also spread its evil tentacles to the North to control provinces bordering Russia and China. The group wanted to infiltrate into Chinese Muslim province and parts of Central Asia and challenge the authority of local governments there. The civilian deaths in Afghanistan became a routine as innocent women and girls were kidnapped, raped and tortured in the group's secret prisons in Kunar and Jalalabad provinces. The Islamic State fighters were being facilitated by the corrupt commanders of the Afghan army. They were sheltered, armed and transported by them to their destination. Editor Iain Overton and researchers, Aman Bezreh, Chris Hitchcock, Jacob Berntson, Jen Wilton, Jennifer Dathan, Khalil Dewan,

Leyla Slama, Michael Hart, Shaza Alsalmoni, Sophie Akram and Tim Hulse in their paper (Understanding the Rising Cult of Suicide Bomber. Action on Armed Violence (AOAV) have highlighted some aspects of suicide terrorism in Tunisia and the Arab world:

"Jihadi organisations have been very effective in targeting grievances created by lack of economic opportunities in Tunisia, and have according to the people AOAV has spoken with in areas like Ettadhamen managed to recruit youth by offering them a way out of poverty. Besides the salaries that some organisations pay, joining a jihadi group might also function as revenge against the state which has failed to provide opportunities for its citizens. Moreover, given the traditional antagonism between the Tunisian state and conservative strands of Islam, joining a radical Salafist serves as act of ultimate rebellion. Last but not least, groups like IS also offer recruits a standing in which they enjoy status and a sense of fulfilment, which is the direct opposite of what many young unemployed Tunisians feel. Much of these sentiments and perceptions are found in the case of Houssam Abdelli, who was 28 years old when he detonated himself on the bus in Tunis in 2015. Abdelli was from a poor family, and neighbours and friends that AOAV spoke with said that he was worried about their financial well-being. From Ettadhamen, Abdelli worked as a street seller, selling plants and clothes. According to his friends, he had tried to find a better job, but had had no success. He reportedly drank alcohol and smoked hashish several times per week".[11]

Chapter 4

The Taliban, IS-K, TTP and their War against Women, Children and Hazara Muslims in Afghanistan and Pakistan

In Afghanistan, every tired face and pair of eyes have a gory story to narrate but who cares and listens? Women are being stoned to death and raped by Taliban leadership. Kidnapping has become a profitable business across the country in which Ministers, security officials and parliamentarians have been deeply involved. Children are barred from education and youngsters were being pushed into forced labour. In Nuristan province, the Taliban hanged seven men. People were imprisoned and tortured in private homes and private prisons. Women were treated like animals in the Shinwari Pashtun tribe where they were sold like goat or sheep. Human Rights activist, Sabrina Hamidi confirmed to news reporters that women were sold like animals in different districts of the Shinwari area of Jalalabad. Sabrina revealed that the price depends on the beauty of the girl and can range from around 80,000 in Afghan currency to 2,000 $ US. NGOs and rights groups have registered numerous complaints with government authorities about the mistreatment of women by the police force. Journalist Atal Ahmadzai and Faten Ghosn in their Asia Times analysis (published on 19 January 2022), highlighted the difficulties women faced in Afghanistan:

"The Taliban has banned women from travelling more than 72 kilometres from home without a male relative. In early December, the Taliban released a decree saying a woman is a "noble and free human being" and should not be forced into a marriage. The international community largely welcomed the announcement. However, a closer look at the decree reveals that the Taliban formalizes the regime's right to determine whether a woman actually consents to a union. The Taliban have systematically reinstated old restrictions on girls' education and female employment. Most primary girls' schools are closed across the country and secondary and tertiary education is completely banned for girls. In 2017, UN Children's Fund figures showed that 3.7 million Afghan children were out of school, 60% of them girls. This percentage is now likely much greater with the Taliban's ban on girls' education. This differs from the Taliban's recent public messaging on girls' and women's "right to education and work." To the domestic audience, the regime's messages are vague. Leaders say, for example, that reopening girls' education depends upon economic and moral conditions that are not made clear. Deputy Prime Minister Mullah Abdul Ghani Baradar said recently that once "economic challenges are resolved, we will provide education for all those who want to pursue their studies."[1]

Recent research shows that Afghan women and children encountered numerous challenges while trying to access justice, education and work places. In remote villages, due to the lack of women prisons, women prisoners were handed over to Maliks and the opulent who sexually abused and shared them with friends. The painful story of Afghan women subjected to sexual harassment, torture and authoritarian treatment has not yet changed under the Taliban government. In fact, women in Afghanistan are being burnt, tortured, harassed and traded with commodities, sold like goats and treated like dogs. Their torture and sexual abuse in workplaces, prisons, private jails, police stations, homes, streets, in armed forces barracks, and government offices in all major provinces of Afghanistan continued with impunity. There are numerous accounts of Bachabazi in world media that diverted the attention of authorities to the vulnerability of homeless and orphan children whose parents were killed in civil wars. The practice of male-child prostitution is a serious lingering social issue that is rarely discussed in the print and electronic media of Afghanistan. This tradition has deep rooted in the war-torn society.

The Taliban humiliated women by imposing un-Islamic culture of hijab. This is a new mental and physical torture of women in Afghanistan. The terrorists banned young girls from school, tortured women when they were travelling alone in buses in cities, but never intercepted trade of women and children in Shinwari district of Jalalabad province. On 08 May 2022, Afghanistan Times reported the Taliban atrocities against women and girls in Afghanistan. In May 2022, Taliban announced new rules regarding women's covering or hijab, saying it would be implemented in two steps-encouragement and punishment, and specified the types of dress that women will need to wear when stepping out of home. The UN Secretary General Antonio Guterres said he was "alarmed" that "women must cover their faces in public and leave home only in cases of necessity. "I once again urge the Taliban to keep their promises to Afghan women and girls, and their obligations under international human rights law."[2]

In the European Asylum Support Office Report, Afghanistan Country focus, Country of Origin Information Report", published in 2022, atrocities of Taliban against women in different provinces of Afghanistan is well documented: "In Kandahar most women had reportedly been barred from resuming work or education. Taliban officials in Helmand reportedly banned barbers from shaving or cutting beards, and issued a warning that those violating the rule would be punished by the religious police. There were also reports on similar restrictions in Ghor, Kabul, Uruzgan, Kapisa and Takhar, although this information could not be verified through other sources. According to TOLO news, these restrictions also prohibited women to own smartphones in Helmand, Takhar and Kapisa. TOLO news also reported that Ministry of Culture and Information officials stated that limitations on shaving beards and smartphones were not in line with the Taliban's official position. According to WSJ, the Taliban authorities in Kabul 'overruled' decisions in Helmand on cutting hair or shaving beards. A report of Human Rights Watch and the San Jose State University (SJSU) Human Rights Institute suggested a dire situation for women and girls in Herat city, claiming that the Taliban committed 'widespread and serious human rights violations against women and girls' and had instilled fear among them. Seven women activists, educators and university students in Herat were interviewed about their life under the Taliban, and, in sum, they said that their lives had completely changed, being trapped indoors and afraid to leave their houses without a male family member."[3]

The UN Assistance Mission in Afghanistan (UNAMA) in a statement expressed concerns on violations of women rights. Moreover, on 13 May 2022, in a press release, British Foreign, Commonwealth & Development Office said, "We remain deeply concerned by the continued restrictions on girls' access to education in Afghanistan, and call on the Taliban to respect the right to education and adhere to their commitments to reopen schools for all female students. We are deeply disappointed about escalating restrictions imposed by the Taliban that impact on the human rights of Afghan women". Associate Women's Rights Director at Human Rights Watch and expert, Heather Barr in her recent article (Speak Up on Behalf of Afghan Women: What is happening right now in Afghanistan is the most serious women's rights crisis in the world today, published in The Diplomat, on May 12, 2022) noted:

"The list of Taliban violations of the rights of women and girls is long and growing. The Taliban appointed an all-male cabinet. They abolished the Ministry of Women's Affairs and replaced it with the Ministry of Vice and Virtue, which issued the most recent order. They banned secondary education for girls and banned women from almost all jobs. They blocked women from traveling long distances or leaving the country alone. They dismantled the system to protect women and girls from violence and made it difficult for them to get health care. They issued new rules for how women must dress and behave. They enforce these rules through violence. Women – with extraordinary courage – took to the streets in protest. The Taliban beat, threatened, pepper sprayed, abducted, and detained them. The latest order is a chilling escalation. Not only does it make every woman or girl who is outside her home a suspect, but it also strips women and girls of the shreds of autonomy they still had, the ability to resist. The order states that if a woman or girl disobeys, the punishment — including imprisonment — will be inflicted on her male guardian. In this way the Taliban coerce every man to become complicit in their abuse, each man the jailer of his female relatives".[4]

The Conversation on February 4, 2022 also noted, "Taliban captured 40 people in Mazar-e-Sharif, then allegedly gang-raped eight of the women. The women who survived the gang rape were subsequently killed by their families. The fact that the women had been raped violated a societal honour code called Pashtunwalli, which prohibits women from engaging in sex outside of marriage". Under the Taliban's latest rule, lesbian, gay, bisexual and transgender people in Afghanistan are facing "grave threats" of violence and death, according to new findings by the research and advocacy nonprofit organization Human Rights Watch". Former Afghan President Hamid Karzai condemned the closure of girls schools, Afghanistan Times reported. Experts and writers, Shamil Shams, and Shabnam von Hein in their DW article (How the Taliban are 'eliminating women' in Afghanistan, published in DW News, on 09 May 2022) have documented Taliban atrocities against the women in Afghanistan:

"Following the US-led invasion of Afghanistan in 2001, Afghan women earned many rights, which the Taliban had taken away from 1996 to 2001. The hard-earned rights included the right to choose how they dress, and the right to employment and education. Since they retook power, the international community has been urging the Taliban to allow girls to go to school and give them more freedom in society. Instead, the new Afghan rulers have done the contrary and backslide on women's rights.

Daud Naji, a former Afghan government official, wrote on Twitter that the Taliban have imposed a type of Hijab that is not suitable for working in office or in the field. "The Taliban have imposed the burqa, which abolishes [a woman's] identity... The issue is not the hijab but the elimination of women," he said. Nahid Farid, a former Afghan Member of Parliament and women's rights activist, has dubbed the veil mandate a "symbol of gender apartheid." "The dress code for women, and putting men as executors of this plan, along with the Taliban's restrictions on girls' education, prove that the group seeks to control the body and mind of half of the population," she wrote on Facebook. Instead, the Islamist militant group has decided to focus on setting up rules of conduct and dress codes for women based on a fundamentalist interpretation of Islam. New, stricter rules are announced almost every day. For example, since the end of March, women are only allowed to board an airplane in the company of a man. The Taliban also recently backtracked on a promise to allow girls to attend school. Secondary schools for girls will be opened once "appropriate dress codes" are agreed upon for students aged 12 and older, according to a statement issued last week by the Ministry for the "Promotion of Virtue and Prevention of Vice."[5]

Amidst Taliban atrocities against women, hunger further added to the pain of Afghan mothers. Ariana News (10 May 2022) reported that half of Afghanistan's population were facing acute hunger. Lingering drought and the deep economic crisis meant that unprecedented hunger would continue to threaten the lives and livelihoods of millions of people across Afghanistan. "Of particular concern – and for the first time since the introduction of the IPC in Afghanistan in 2001–a small pocket of 'catastrophic' levels of food insecurity–or IPC Phase-5 has been detected in the country," the World Food Program (WFP) reported. "More than 20,000 people in the north-eastern province of Ghor were facing catastrophic levels of hunger because of a long period of harsh winter and disastrous agricultural conditions.[6] However, on 12 May 2022, Ariana News reported United Nations Secretary-General Antonio Guterres warning that the continued expansion of Daesh and Al-Qaeda in Africa and resurgent terrorism in Afghanistan posed a growing threat to global peace and security. Addressing an UN-backed counter-terrorism meeting in Malaga, Spain, this week he said: "Responses to terrorism must be anchored in the rule of law, human rights, and gender equality to ensure their effectiveness..."In the name of security, humanitarian aid is often blocked–increasing human suffering. Civil society and human rights defenders are silenced – particularly women. And survivors of terrorism and violence are left without the support and access to justice they need to rebuild their lives," United Nations Secretary-General Antonio Guterres said.[7]

This business is more widespread in Afghanistan than it is in Pakistan and Iran, as the trafficking of young boys for paedophilic sexual violence has reached its peak. The practice is increasingly becoming a national shame. This culture has spread to all sections of society. Children are sexually abused in safe houses, jails, police stations, guest houses and on streets. They are kidnapped from school, streets and parks and sold into male prostitution. Ariana News reported the announcement of Taliban regarding women's covering or hijab and said it would be implemented in two steps-encouragement and punishment – and defining the types of dress that women will need to wear when stepping out of home. The plan was confirmed by Mawlawi Hibatullah Akhundzada-leader of the terrorist group, and leader of the so called Islamic Emirate. "If a woman doesn't wear a hijab, first, her house will be located and her guardian will be advised and warned. Next, if the hijab is not considered, her guardian will be summoned. If repeated, her guardian (father, brother or husband) will be imprisoned for three days. If repeated again, her guardian will be sent to court for further punishment, the plan reads," said Akif Mahajar, a spokesman for the Ministry of Vice and Virtue. A statement from the Vice and Virtue Ministry of the Islamic Emirate said that hijab was an obligation in Islam and that any dress that covers the body can be considered as hijab given that it was not "thin and tight." When it comes to the type of the covering or hijab that women will need to wear, the statement said that burka was the best type of hijab/covering "as it is part of Afghan culture and it has been used for ages." It adds that another preferred type of hijab was a long black veil and dress that "should not be thin or tight."

The statement, called "the descriptive and accomplishable plan on legitimate hijab," also instructs women not to step out of home unless necessary, calling it one of the best ways of observing hijab. The rules were published in a two-page statement and were approved by a seven-member team whose names and signatures were on the second page. Moreover, the UN Secretary-General, Guterres said this was 'alarming' that "women must cover their faces in public and leave home only in cases of necessity. The US special envoy for Afghan women and girls and human rights, Rina Amiri, said the "Taliban continue to adopt policies oppressing women and girls as a substitute for addressing the economic crisis and need for inclusive government. The UNAMA in a statement expressed concerns and said it will immediately request meetings with the officials of the current government to seek clarification on the status of the decision.

The recent news stories about women, men and children trafficking in Afghanistan under the Taliban government have become a hot topic in print and electronic media. The heart-breaking stories of helpless, poor and vulnerable girls and women of Afghanistan are in trouble. Every month, hundreds of Afghan children, women and unemployed young men are kidnapped, imprisoned or sexually abused. Afghanistan Independent Human Rights Commission (AIHRC) recently voiced about the surge in women and child trafficking in the country. In its latest report, it has warned that the human traffickers used coordinated methods to allure women and children to take them outside the country. Poverty, unemployment, corruption and insecurity as the factors behind an increase in human trafficking.

The recent debate in Europe-based think tanks suggested that, as the ISIS group retrieved nuclear and biological material from the Mosul University in Iraq, it can possibly make nuclear explosive devices with less than eight kilograms of plutonium. The debate about bioterrorism and biodefense was not entirely new in the military circles of South Asia. The involvement of ISIS in using biological weapons against the Kurdish army in Kobane was a lesson for Pakistan and Afghanistan to deeply concentrate on the proliferation of these weapons in the region. Editor Iain Overton and researchers, Aman Bezreh, Chris Hitchcock, Jacob Berntson, Jen Wilton, Jennifer Dathan, Khalil Dewan, Leyla Slama, Michael Hart, Shaza Alsalmoni, Sophie Akram and Tim Hulse in their paper (Understanding the Rising Cult of Suicide Bomber. Action on Armed Violence (AOAV) have documented cultures of suicide terrorism in Afghanistan, Pakistan, Syria, Iraq, Algeria, Nigeria, Saudi Arabia's Wahhabism, violence, and Saudi suicide bombings. Exporting suicide bombers? And in Yemen SIED attacks in Yemen, Tunisia terrorism of Salafi-Jihadism in Tunisia and Tunisian suicide bombers:

"The vast majority of suicide attacks take place in three major geographical hotspots crossing national borders: Iraq-Syria, Nigeria and Afghanistan-Pakistan. These hotspots are associated with specific conflicts and groups which operate in several countries at once. Some of these groups–in particular al-Qaeda offshoots in Iraq and Syria, foremost among them IS–have proven themselves to have the ambition and the resources to carry out attacks as far afield as Europe. Together, attacks in these three areas caused 7853 civilian deaths and injuries in 2015–86% of civilian deaths and injuries from suicide bombings worldwide. In the same year Yemen–which lies outside these three hotspots – accounted for another 7% (644 civilian deaths and injuries). No other country saw more than 200 civilian deaths and injuries or more than a handful of incidents. Iraq has between 2011 and 2015 seen 382 SIED attacks, as reported in English language media sources. These attacks have claimed a reported 13,736 casualties (killed or injured), 76% of whom were civilians. Suicide bombings in the country reached their peak in 2013, but decreased in 2014 and 2015. However, 2016 has witnessed more SIED attacks than 2015, suggesting that suicide bombings do not show any signs of disappearing from Iraq. The geographical spread of suicide bombings in Iraq reinforces the idea that suicide bombings are used predominantly in military battles, or at least in areas in the vicinity of them."[8] Like Syria and Libya, Yemen has found itself facing violence in the aftermath of political change in the country after the Arab Spring.

The problem of nuclear and biological terrorism deserves special attention from the governments of Pakistan and Afghanistan because the army of IS-K can develop a dirty bomb in which explosives can be combined with a radioactive source like those commonly used in hospitals or extractive industries. The use of this weapon might have severe health effects, causing more disruption than destruction. Political and military circles in Pakistan fear that, as ISIS has already seized chemical weapons in Al Muthanna, in northern Iraq, some disgruntled retired military officers or experts in nuclear explosive devices might help the Pakistan chapter of the group to deploy biological and chemical weapons. A letter by the Iraqi government to the UN warned that the militant-captured chemical weapons site contains 2,500 chemical rockets filled with the nerve agent Sarin. On 15 August 2015, the ISIS-K terrorists attacked Mawdoud Education Center. They targeted schools and killed girls and boy students. Mohammad Hussain Hasrat noted that; "religious centres were also changed to be the frontline of terrorist attacks by the Taliban and IS-KP in recent years."[9]

One of the deadliest targets of such attacks was at a mosque, Imam-e-Zaman on 20 November 2017 which is located in western part of Kabul. According to Media's coverage, the attack on Imam-e-Zaman mosque resulted in 111 civilian casualties. The Hazara Muslims were tortured by nomads, Taliban and extremist mujahideen. On 18 January 2018, Human Rights Watch (HRW) and Amnesty international reported widespread atrocities against Hazara population in Afghanistan: "A number of particularly deadly suicide attacks in urban areas, some claimed by IS-KP, killed and wounded more than 2,000 people across the country".[4] However,

Reuter reported the killing of 35 people by a Taliban group: More than 7,000 people have fled from Jaghori and Malistan either to Ghazni or into neighbouring Bamiyan and more than 3,000 homes had been razed. Expert and analyst, Mohammad Hussain Hasrat, in his research paper (Over a Century of Persecution: Massive Human Rights Violation against Hazaras in Afghanistan. Concentration on attacks occurred during the National Unity Government, published in February, 2019) documented Taliban atrocities against the Hazara Muslims and different provinces of Afghanistan:

"The Taliban orchestrated massive attacks on several Hazara areas beginning from a place called Kondolan located in Uruzgan Khas on 27 October 2018. At the outset, the Taliban's attack was reported to target only an opponent, anti-Taliban commander. Expansion of Taliban attacks in the following days left unprecedented civilian casualties, displacement and humanitarian crisis to Hazaras of targeted sites. After Uruzgan, the Taliban expanded their attacks and killed 11 Hazara civilians in three villages of Malistan district namely Shirdagh, Pashi and Zardak Zawli....The twin suicide attacks on Hazara peaceful demonstration in Dehmazang square was the deadliest and horrific incident in recent decades in Afghanistan. The first coverage of the public media and the UNAMA's investigation recorded at least 85 deaths and around 413 injured of Hazara civilians. Another report published after the event recorded around 100 deaths and several hundred injured in Dehmazang attacks. As an eyewitness, along with the supporter team, enumerated 84 deaths and 500 injuries only in hospitals of the western part of Kabul hours later after the incident. Some families transferred coffins of their victims to their birthplaces as soon as possible according to Islamic burying rituals. Tens of other deaths were buried in subsequent days which made it hard to know the real figure of casualties except those available in the official record. The Taliban, the IS-KP and other similar groups increased and expanded their direct threats and Intimidation against Hazaras in recent years. Not only had the conventional intimidation remained as usual, new sorts of threats and intimidation arose. In rural areas, the Taliban wielded their violence machinery to put the Hazara people into severe pressure".[10]

The Taliban government killed thousands of civilians including women and children, and looted their houses. These killing could constitute war crimes. Taliban committed war crimes in area of Spin boldak. After AIHRC's revelation, the US and UK condemned that massacre. The AIHRC called the Taliban's terrorism against the Afghan civilian population a war crime. Amnesty International also reported the Taliban war crimes by targeting civilians. Amnesty International reported in 2015 the Taliban mass murder sexual exploitation of women. In Kandahar province, in 2021, Taliban killed people in the pretext that they were working with the former Afghan government. During the Panjshir operation, Taliban killed people and blocked their food supply. They also killed women in Kabul and extra judicially murdered hundreds of former Afghan army officers in different provinces. The Global Centre for the Responsibility to Protect in 01 March 2022 noted the Taliban capture of Kabul and violation of human rights abuses-targeting vulnerable population:

"On 15 August 2021 Taliban forces entered Kabul, effectively overthrowing the Afghan government. Since then, the Taliban have perpetrated human rights abuses targeting vulnerable populations, including religious minorities and women and girls. The UNAMA and the Office of the UN High Commissioner for Human Rights (OHCHR) have received over 110 credible reports of extrajudicial killings of former Afghan security personnel and 50 credible reports of arbitrary detentions, beatings and threats of previous Afghan government officials, political opponents, journalists, civil society activists and human rights defenders. According to Human Rights Watch, Taliban officials have forcibly displaced residents in several provinces, including Shia Hazara and people associated with the former government, as a form of collective punishment. The Taliban have severely restricted fundamental rights, including freedom of religion and expression. The Taliban have also dissolved key government agencies, including the Independent Election Commission, the Ministry of Peace and the Ministry of Parliamentary Affairs. Reports also indicated pattern of institutionalizing large scale and systematic gender-based discrimination and violence against women and girls, including forced marriage, as well as restrictions on freedom of movement, freedom of expression, employment opportunities and access to education and healthcare".[11]

In another report (Atrocity Alert No. 298: Ukraine, Sudan and Afghanistan, published on 27 April 2022), the Global Centre for the Responsibility to Protect has reported atrocities of Taliban terrorist group in Northern Afghanistan: "On 19 April, 2022, at least 75 civilians have been killed in two improvised explosive devices (IEDs) detonated outside the Abdul Rahim-e Shahid High School and Mumtaz Education Centre in the predominantly Hazara neighbourhood of Dasht-e-Barchi in Kabul, killing six people and injuring 25, including students. On 21 April, 2022, IED explosions targeted the Shia Seh Dokan Mosque in Mazar-e-Sharif, killing 17 people and injuring at least 52, many of whom were Hazara".[7] In 2016, the amount of sexual abuse and violence culminated while the culture of entering marriage with two or three women at one time has become a national shame. Unfortunately, in Northern Afghanistan, women and girls were facing countless challenges including forced abortion, forced prostitution, the demand for illegitimate sexual acts, husband's extramarital relations, and forced watching of pornographic films. An Afghan female pilot, Miss Nelofer Rahmani claimed asylum in the United States and refused to return to her country due to her fear of persecution. She hammered the leadership of Afghan national army for harassment and sexual abuse. The unity government is a conglomeration of different war criminals, private militias, and ethno-sectarian mafia groups who have been involved in war crimes, sexual abuse and male prostitution during the last 30 years' civil war.

The United States, the UK and European Union member states have treated Afghanistan like a terrorist state, while they have established their proxy government of Taliban who maintain suicide brigades and support and train Pakistani and Central Asian terrorist organizations to create war like situation in the region. The United States looted and plundered the country's menial resource and transported more than 350,000 container full of Talc, Lazuli, Gold and uranium, bauxite, coal, iron ore, lithium, chromium, zinc, gemstones, sulphur, travertine, gypsum and marble during the past 20 years. The US committed war crimes by killing women and children. Afghanistan's vast mineral wealth is estimated to exceed one trillion dollars. The US Geological Survey argued that Afghanistan holds 60 million metric tons of copper, 2.2 billion tons of iron ore, 1.4 million tons of rare earth elements (REEs) such as lanthanum, cerium, neodymium, and veins of aluminium, gold, silver, zinc, mercury, and lithium. With the establishment of the Taliban government in August 2021, different communities refused to accept their government and denominated it as a Pakistan's proxy regime. In Panjshir valley National Resistance Front organized fighters and former ANA officers and soldiers to challenge the Taliban government. Expert and writer, Peter Mills in his research paper (Afghanistan-in-Review: Institute for the Study of War, January 3–January 25, 2022) has documented activities of National Desistence Front of Afghanistan, their Russian made weapons and the IS-K campaign of suicide attacks against Hazara Muslims in various provinces of Afghanistan:

"The National Resistance Front militants have recently been spotted with newer weapons, possibly Russian-made PG-7VR's and SVDS DMRs, which could indicate external support. The Russian Ministry of Foreign Affairs explicitly denied that these weapons had come from Russia. There were also reports that Uzbek Afghan warlord, Abdul Rashid Dostum, told his commanders that he will launch a spring offensive against the Taliban. It is unclear what capabilities Dostum can deploy inside Afghanistan and to what extent he will work with the NRF. The NRF engaged in skirmishes with the Taliban in Kapisa Province on January 16, Panjshir Province on January 18, and Balkh Province on January 21. There are reports of ongoing battles between the NRF and the Taliban in Khost wa Fereng District, Baghlan Province. These battles resulted in mostly minor casualties, but they indicate that the NRF maintains the ability to carry out insurgent attacks and that they may be expanding this capability to other parts of Afghanistan.....IS-KP carried out at least eight attacks in Kabul, mostly targeting Taliban soldiers, though at least one targeted a bus carrying Shi'a civilians. IS-KP also attacked local Taliban officials in several districts in Nangarhar and Kunar Province in eastern Afghanistan. In Kunar Province, likely IS-KP militants attacked the home of a local Taliban intelligence commander in Sawkay District on January 16. On January 19, likely IS-KP militants attacked and killed a local Taliban commander in neighbouring Narang district".[12]

On 17 August 2021, former Vice President of Afghanistan, Amrullah Saleh declared himself the "caretaker" President of Afghanistan and announced the resistance. As of 3 September 2021, in addition to the opposition in the Panjshir, there were also districts in the centre of Afghanistan that still were resisting the Taliban, supported by ethnic and religious minorities. Prior to the fall of Kabul, the National Resistance Front (NRF) began moving military equipment including helicopters, into Panisher. On 31 August 2021, Taliban commenced an offensive against the NRF in the provinces of Baghlan, Panjshir, and Parwan and crushed their military strength. On 06 September, 2021, Pakistan Air Force's CH-4 Drones targeted Forces in Panjshir. Ahmad Massoud warned that the Taliban were backed by the PAF. The NRF, also known as the Second Resistance is a military alliance of former Northern Alliance members and other anti-Taliban fighters who remain loyal to the Islamic Republic of Afghanistan. Expert Ananya Varma in the article (In Afghanistan, NRF Continues Training in Panjshir; New Resistance Formed against Taliban) asserted that The NRF member were being trained in Panjshir:

"Just weeks ago, the brave fighters of NRFA had issued a video message to the people of Afghanistan urging them to not be silent. Condemning the brutality against women, the group stated that such acts will not be tolerated. In the message, NRFA also stated that they wouldn't be remembered as a 'spy or as someone who sold their land' in the eyes of the world. They will fight, and hope that the world remembers their good deeds as Afghan's National Hero Ahmad Shah Masoud and General Raziq did in defending their homeland, the group stated. On August 15, the Taliban took control of Afghanistan, putting an end to more than two months of military blitz. Since then, the law and order situation in the war-ravaged country has remained shaky with a shrinking economy and an unpredictable security situation for people. The terror group is under the clutches of its toughest challenges as it attempts to manage the national leadership, side-lined by the international community as a "rogue state".[13] On 23 August 2021, BBC reported Amrullah Saleh presence in Panjshir, who tweeted that the Taliban had massed forces near the entrance to the valley.[14] Expert and analyst, Nilly Kohzad an Afghan American economist and journalist in her article (What Does the National Resistance Front of Afghanistan Have to Offer? The NRF says it is pushing for a new trajectory in Afghanistan. The Diplomat December 15, 2021) noted efforts of NRF to challenge the Taliban government:

The NRF, a grassroots resistance movement that emerged from the rugged terrain of the Panjshir Valley, has vowed to keep its momentum strong against Taliban aggression, despite the group's rise to power with its taking of Kabul four months ago…Today, the NRF finds itself trapped in a deja-vu moment as it grapples with the challenges of ridding Afghanistan of the Taliban once again, and this time alone. The NRF is led by Ahmad Massoud, son of Ahmad Shah Massoud or the "Lion of Panjshir," a key figure who led multiple offensives against the Taliban in the 1990s. Ahmad Shah Massoud played a critical role in forming an anti-Taliban resistance after the group's first rise to power in 1996. The powerful commander was known for his larger-than-life personality and keen leadership. He was assassinated by al-Qaeda just two days before the 9/11 attacks. For his now 32-year-old son, Massoud junior, the apple doesn't fall far from the tree. Ahmad Massoud is closely following in his late father's footsteps through the formation of his own resistance movement…. "We resist for freedom, justice, and independence and for the welfare of every single citizen inside the country. The NRF was formed by people, not political parties and its platform is not for a specific region or a specific ethnic group. We are fighting for everyone in the country. The only resistance group that has a legitimate presence inside Afghanistan at the moment is the NRF," said Nazary. "In Panjshir we have around 17 bases and it's well protected with ground and aerial forces. Same with Parwan, Kapisa, Badakhshan, Balkh and Takhar. People are also reaching out to us from the east and the south but it's going to take time for them to announce their forces, it's because you have the Taliban oppressing many Pashtuns, the Achakzai tribe is a good example," said Nazary."[15]

However, expert and writer, David Loyn in his analysis (The Spectator, published on 6 February 2022) noted that Taliban tried to present themselves as a moderate but their hardliner policies reflect their psychology: "But there is mounting fear of their rule. Dozens of Afghan media organisations have closed; Afghan journalists have been beaten and imprisoned; leaders of women's opposition groups are being taken from their homes every day". The BBC Chief Correspondent, Lyse Doucet on 29 April 2022, reported that former Lt Gen Sami Sadat's statement in which he said that eight months of Taliban rule convinced many Afghans that military action was the only way forward. "Speaking for the first time about the plans, Lt Gen Sadat told the BBC he and others would "do anything and everything in our powers to make sure Afghanistan is freed from the Taliban and a democratic system is re-established". "Until we get our freedom, until we get our free will, we will continue to fight," he said, while refusing to be drawn on a specific timeline. Lyse noted.[16] The USAF, Retired; and CPT Joshua Fruth, US Army Reserves, Maj Gen Buck Elton and Dr. Vanessa Neumann in their paper (Evacuation Operations, Great-Power Competition, and External Operations Terror Threats in Post-Drawdown Afghanistan: Mapping out the Path Ahead- Journal of Indo-Pacific Affairs, published on 01 November, 2021) noted great powers competitions and evacuation operation of the US Army:

"Under its strict Deobandi Salafist interpretation of Islam, the Taliban's 'Islamic Emirate' regime has implemented the most significant gender inequality measures anywhere in the world. Women and girls have lost basic rights, face education and employment restrictions, and have been subjected to increased physical abuse, sexual violence, and human trafficking. Members of the LGBTQ community; religious/ethnic/racial minorities, such as the Shia Hazaras, Uighurs, and population groups from the Panjshir; and individuals who worked with US and NATO forces as diplomats, interpreters, law enforcement officers, and members of the military, all face an extraordinary risk of violence, torture, human trafficking, and execution. The most immediate risk ahead of us is a ripe kidnap-for-ransom (KFR) environment, wherein the Taliban utilize other Sunni violent extremist organizations (VEO) as proxies to leverage a humanitarian crisis by holding American citizens and our Special Immigrant Visa (SIV) ally's hostage. This offers the Taliban the opportunity to enrich their coffers and gives its Chinese and Pakistani partners hostage-negotiating leverage in other major policy issues. In line with current US government policies on gender equality, violence against women, LGBTQ rights, and human trafficking, we should also prioritize evacuation of these population groups—lest we lose legitimacy in the international community for not defending underserved communities when it counts the most".[17]

The term Punjabi Taliban or Jaish-e-Muhammad has come to be widely used for militants in recent times, but the militancy of the Punjabi Taliban has long been a destabilising factor for civil society. Earlier, recruits from Pakistan's Punjab were used for jihad in Afghanistan and Kashmir. Some Punjab-based political leaders and police officials, at the behest of their political bosses, tried to blame the attacks on FATA-based Taliban or on Indian agents, but it was generally accepted that there were some extremists from Punjab. The Punjabi Taliban were more lethal than the so-called Pashtun Taliban, as they carried out attacks that needed much higher levels of training and coordination. Operations in Swat, Balochistan and Waziristan suggested that the military establishment remained largely unwilling to hold itself accountable to the public. Army was reluctant to be more transparent to civilian authorities. Army was not in full control of the Balochistan province. Conditions in Balochistan had worsen and the exploited people were feeling insecure and frightened. Operations in Swat, Bajour, Mohmand, Tirah Valley and Waziristan did nothing to raise the credibility of the armed forces. The issue of extra-judicial killing needed to be settled as world's human rights groups, the HRCP and newspapers reported human rights violations in Swat.

On January 16, 2013, BBC reported that hundreds of protesters in Khyber Pakhtunkhwa displayed the bodies of at least 14 people who they said were victims of extra-judicial killings outside government office in Peshawar. Military leaders should have realized that attacks on military convoys were revenge attacks of Pashtuns whose houses were targeted by army gunship helicopters. In Balochistan, the Army used helicopter gunships, bombarded villages and destroyed the houses of the poor Baloch people. The Asian Human Rights Commission in its report (2013) thus recorded army's atrocities in Balochistan: "The main military sweep took place in Awaran, Panjur and Makran districts of Baluchistan. Hundreds of villagers were rounded up and interrogated. Many since have disappeared. Some were later found dead, with their mutilated bodies showing signs of torture."

This way of tackling insurgency in Baluchistan and forceful disappearances affected the credibility of the armed forces in the eyes of the public.

Fighting against the state of Pakistan, Tehrik-e-Taliban Pakistan (TTP) is assortment of more than 40 sectarian, nationalist and extremist organizations who trained their fighters during the Afghan Mujahideen fight against Soviet Union in 1980s and 1990s in Afghanistan and Pakistan. During the war criminal General Raheel Sharif's military operation in North Waziristan, the TTP experienced huge loss and bad luck, and vanished hundreds of professional fighters. Raheel Sharif never pardoned women and children while hundreds of women and girls were kidnapped by his rogue army. The TTP was established in 2007 by elders of Waziristan. TTP militants regularly conduct attacks against Pakistan Army within Pakistan, using everything from small arms to IEDs to suicide bombers. The appointment of Maulana Fazlullah as the new commander of the TTP's (divided) Shura Council led to major internal divisions and defections in 2013, 2014, and 2015. Expert and writer, Abdul Sayed in his paper (The Evolution and Future of Tehrik-e-Taliban Pakistan. Carnegie endowment for international peace, published on 21 December, 2021) has documented prospect and evolution of the TTP:

"The TTP is a by-product of the intra-jihadi politics that followed the 2001 US invasion of Afghanistan. The TTP claims that its armed struggle aims to establish an Islamic political system in Pakistan based on the group's interpretation of sharia, a task it says was the main goal for establishing Pakistan in 1947. At the time of the US invasion, many Pakistani jihadists who had fought on behalf of the Pakistani government in Afghanistan and in Indian Kashmir turned against the Pakistani state for its support of the United States' so-called global War on Terror, among other grievances. TTP members thus began sheltering the Afghan Taliban, al-Qaeda, and other militant allies who were fleeing the Afghanistan conflict. Yielding to US pressure, the Pakistani government eventually cracked down on the safe havens, but its violent response ultimately prompted these Pakistani jihadists to band together and more formally ally with al-Qaeda and the Afghan Taliban. This eventually led to the establishment of the TTP in 2007. The TTP is the largest militant organization fighting against the state in Pakistan. According to the UN, the TTP also boasts several thousand fighters in Afghanistan, with strongholds on both sides of the Afghanistan-Pakistan border. Although Pakistani military actions, US drone warfare, and factional infighting led to the TTP's decline from 2014 to 2018, the militant group has been experiencing a strong resurgence since the Afghan

Taliban and US government signed a peace deal in February 2020. In fact, since July 2020, ten militant groups opposed to the Pakistani state have merged with the TTP, including, among others, three Pakistani affiliates of al-Qaeda and four major factions that had separated from the TTP in 2014".[18]

The TTP is the original voice of the people of Waziristan where Pakistan Army committed war crimes-killed thousands of women and children, kidnapped tribal leaders, and looted houses and markets of Wazirs and Mehsuds. The TTP has no link with al Qaeda and the IS-K terrorist organizations. The US intelligence assessment misled writers and scholars about the TTP fight for the rights of the people of Waziristan. "Though the TTP framed its militant campaign as a defensive war against Pakistan's military operations, the group hoped to follow in the Afghan Taliban's footsteps and establish a sharia system in Pakistan, freeing the country from the "American stooges" who supposedly governed it". Abdul Sayed noted. However, in 2020, the TTP asserted that the group no longer wanted to design global agenda beyond Pakistan. Its organizational infrastructure suffered bad luck when some allied groups changed their loyalties and surrendered to Pakistan Army. The disgruntled commanders had been involved in jihad in Afghanistan and Kashmir. They were secretly in contact with some units of the army and intelligence agencies. Expert and writer, Abdul Sayed in his paper (The Evolution and Future of Tahrik-e-Taliban Pakistan, published on 21 December 2021), documented the prospect challenges of the TTP in Waziristan: "The TTP leaders pursued four political objectives. First, the group's leadership strengthened its alliances with the Afghan Taliban and al-Qaeda to increase its local and international legitimacy. Pakistani Pashtun tribesmen as well as Deobandi and Salafist seminaries, Islamist parties, and other jihadi groups all supported the Afghan Taliban's insurgency against the United States and its allies, seeing the campaign as a legitimate jihad to expel foreign infidels. Thus, as the TTP supported the Afghan jihad by offering material provisions, the group's legitimacy was enhanced. This strategy helped the TTP recruit a large number of young recruits for its war against the Pakistani state. The TTP provided the Afghan Taliban with bases in the Pashtun tribal regions bordering Afghanistan, eventually earning an official endorsement from its Afghan ally."[19]

After the Taliban took control of Afghanistan in August 15, 2021, they rolled back women's rights and media freedom, the foremost achievements of the post-2001 reconstruction effort. "Afghans were caught between

Taliban oppression and the spectre of starvation," said Patricia Gossman, Associate Asia Director at Human Rights Watch.[20] "Governments involved in Afghanistan over the past two decades should provide humanitarian aid and fund basic services, including health and education, while using their leverage to press for an end to Taliban rights violations." She said.[17] During the first ten days in August 2021, the Taliban was reported to have committed several high-profile killings. The British House of Lords re called to debate the situation in Afghanistan in 18 August 2021. However, the Afghan Taliban rise to power set forth and accorded military power of the TTP group in Pakistan. Pakistani establishment abruptly changed its narrative and demanded for talks with TTP, but its attitude changed by bombing innocent people in Waziristan and Khost province of Afghanistan.[18] Expert and research scholar, Madiha Afzal in her commentary (Pakistan's ambivalent approach toward a resurgent Tehrik-e-Taliban Pakistan, published on February 11, 2022) noted important points of the TTP's negotiation with government, its strategies and planning of attacks against Pakistan army:

"In October, former Prime Minister Imran Khan revealed during a television interview that his government was talking with the TTP, saying that "there are different groups which form the TTP and some of them want to talk to our government for peace. So, we are in talks with them. It's a reconciliation process." He noted that the talks were taking place in Afghanistan. That talks were underway came as a surprise to parliament as well as the public, although in September the foreign minister had also hinted in an interview that Islamabad would be open to pardoning TTP members if they laid down arms and submitted to Pakistan's constitution.... But the news was criticized widely by opposition parties, especially given the secrecy of the process and lack of consultation with parliament. The Afghan Taliban reportedly helped with the negotiations, per Pakistani national security officials, though it denied official involvement. One outlet reported that the Taliban interior minister, Sirajuddin Haqqani (head of the Haqqani Network and designated as a terrorist by the United States), was the mediator. In November, the Pakistani government announced a month-long cease-fire with the TTP — though it was unclear with what concessions to the insurgents".[21]

Chapter 5

Al Qaeda, the Haqqani Terrorist Network, Lashkar-e-Taiba, Taliban and the Islamic State of Khorasan's Plundering of Mineral Resources in Afghanistan and their Expedition Towards Central Asia

They are rolling again with punches to Afghanistan, with blood stained faces, lethal technology, nuclear technology, and strategies of destruction. They want to terminate more Afghan women and children, destroy more houses, more bridges and more buildings, but this time Afghan will never support their war crimes, and will never support their military operations. The Ukraine War has lidded and covered transmogrifies faces and blood stained hands of US and NATO war mongers who killed thousands in Afghanistan. The US House of Republicans went on the offensive against President Joe Biden, attacking his handling of the situation in Afghanistan. Mr. Michael McCaul said President Biden had blood on his hands". Former President Donald Trump and Republican lawmakers' slammed Joe Biden after the Kabul blasts. "Joe Biden's hands are drenched with blood after the botched withdrawal from Afghanistan". Lawmaker said. Now these war criminals want to return on the pretext that Afghanistan has become nest of terrorism. What do they want from a poor country? They want to use Afghanistan against Russia and China, or Pakistan. Their intentions are not clear. Writer David Markichok (Asia Times, 22 April 2021) warned that as London left the door open for NATO allies to return to Afghanistan in the event any "threat" re-emerges to the free world. Analyst and expert, Ashok K. Behuria in (Fighting the Taliban: Pakistan at war with itself, published in 2007, in Australian Journal of International Affairs, 61:4, 529-543) has noted Former Pakistani Army Chief General Musharaf's concerns about shift of centre of gravity of terrorism from al Qaeda to Taliban:

"General Pervez Musharraf, President of Pakistan, admitted on 15 September 2006 that the "centre of gravity of terrorism" had shifted from Al Qaeda to the Taliban and that the Taliban was a "more dangerous element because it has roots in the people" unlike Al Qaeda and was "more organised". He regarded the Taliban as an "obscurantist social concept" and argued that the real danger lay in the emerging strength of the Taliban and in the possibility of converting their resistance "into a national war by the [Pashtuns] against ... all foreign forces". The resurgence of the Taliban was the pet theme of analysts and observers who tracked developments in Afghanistan since 2004-2005. In Kabul in August 2007, Musharraf expressed his concern about "a particularly dark form" of terrorism confronting the region and said that people of Pakistan and Afghanistan faced "a great danger in the shape of fringe groups, a small minority that preaches hate, violence and backwardness".....The case of pro-Taliban militants laying siege on the Red Mosque at the heart of the Pakistani capital, in February 2007, until they were flushed out through military action, along with the rising incidence of suicide attacks against security forces in the tribal areas of Pakistan and the spread of the influence of the Taliban beyond the tribal areas in recent years, suggest that the Taliban phenomenon will affect Pakistan for a prolonged period and warrants a deeper analysis of the malaise that is affecting the Pakistani state at the moment".[1]

The Taliban and Haqqani terrorist organizations failed to stabilise Afghanistan. They imposed restrictions on women and journalist, on politicians to hide their crimes of sexual exploitation, murder of innocent Afghans including former army and police officers and soldiers. They are molesting transgender, gays, women and young girls and torturing them in secret torture cells. Taliban and Haqqani terrorist group nothing know how to govern Afghanistan and how to reinvent state institutions. They are recruiting young generation for suicide mission and intimidating Tajikistan, Iran and Uzbekistan by firing missiles across the borders and deploying suicide brigades along with their borders. They are sex hungary and train terrorist organizations of Central Asia, Pakistan and the Arab world, and adorn them with sophisticated arms and suicide jackets. Haqqani has a long history in Afghan politics and militancy stretching back to 1970s and was a major recipient of foreign funding during the Soviet jihad; during this period, Haqqani was regarded as a valuable asset by the CIA. On 16 May 2022, online media outlet journalist Jawad Etimad told ToloNews that Taliban arrested him while covering a blast in PD5 of Kabul city. Mr. Etimad said he spent two days in a cell of Islamic Emirate. "They prevented me from making footage. They beat me with kicks and punches. And then they arrested me," he said. Journalists voiced criticisms that the Islamic Emirate's forces prevent them from covering the security incidents in Kabul. "When a security incident happens in an area we go there to cover the incident. Unfortunately, we are not being allowed to cover the incident," said Farogh Faizy, a journalist. "The media has the right to make footage. Whenever there are restrictions on access to information, it is a violation of the law", said Masroor Lutfi, head of the Afghanistan National Journalists Union.

Pakistan once more wants to wash hands with the blood of Afghan citizens by allowing US and NATO to establish military bases in the country. They have trained strong armies of the IS-K and Taliban who will further their hegemonic agendas in Central Asia, Pakistan and China. They will make Central Asia and Afghanistan the nether regions and may possibly use weapons of mass destruction. They de novo and over again need the £3-trillion mineral resources to stabilize their economies, but this time, things will shape differently. Russia and China will interfere, and India will be supporting and Pakistan will play as a proxy. Russian Today reported that the UK intention to entre Afghanistan if realised threatening situation coming from the country again, UK under Secretary for the Armed Forces James Heappey told MPs. "If some part of the Afghan territory turns into "an ungoverned space" providing safe haven to international terrorists and threatening "the UK homeland or to the interests of our allies," London would not hesitate to act "unilaterally and multilaterally through NATO," a former Afghan Army officer said. Expert and analyst, Cosmin Timofte in his paper (Unlikely Friends: What role would the USA play in the fight between ISIS K and the Taliban? The Institute of New Europe's Work, published on 29 November 2021) has reviewed the UK withdrawn from Afghanistan after 20 years of fighting, which then paved the way for the Taliban to return to power. The US and NATO will arm both Taliban the ISIS to keep ignite the fire in order to easily plunder mineral resources of Afghanistan. They will bomb positions of Taliban in order to push them to the brink and make the country vanquish at the hands of the IS-K terrorist group. Recent engagement between Pakistan and the United States is crystal clear that they want to take the war inside China, or Russia:

The United States has withdrawn from Afghanistan after 20 years of fighting, which then paved the way for the Taliban to return to power at a speed that exceeded many estimations; reaching Kabul in around 10 days since the retreat started. The evacuation was made on the basis of the peace deal the US and the organisation forged under Trump. During the evacuation, the Taliban were declared as and "by Biden's Administration, which is a positive signal for the relationship the two parties may have. However, the emerging chaos from the evacuation and the change in government has prompted the Islamic State Khorasan Province (to s trike with the intent of establishing and empowering themselves and destabilising the new Taliban rule. This is most accurately acknowledged when one considers the timing of the Kabul airport attack, which killed over 100 people during the evacuation. With the Taliban striking back against IS-K, who is perhaps their biggest contester in the region at the moment, the United States is put in a position where it must consider its post war role in Afghanistan. It is a not question of whether the US might intervene, but in what measure it will. Chairman of the US Joint Chief of Staff General Milley said "it's possible" for the US to work with the Taliban against ISKP. If cooperation between the US and the Taliban is possible, then one must take a look into how will it materialise. It is not simply a question of eradicating a common enemy, but also the first glimpse over the new relationship between the two will have in the future".[2] Expert and commentator, Hassan Abu Haniyeh in his commentary (Daesh's Organisational Structure, published on 03 December 2014) has documented organisational infrastructure of the Islamic State in Iraq and Syria:

"On the eve of the US invasion and subsequent 2003 occupation of Iraq, Zarqawi worked hard to rebuild his jihadi network from a solid foundation that had already been established in the Afghanistan's Herat province. He began by building an inner circle of his most loyal followers. The most prominent among them were Abu Hamza al-Muhajir, an Egyptian national who took over the group after Zarqawi's demise; Abu Anas al-Shami, a Jordanian who became the group's first spiritual advisor; Nidhal Mohammed Arabiat, another Jordanian from the city of Salt, who was considered the group's top bomb maker and thought to be responsible for most of the group's car bombs; Mustafa Ramadan Darwish (also known as Abu Mohammed al-Libnani), a Lebanese national; Abu Omar al-Kurdi; Thamer al-Atrouz al-Rishawi, a former Iraqi military officer; Abdullah al-Jabouri (also known as Abu Azzam,) also an Iraqi; Abu Nasser al-Libi; and Abu Osama al-Tunisi. All of them were killed in 2003 except Abu Azzam, who was killed in 2005. Among the Jordanians most trusted by Zarqawi were Mowaffaq Odwan, Jamal al-Otaibi, Salahuddin al-Otaibi, Mohammed al-Safadi, Moath al-Msoor, Shehadah al-Kilani, Mohammed Qutaishat, Munther Shihah, Munther al-Tamuni, and Omar al-Otaibi. To rebuild his network, Zarqawi employed the ideology, ideas and jurisprudence he had learned at the hands of his mentor, Abu Abdullah al-Muhajir, who had a profound impact on Zarqawi's fighting doctrine and approach to jurisprudence. Zarqawi's network grew and developed quickly, but never had a specific name and did not adhere to a clearly defined structure".[3]

The United States illegitimate invasion of Iraq was with the motive to destroy the country and plunder its oil and mineral resources. That invasion generated several suicide terrorist organizations that killed thousands of women and children with impunity. Iraqi Muslims were beheaded, tortured, sexually abused and killed by these terrorist groups who received funds and weapons from the US Army. Since 2003, these terrorist groups carried out 900 suicide attacks against Iraqi civilians, killed over 10,000 women and children. They used female suicide bombers because they were easily crossing police and army checkpoints. The bomber women were motivated to attack US forces. According to the Action on Armed Violence report, dated 01 January 2017, actual knowledge about the education level of these bombers were difficult to find but one thing is clear that they were educated and brainwashed. There was also no real correlation between education and suicide bombers in Iraq and Syria. In areas where communal support for suicide bombing exists it can also help to motivate individual bombers. Most Salafi-Jihadi propaganda includes continuous, general references to the importance and nobility of martyrdom and martyrs, which likely translates to increased social status.

Suicide bombers in Syria and Afghanistan died in Vehicle-Borne operations. In Iraq, they proved to be ideal for launching against advancing ISF units from concealed garages. On 21 January 2021, VoA reported Islamic State suicide bombers attacks in a market in Iraq's capital killing at least 32 people and wounding 110 others. Expert and analyst Ellen Tveteraas "Department of Politics and International Relations, University of Oxford, Oxfordshire, United Kingdom" has highlighted operational mechanism of the ISIS terrorist group in Iraq, and performance of Martyrdom Operatives Battalion (Katibat al-Istishadiin), and its associates in her paper (Under the Hood–Learning and Innovation in the Islamic State's Suicide Vehicle Industry. Studies in Conflict & Terrorism, published on 13 February, 2022). She also noted that suicide operatives were the purview of the special skills bureau:

"Suicide operatives were the purview of the special skills bureau, with prospective bombers organized in a section called the Martyrdom Operatives Battalion (Katibat al-Istishadiin). Members of the suicide battalion would normally arrive at the area of operation shortly before the execution of an attack and spend the preparation period in isolation with clerics to build the mental fortitude required to execute this type of mission. The battalion had no shortage of volunteers and, following the group's acquisition of territory, its size far outgrew the tactical demand for suicide operations. The Islamic State was not the first group to find itself in this situation. Around 2006, an ISI document shows that it too had more suicide bombers than the group was able to deploy. However, while ISI was unable to utilize aspiring bombers for logistical reasons, the Islamic State was arguably unwilling to waste them. Winter's analysis of suicide attack use in 2015-16, suggests that the group appeared reluctant to use bombers in campaigns where it did not feel it could win. While this changed during the Battle of Mosul in 2016–2017, it corresponded with the impression of several interviewees, one of whom remarked, "The Islamic State does not use suicide bombers unnecessarily, they are cheap, but they are also indispensable. "While the Islamic State kept using inconspicuous suicide vehicles in clandestine operations, it also designed a new type with an emphasis on repelling, rather than avoiding, incoming fire. This expanded the tactical functions of suicide vehicles. In addition to their utility in guerrilla assaults and as symbolic acts of terrorism, they could now be integrated into battlefield operations to weaken enemy defence positions in advance of ground-troop assaults, in some ways paralleling the use of traditional artillery. This capability became particularly pertinent following the fall of Mosul in June 2014, when the Islamic State obtained enough arms to equip nearly 50,000 soldiers from Iraqi military stocks and sought to further expand the state."[4]

Writer Pepe Escobar in his article (Who profits from Kabul suicide bombing? ISIS-Khorasan aims to prove to Afghans and to the outside world that the Taliban cannot secure the capital, published on 30 August, 2021) documented links between the Haqqani terrorist group and the IS-K of Khorasan. However, he also noted that the suicide bomber who carried out the Kabul airport attack was identified Abdul Rahman Logari and his attack was organised by an IS-K sleeper cell: "Founded in 2015 by emigré jihadists dispatched to southwest Pakistan, IS-K is a dodgy beast. Its current head is one Shahab al-Mujahir, who was a mid-level commander of the Haqqani network headquartered in North Waziristan in the Pakistani tribal areas, itself a collection of disparate mujahideen and would-be jihadis under the family umbrella. Washington branded the Haqqani network as a terrorist organization way back in 2010, and treats several members as global terrorists, including Sirajuddin Haqqani, the head of the family after the death of the founder Jalaluddin Haqqani. Up to now, Sirajuddin was the Taliban deputy leader for the eastern provinces–on the same level with Mullah Baradar, the head of the political office in Doha, who was actually released from Guantanamo in 2014. Crucially, Sirajuddin's uncle, Khalil Haqqani, formerly in charge of the network's foreign financing, is now in charge of Kabul security and working as a diplomat 24/7. The previous ISIS-K leaders were snuffed out by US airstrikes in 2015 and 2016. ISIS-K started to become a real destabilizing force in 2020 when the regrouped band attacked Kabul University, a Doctor without Borders maternity ward, the Presidential palace and the airport. NATO intelligence picked up by a UN report attributes a maximum of 2,200 jihadists to ISIS-K, split into small cells."[5]

The IS-K is militarily strongest terrorist organization in Afghanistan that not only challenged the Taliban government, but Central Asian states as well. Having established centres across Afghanistan and some Central Asian state to recruit thousands of fighters and adorn them with modern technology and weapons, the IS-K needs a strong military infrastructure to commence its military campaign. In Syria and Iraq, the ISIS killed thousands of civilians and generated a strong revenue by transporting oil and narcotics drugs across Africa and Europe. In yesteryears, in Afghanistan, IS-K controlled rich mineral wealth, especially talc, chromite and marble. In 2017, Global Witness reported displacement of more than 60,000 people by fighting between IS-K and the Taliban for control of other mineral-rich districts close to Achin. A Taliban official explicitly linked the ferocity of the battle to the struggle over the mines. The IS-K's interest in Afghanistan's minerals should be an urgent wake-up call not just for the fight against extremist armed groups, but for the wider reform that the sector has been lacking so far. In each case, the Islamic State opportunistically sought to establish itself in an area primed for insurgency by both poor governance and a population susceptible to religious extremism. Global Witness noted. Expert and analyst, Michael Rubin in his commentary (Biden ignores Afghanistan at America's peril, The National Interest, 28 April, 2022) has raised the question of President Niden abandonment of Afghanistan and recent wave of terrorism:

"Recent mosque bombings are ominous because they suggest terror is about to get much worse. In the past, the Afghanistan fighting season began in April when winter snows melted enough to allow movement. The White House and Pentagon appear to have misinterpreted the relative calm which followed the U.S. withdrawal as a sign that the Taliban could consolidate control and, if provided enough aid, govern. In reality, the calm was illusionary. While Uzbekistan denies that there was a cross-border rocket attack into Termez on April 11, 2022, locals confirm the strike and say a diplomatic convenience motivates the denials. Also naive was the notion that the Taliban's desire for legitimacy would give the international community leverage. Two weeks ago, the Russian government quietly handed the Afghanistan embassy in Moscow over to a Taliban diplomat. Videos circulating on Telegram and Signal showing the Taliban flag now draped inside the building, with diplomats loyal to the former government unceremoniously booted from the embassy by the Russian government. The Russian move shows the gullibility of those who believed international opprobrium would be enough to ensure the Taliban respected women's rights. An even greater error—the blame for which transcends administrations—was the belief that the United States could co-opt the Taliban as an ally in the fight against even worse terror groups".[6]

The establishment of the ISIS networks in Tajikistan and Uzbekistan raised several questions including the failure of Tajik law enforcement agencies to intercept infiltration of ISIS fighters into the country. The Islamic State is now recruiting young people into its ranks, and supports them financially. In view of this development, Tajikistan introduced new legislation in 2015 allowing authorities to pardon citizens who voluntarily return home and express regret that they joined militant groups abroad, but, notwithstanding this legislation, people of all walks of life are joining Daesh consecutively. On 06 November 2019, BBC reported terror attack of the ISIS fighters on Checkpost of Tajik border with Uzbekistan, and killed 17 people. Analyst Damon Mehl in his paper (Damon Mehl, CTC Sentinel, November 2018, Volume-11, Issue-10), noted some aspects of the development of ISIS networks in Tajikistan:

"Jamaat Ansarullah, an Afghanistan-based Tajikistani terrorist group, was formed in 2010 with likely fewer than 100 members and has since received support from the Islamic Movement of Uzbekistan (IMU), the Taliban, and al-Qaeda. The group's stated mission is to bring an 'Islamic' government to Tajikistan. Beginning with its foundation, Jamaat Ansarullah sporadically published videos and disseminated messages through its website, which has been inactive since 2016. The group's leader Amriddin Tabarov was killed in Afghanistan in December 2015 and Tabarov's son-in-law Mavlavif Salmon was appointed as the new leader by the end of 2016. In 2014, Jamaat Ansarullah sent some of its members to fight in Syria with Jabhat al-Nusra, an al-Qaeda-aligned group now known as Hayat Tahrir al-Sham. At a point in 2014 or 2015, some Jamaat Ansarullah members ended up fighting alongside the Islamic State. The Islamic State subsequently began financially supporting Ansarullah, according to Afghanistan expert Antonio Giustozzi, citing a Jamaat Ansarullah commander. This support reportedly caused fissures between Jamaat Ansarullah and al-Qaeda, and by 2015, Ansarullah received 50 percent of its financial backing from the Islamic State. In October 2014, a Jamaat Ansarullah member going by the name Mansur stated on the group's website that Jamaat Ansarullah considered the Islamic State a jihadi organization, but had paused its decision on whether to accept the Islamic State's claim of being the caliphate".[7]

The Chechen fighters have also established networks across the Russian Federation and want to retrieve sophisticated weapons and weapons of mass destruction. The group in Afghanistan receives military training to strengthen its army for the future war against Russia. Pakistan have also trained Chechen commanders years ago, while during their jihad against Russia, some reports confirmed the participation of over 1000 Pakistani jihadists and retired military officers in fighting alongside their fighters. Analyst and researcher, Christian Bleuer (Chechens in Afghanistan: A Battlefield Myth That Will Not Die, published on 27 June 2016) noted the presence of Chechen leadership in Afghanistan: "Extremist members of Chechnya's rebel movement adhere to ideas tied to jihad and the creation of an Islamist state. Afghan and foreign officials say as many as 7,000 Chechens and other foreign fighters could be operating in the country, loosely allied with the Taliban and other militant groups. Local reporting by Pajhwok News, sourced to the Logar governor's spokesman, was slightly different, naming the targets as "Taliban Commanders Mullah Saber, Mullah Sabawon and Mullah Bashir," but also noting the presence of Chechens–in this case, three Chechen women who were allegedly killed. Khaama Press also reported the incident, noting that "[f]oreign insurgents fighting the Afghan forces is not new as scores of militants from Chechnya and other countries are routinely reported killed during the fight with the Afghan forces," with the caveat that "[t]he anti-government armed militant groups have not commented regarding the report so far."[8]

The 2021 Kabul bombing killed 103 people, while at least 1,300 persons were injured, Afghan Health Ministry noted. Writer and expert, Pepe Escobar (Who profits from the Kabul suicide bombing? ISIS-Khorasan aims to prove to Afghans and to the outside world that the Taliban cannot secure the capital. Asia Times, published on 27 August 2021) noted in his article that "responsibility for the bombing came via a statement on the Telegram channel of Amaq Media, the official Islamic State (ISIS) news agency. This means it came from centralized ISIS command, even as the perpetrators were members of ISIS-Khorasan". Expert and analyst, Michael W. S. Ryan in his research paper (ISIS: The Terrorist Group That Would Be a State, published in U.S. Naval War College) has described historical journey of the ISIS in Iraq and Syria. He also noted that the "ISIS developed its strategic approach within the modern jihadist tradition, which al Qaeda violently introduced to the United States with a series of escalating attacks, culminating in the attacks of September 11, 2001". Michael W. S. Ryan has argued that the 'ISIS used a strategic plan for establishing an Islamic Emirate, as presented in broad strokes by another al Qaeda strategist with the pseudonym Abu Bakr Naji and learned from U.S. operations, especially from the use of Sunni tribes during the successful "surge" in Iraq, which came close to destroying al Qaeda in Iraq.[9]

After the Taliban takeover, smuggling of narcotics drug, money extortion, and illegal extraction of minerals resources exacerbated. Taliban profited from minerals in Jalalabad, Badakhshan and Helmand provinces. Global Witness noted how local elites had to control extraction and employ people mainly from their own families, paying a set amount to the Taliban, which the source estimated at ($1,900-$4,770) a month. Taliban also collect taxes of ushr and zakat. They took a third of the value of the output this way. The Taliban searched for international recognition, as well as assistance to avoid a humanitarian and economic disaster in Afghanistan. However, no country officially recognised the Emirate, and the UN referred to the Taliban as the 'de facto' authorities. With its extensive territorial control and reach all over the country, the Taliban has taxed cultivation, processing, and smuggling of drugs; and units and members of the Taliban have been intensely involved in all these elements. The Taliban basically now controls one of the largest reserves of natural resources that the world very much needs. These comprise materials such as copper, iron, gold, and lithium. This gives the Taliban considerable leverage when dealing with external interests and possibly gives them political capital with which to negotiate. The Taliban derived income from mining directly under their control and are measured to stem further incomes from at least some of the mining areas controlled by the warlords."[10]

The IS-K was in control of Achin from late 2014 to 2018, but Taliban couldn't tolerate and declared war against the group, but the US Army airstrikes caused further widespread destruction in the area. The Taliban defeated Daesh in Achin. Now the US government wants to send its army back to Afghanistan to control all mineral sites in order to support its economy. The

Biden government wants to stabilize its economy be containerising more than $1 trillion mineral resources of Afghanistan. Moreover, in its press release (06 June 2016) Global Witness warned that Afghanistan's famous lapis mines are source of funding for the Taliban and armed groups. A new investigation reveals how Afghanistan's 6,500 year old lapis mines were driving corruption, conflict and extremism in the country. Global Witness found that the Taliban and other armed groups were earning up to 20 million dollars per year from Afghanistan's lapis mines, the world's main source of the brilliant blue lapis lazuli stone, which was used in jewellery around the world. As a result, the Afghan lapis lazuli stone should now be classified as a conflict mineral. Global Witness warned. The Global Witness' investigation also warned that the "Badakhshan mines were a strategic priority for the so-called Islamic State. Unless the Afghan government acts rapidly to regain control, the battle for the lapis mines was set to intensify and further destabilise the country, as well as fund extremism".[11]

Writer Asad Mirza (For quick revenue, Afghan mining wealth is the best option for Taliban: A decade back some US geologists had calculated the mineral reserves in Afghanistan to be in excess of $1 trillion, published on 14 March 2022) has noted that Afghan mining wealth was the best option for Taliban and the current Taliban administration, its Mining Ministry was apparently engaged in a lot of activities. However, Mirza argued that countering the deeds of the past Taliban administration, which blasted the two Bamiyan statues in 2001, this time Dilawar tried to assure by saying that these antiquities would be protected but how it hasn't been decided: "His preference would be to move the whole city to somewhere nearby and reconstruct it. Many prize artefacts have been shifted to the Kabul Museum. Mes Aynak flourished between the first and seventh centuries. Reportedly there are Buddhist monasteries, stupas, graveyards and wall paintings beneath the mountain. Its eastern flank is covered with antique structures that formed the city".[12] Global Witness interviewed a wide range of relevant sources, including a number from Khogyani and Sherzad and individuals with direct knowledge of the trade. According to Global Witness report, "the most direct of these sources was the Taliban official cited above, who described the revenues from the mines as critical to the group's survival in the district. He put the total daily income just from the major mining area of Ghunday at Rs 500,000 to Rs 1.2m ($4,760-$11,430)". Expert and writer, Nik Martin (Afghanistan: Taliban to reap $1 trillion mineral wealth, published on 18 August 2021) has documented Taliban revenue and financial benefits from illegal extraction of mines in Afghanistan. He also noted that Pakistan was also set to benefit from Afghanistan's minerals wealth because Islamabad supported the Taliban:

"The Taliban have been handed a huge financial and geopolitical edge in relations with the world's biggest powers as the militant group seizes control of Afghanistan for a second time. In 2010, a report by US military experts and geologists estimated that Afghanistan, one of the world's poorest countries, was sitting on nearly $1 trillion (€850 billion) in mineral wealth, thanks to huge iron, copper, lithium, cobalt and rare-earth deposits. In the subsequent decade, most of those resources remained untouched due to ongoing violence in the country. Meanwhile, the value of many of those minerals has skyrocketed, sparked by the global transition to green energy. A follow-up report by the Afghan government in 2017 estimated that Kabul's new mineral wealth may be as high as $3 trillion, including fossil fuels. Lithium, which is used in batteries for electric cars, smartphones and laptops, is facing unprecedented demand, with annual growth of 20% compared to just 5-6% a few years ago. The Pentagon memo called Afghanistan the Saudi Arabia of lithium and projected that the country's lithium deposits could equal Bolivia's-one of the world largest. Copper, too, is benefiting from the post-COVID global economic recovery-up 43% over the past year. More than a quarter of Afghanistan's future mineral wealth could be realized by expanding copper mining activities".[13]

The looting and ransacking of Afghanistan's natural resources by Taliban and criminal militias; such as the IS-K terrorist group, caused a misunderstanding between the Afghans and International Coalition that they all were involved in looting of mineral resources of their country. The IS-K controls large amount of territory in Afghanistan, and that includes parts of the country's rich mineral wealth, especially talc, chromite and marble. According to the Global Witness research report, several insurgents' groups, militias, Taliban and the ISIS are deeply involved in the plunder of these resources. These are the aspects discussed in the book by prominent authors. Now the IS-K has retrieved huge amount of money from illegal mines and the smuggling of narcotics drug, and Taliban also receive billions from drug trafficking and illegal mining. Expert and analyst, Tim McDonnell in his article (The Taliban now controls one of the world's biggest lithium deposits: Illegal mining of lapis lazuli, a gem, is a major source of revenue for the Taliban, 28 December 2021), argued that in 2010, an internal US Department of Defense memo called Afghanistan the Saudi Arabia of lithium:

"Global demand for lithium is projected to skyrocket 40-fold above 2020 levels by 2040, according to the International Energy Agency, along with rare earth elements, copper, cobalt, and other minerals in which Afghanistan is naturally rich. These minerals are concentrated in a small number of pockets around the globe, so the clean energy transition has the potential to yield a substantial payday for Afghanistan. In the past, Afghan government officials have dangled the prospect of lucrative mining contracts in front of their US counterparts as an enticement to prolong the American military presence in the country. With the Taliban in charge, that option is likely off the table.......The Taliban can't simply flick a switch and dive into the global lithium trade, Schoonover said. Years of conflict have left the country's physical infrastructure—roads, power plants, railways— in tatters. And at the moment Taliban militants are reportedly struggling even to maintain the provision of basic public services and utilities in the cities they have captured, let alone carry out economic policies that can attract international investors. Competing factions within the Taliban would make it very difficult for any company to negotiate mining deals, and China is unlikely to extend to the group the scale of infrastructure loans that would be required to bring any sizable mining operations online, said Nick Crawford, a development economics researcher at the International Institute for Strategic Studies think tank."[14]

Both Sherzad and Khogyani districts of Jalalabad province were entirely under the control of Taliban. In Badakhshan for example, the payments to the Taliban were linked to wider abuses around mining by a local militia. The story of financial source of Taliban and the IS-K terrorist group is complicated but evidences showcase that the three terrorist groups have been looting and plundering mineral resources of Afghanistan since 2015, they have also established a competent international trade networks for selling their plundered precious stones, gold and talc. While they generate money then purchase sophisticated weapons, modern surveillance system and invite young fighter from Pakistan based extremist and terrorist groups in order to strengthen their military positions. The Taliban and Islamic State also received millions of dollars from Europe, the United States, Pakistan and Qatari regime. They also received huge financial assistance from Iran and Saudi Arabia. The US and NATO have betrayed their Afghan proxies, spies and slaves by leaving them maroon and vulnerable in Afghanistan for Taliban to kill them one by one with impunity. After they left, they were dragged from their homes and taken to unknown places and killed shamelessly. Some were killed extra-judicially by terrorists of Haqqani Network and Taliban in front of their relatives, sons and daughters, but champions of human rights never realised their pain and screech, They supported Taliban and the Islamic State financially and militarily, and trained their fighters in their bases.

They purveyed military intelligence and instructed their Afghan spies to transport their suicide bomber to their destinations. Afghan police and the army played a bigger role in protecting the IS-K and Taliban suicide bombers in their bases and houses. The rise of ISIS in Afghanistan posed serious security concerns. According to a September 2016, Russian Foreign Ministry's Director of the Second Asian Department in Afghanistan, Kabulov claimed that about 2,500 ISIS combatants were in Afghanistan and the organization was preparing to expand from Afghanistan into other Central Asian countries and Russia, giving Moscow reasons to worry. Nuclear terrorism in Central Asia and Russia has risen important questions about the US and NATO policy towards Russia that without using biological and nuclear weapons against the country, its dream of supreme power will vanish. Authors Christopher McIntosh and Ian Storey (20 November 2019) in their well-written analysis have elucidated the real motive of US and NATO hegemonic design:

"While terrorist organizations vary widely in their internal organization and structure, almost all are highly sensitive to benefits and costs, both external and internal. By examining these, it will become clear that terrorists might have more to lose than gain by proceeding directly to an attack. Doing so might alienate their supporters, cause dissent among the ranks, and give away a bargaining chip without getting anything in return. While there is any number of far more likely scenarios for nuclear terrorism broadly understood, we focus only on groups with a working nuclear device, not a radiological dispersal device or the ability to attack a nuclear reactor. The threat posed by an operational device is fundamentally different, not least because possession would radically change the nature of the organisation as a strategic, warfighting group. A large body of work in terrorism studies teaches us that terrorist groups do behave strategically.[15]

Scholar and Lecturer Department of Social Sciences, Lahore Garrison University Pakistan, Dr. Yunis Khushi in his research paper (A Critical Analysis of Factors and Implications of ISIS Recruitments and Concept of Jihad-Bil-Nikah, published on 26 June 2017) noted important aspects of the ISIS training bases, and activities of women brigade of the Daesh-including Jihad-Bil-Nikah:

"The recruitment for ISIS has been going on in Pakistan for the past more than 3 years, but the Foreign and the Interior Ministries of Pakistan have been constantly denying the presence and activities of ISIS in Pakistan. Law Enforcement agencies have very recently arrested many people from Lahore, Islamabad, Karachi and Sialkot who were associated with ISIS networks. Men have been recruited as jihadis or mujahids and women as jihadi wives to provide sexual needs of fighters who are fighting in Syria, Iraq and Afghanistan. Many women, impressed and convinced through brainwashing with the concept of Jihad-Bil-Nikah, got a divorce from their Pakistani husbands and went to marry a Mujahid of ISIS for a certain period, came back gave birth to the child of Mujahid, and remarried their former husband. Some decide to continue that marriage for the rest of their lives. All of this is being done to obtain worldly wealth and later eternal life in Heaven because ISIS is paying something around 50,000 to 60,000 Pakistani currency per month to every warrior, which is a hefty amount for an unemployed youth suffering in unemployment, poverty and inflation in Pakistan, which is ruled by corrupt ruling elite for the past 68 years and masses only got poverty for being true Muslims and patriot Pakistanis. Most secret and law-enforcement agencies have behaved like silent bystanders to the activities of ISIS in the country. Is this an unofficial channel of providing soldiers to provide the Saudi demands for fighters to fight on behalf of Saudi armies in Yemen and Syria?"[15]

These trained terrorists managing attacks on civilian and government installations in Central Asia. Tajikistan's long, porous border with Afghanistan is a source of security concerns the reason for that transnational threats such as violent extremism and narcotics trafficking have intensified. Tajik nationals are present in Afghanistan and sometimes cross the border for terrorist attacks. Tajikistan has experienced several violent incidents attributed to IS-K, including prison riots in 2018 and 2019 and a 2019 attack on a border post. Taliban, the IS-K and Pakistan bases terrorist organizations are trying to expand their networks to Central Asia and Africa. Muslim were forced by the US army and CIA to join al Qaeda and ISIS terrorist groups and the ISIS sought the allegiance of the aggrieved communities. The US strike in Jalalabad killed 36 innocent people. The blast destroyed three underground tunnels as well as weapons and ammunition. However, ISIS denied that any of its fighters were killed or injured, according to a statement in Arabic distributed by the terror group's media wing, Amaq News Agency. "This was the right weapon against the right target," Gen. John Nicholson, commander for US forces in Afghanistan, told a press conference. Expert and writer Rushni Kapur in her paper (The Persistent

ISKP Threat to Afghanistan: On China's Doorstep, Middle East Institute, published on January 6, 2022) has documented atrocities of the Islamic State of Khorasan in Afghanistan:

"Two separate bombs were detonated in Dasht-e-Barchi in Kabul on December 10, killing two and injuring three others. Although no group has claimed responsibility for the attack, the Islamic State of Khorasan Province (ISKP) is likely behind the latest bout of violence. ISKP's fingerprints have been on other attacks. One of the worst, which killed over 180 people and injured hundreds, took place outside the Kabul airport in August 2021 during the final days of evacuations. The increasing number of attacks demonstrates the growing threat posed by the ISKP. ISKP has been emboldened by the withdrawal of foreign forces whose previous counterterrorism measures had constrained their activities in Afghanistan. The group is leveraging the power vacuum and lack of political stability to increase their foothold and mount a challenge to the Taliban's rule, monopoly on violence, and efforts to gain international recognition. Moreover, ISKP is trying to absorb disillusioned Taliban fighters and other smaller militant groups into its fold. Although the Taliban has given assurances that Afghanistan will not be used as a launchpad for incursions into neighbouring countries, the growing number of attacks claimed by or attributed to ISKP raise concerns about whether the former has a firm hold on the country. Despite capturing ISKP-held districts in the past, countering the group is proving to be harder this time for the Taliban as they transition from a guerrilla-style insurgency to a government. Beijing's overriding security concerns are spill over effects from the Taliban's takeover of Kabul to other militant groups, the absorption of East Turkestan Islamic Movement (ETIM) fighters into ISKP fold, and possibility of orchestrating attacks in Xinjiang province".[16]

The Islamic State has been more influential during the past decade in Afghanistan and captured several districts where Taliban were unable to penetrate. All jihadist groups, including the ISIS Philippines, the ISIS in Indonesia, Thailand and Bangladesh have direct and indirect presence in Afghanistan. In 2017, ISIS was able to overrun the city of Marawi. ISIS-Philippines. Both the al-Qaeda and ISIS core groups and their franchises have the capacity to use terrorist tactics ranging from improvised explosive devices, vehicle borne improvised explosive devices, suicide bombings, drone attacks, and mortar launchings. An ISIS franchise in Sri Lanka, the National Tawheed Jamaah, was the perpetrator of the 2018 Easter Day attacks that killed more than 300 people in seven separate targets.[17]

Assistant Professor and Research Faculty with Terrorism, Transnational Crime and Corruption Center (TraCCC) and the Schar School of Policy and Government at George Mason University, Mahmut Cengiz, in his paper (ISIS or al-Qaeda: Which Looms as the Greater Threat to Global Security? Small War Journal, published on 01 October, 2022) has noted some aspects of the ISIS presence and operational mechanism in Libya and Egypt:

"The ISIS-Libya emerged in Derna, a port city in eastern Libya, in 2014 when a group of 300 former Libyan members of the Battar Brigade returned to their country after fighting in Syria and allied with the Ansar al-Sharia terrorist group. ISIS-Tunisia emerged in 2015 when the group was involved in attacks in Sousse, Tunisia, including the targeting of the Bardo Museum. ISIS-Tunisia has maintained its capacity to carry out attacks in the country, where the group executed two suicide attacks in 2019. In Egypt, which also hosts many jihadist terrorist groups, most of the attacks by these groups have occurred in the northern Sinai area. ISIS-Sinai was to blame for 320 terrorist attacks between 2013 and 2017. This ISIS franchise originated from the Sunni Salafist Ansar Bayt al-Maqdis terrorist group that declared war against the Egyptian government immediately after the ouster of President Mohamed Morsi in a July 2013 military coup. The origin of the ISIS-Somalia franchise dates to 2012 when al-Shabaab assigned Abdul Qadir Mumin to operate in its remote outpost in Puntland in northeastern Somalia. ISIS-Democratic Republic of Congo (ISIS-DRC) emerged in 2017 in the Democratic Republic of Congo when militants from a new brand of the rebel group Allied Democratic Forces (ADF). Known as the City of Monotheism and Monotheists, the group leaned toward ISIS. The ADF is an Islamist group that has fought against the governments of the DRC and Uganda for several years. The US Department of State designated ISIS-DRC as a foreign terrorist organization in 2021 along with the ISIS branch in Mozambique (ISIS-Mozambique)".[18]

Chapter 6

The IS-K, Central Asian Terrorist Groups, Taliban and Prospect of Nuclear Terrorism

The Islamic State of Khorasan expedition towards Central Asia is causing consternation and fear in the region. In May 2022, Tajik media quoted security officials that four BM-1 missiles had been fired at Tajikistan from Afghanistan. However, Afghan media, quoted the Taliban-led government attributed the attack to the ISIL while local Tajik officials at the Afghan border claimed that the terrorist act was carried out by anti-government militants in Tajikistan. That was the second missile attack from Afghanistan on Central Asia. The Taliban government said the missile attack was investigated. The Afghan Islamic Press (AIP) news agency quoted an IS press release claiming the militants had fired the rockets from the Khawaja Ghar district of Afghanistan's Takhar Province toward unspecified military targets in Tajikistan. However, on 29 April 2022, in their Diplomat magazine article, (Islamic State in Afghanistan Looks to Recruit Regional Tajiks, Inflict Violence Against Tajikistan: ISKP's expanded media campaign seeks to recruit ethnic Tajik and nationals as well as incite militant violence against Tajikistan) experts Lucas Webber and Riccardo Valle argued that the IS-K wants to recruit more Tajik and Uzbek national to commence war against Tajikistan:

"Shortly after the Islamic State Khorasan Province's (ISKP) first reported an attack targeting Uzbek territory on April 18, one Tajik-speaking supporter on Telegram, feeling particularly inspired, urged similar operations against Tajikistan. Likewise, the official ISKP branch media outlet al-Azaim released an Uzbek-language audio statement celebrating the act, declaring it the opening salvo in the "great jihad to Central Asia." These hostilities have been festering for some time, as displayed in a July 2021 Islamic State (IS) video from the "Makers of Epic Battles Series" featuring a Tajik ISKP militant threatening the "taghuti" (tyrannical) government in Dushanbe, explicitly naming Tajikistan President Emomali Rahmon. The animosity has also manifested in a series of IS attacks against Tajikistan over the last few years. ISKP seeks to further exploit such sentiments and, recently, has markedly intensified its propaganda outreach to speakers of Central Asian languages inside Afghanistan and throughout the region. The Islamic State sees fertile opportunity in Central Asia and has placed an increased focus on appealing to ethnic Tajiks and criticizing Tajikistan's government. This strategic calculation based in part on the Islamic State's success in attracting and integrating Tajik jihadists in Iraq and Syria with the founding of the caliphate in 2014 and in Afghanistan since the branch's emergence in 2015. ISKP's expanded media campaign seeks to recruit ethnic Tajik and nationals as well as incite militant violence against Tajikistan. It is also purposed to discredit the Taliban as a governing body and discredit it as a religious authority in the eyes of potential Tajik supporters".[1]

On 06 November 2019, IS-K had attacked outpost in Tajikistan in which 17 people were killed. In their New York Times article (ISIS Fighters Attack Outpost in Tajikistan: The violence points to the resilience of the Islamic State and its longstanding aim to spread from its enclave in Afghanistan) writers and experts, Thomas Gibbons-Neff and Najim Rahim have noted recent attacks of the IS-K in Tajikistan and discussed that the attack pointed to the resilience of the Islamic State and its longstanding aim to spread further into Central Asia from its enclave in Afghanistan. They were of the opinion that "it came almost two weeks after the group's leader, Abu Bakr al-Baghdadi, was killed during an American military operation in north-western Syria…" The Islamic State, Thomas Gibbons-Neff and Najim Rahim noted, didn't take responsibility for the clash, which occurred around 50 miles southwest of the capital, Dushanbe.[2] The Takfiri groups of al-Nusra Front and the so-called Islamic Jihad Union are also employing nationals from Central Asia. In some countries, the process of employment is done through indigenous people. Efforts of terrorists to get access to nuclear materials and technologies appear to be increasing at the same time as there is a race for developing nuclear power projects in the Middle East, Africa and Asia. This might create fertile soil for the rise of nuclear terrorism on a global scale.

There is evidence that terrorist groups have tried to acquire the material needed to construct a crude nuclear explosive device, or a dirty bomb. Terrorists use biological agents because they are often difficult to detect. In 2016, after the two ISIS brothers involved in the Brussels bombings, Khalid and Ibrahim el-Bakraoui, were captured and killed, authorities discovered they had been secretly watching a Belgian nuclear scientist who worked at the Tihange Nuclear Power Station. Nuclear terrorism remains a constant threat to global peace. Access to terrorist organizations to nuclear material is a bigger threat to civilian population. Terrorist groups can gain access to highly enriched uranium or plutonium, because they have the potential to create and detonate an improvised nuclear device. Since the ISIS has already retrieved nuclear materials from Mosul city of Iraq, we can assert that terrorist groups like ISIS and Katibat Imam Bukhari, and Chechen extremist groups can make access to biological and nuclear weapons with the help of local experts. Nuclear facilities also often store large amounts of radioactive material, spent fuel, and other nuclear waste products that terrorists could use in a dirty bomb. Without access to such fissile materials, extremist and radicalised groups can turn their attention toward building a simple radiological device.

The most difficult part of making a nuclear bomb is acquiring the nuclear material, but some Muslim and non-Muslim state might facilitate the ISIS, Lashkar-e-Taiba, Chechen extremist groups and Afghanistan and Pakistan based groups to attack nuclear installations in Russia and Central Asia. Information on how to manipulate nuclear material to produce an explosive device—an improvised nuclear device, which would produce a nuclear explosion and a mushroom cloud, or a radiation-dispersal device, which would spread dangerous radioactive material over a substantial area—is now available widely. Daesh (ISIS) seized control of the Iraqi city of Mosul in 2014. Pakistan has also been heavily dependent on outside supply for many key direct- and dual-use goods for its nuclear programs. It maintains smuggling networks and entities willing to break supplier country laws to obtain these goods. Many of these illegal imports have been detected and stopped. These illegal procurements have led to investigations and prosecutions in the supplier states, leading to revelations of important details about Pakistan's complex design to make nuclear explosive materials and nuclear weapons. According to some reports weapons-grade and weapons-usable nuclear materials have been stolen by terrorist groups from some states. Once a crude weapon is in a country, terrorists would transport it in a vehicle to city and then detonate it in a crowded area.

Presence of IS-K in Afghanistan led to escalation of terrorist acts in Central Asia. On 23 April 2022, Tehran Times reported President Raisi's warning that the crimes committed by the Zionist regime against Palestinian worshippers and those committed by ISIS against Afghan worshippers were the result of movements created by the West. Speaking at a religious congregation marking the anniversary of Imam Ali's martyrdom (PBUH),

President Raisi said that the current Afghan authorities were responsible for protecting all Afghans, including Shias. He stated that Imam Ali exhorted Muslims to join with the downtrodden against the oppressors, pointing out that the world is witnessing two crimes against Muslims. A separate blast led to at least 11 more casualties in Kunduz, another northern Afghan city, according to a provincial health official.[3] In 2018, terrorist incidents in Central Asia alerted Russia that the United State and its allies might wanted to commence confrontations in Central Asia. An independent non-profit organization, the Soufan Centre in its report (IntelBrief. Terrorism Trends in Central Asia. The Soufan Center (TSC) November 26, 2018) argued: "Terrorism trends in Central Asia suggest that the region was shifting from primarily an exporter of foreign fighters to one where domestic and regional terrorist attacks may become increasingly more common. Uzbekistan and Tajikistan were two of the countries that had produced the largest number of foreign fighters per capita: 1,500 and 1,300, respectively. Yet, the region had mostly been spared from terrorist attacks and, instead, religious extremists traveling elsewhere. The diaspora had produced several attacks with deadly consequences: the Stockholm and New York truck attacks, the St. Petersburg Metro bombing, and the New Year's Istanbul night club shooting were but a few examples of attacks perpetrated by foreign fighters from Central Asia. Authorities and security services worldwide were fearful of similar attacks in the future".[4]

Communications within Al Qaeda, Princeton Near Eastern Studies expert Michael Doran has shown that the group behaved "almost exclusively according to the principle of realpolitik," and was "virtually compelled " to do so by the "central doctrines of Islamic extremism" itself. Michael Doran noted that it may not appear so based on terrorists' tactics, most groups had all the hallmarks of strategic decision-making, command and control, and sensitivity to costs. Regardless of what one thinks about the debates regarding terrorist organizations and their ability to acquire these weapons—either by theft or gift—acquisition and maintenance was going to be resource-intensive and difficult". Michael Doran noted. If terrorist groups such as ISIS or Lashkar-e-Taiba and Tablighi Jamaat determine to go nuclear, what will be the security preparations in Central Asia to intercept these groups? These and other Pakistan based groups can attempt to manufacture fissile material needed to fuel a nuclear weapon—either highly enriched uranium or plutonium, and then use it. Moreover, there are possibilities that Pakistan, Afghanistan and Central Asia based extremist and jihadist groups can purchase fissile material in black market or steal it from a military or civilian facility and then use that material to construct an improvised nuclear device. Yet today, with Russia rising again as a military power, the grim logic of nuclear statecraft is returning.

The Islamic State and Central Asian terrorist groups seek biological and nuclear weapons to use against security forces in Russia and Central Asia. The modus operandi of ISIS or ISIS inspired individuals are diverse and show no moral restraints, as recent attacks in Brussels and Berlin demonstrated. The use of biological and chemical weapons by terrorists has prompted huge fatalities in Iraq and Syria. However, preventing dangerous materials from falling into the hands of ISIS, Pakistani terrorist groups, and Central Asia extremists is a complex challenge. Since 2013, there has been extensive use of chemical weapons in armed conflicts in Syria by US backed terrorist groups. Since 2015, the IS-K started attacking and beheading innocent civilians in Afghanistan, its way of killing was brutal even by the standards of the Afghan conflict, which has alienated at least some potential supporters, and could be another factor limiting their growth. Global Witness in its research report (At Any Price we Will Take the Mines: The Islamic State, the Taliban and Afghanistan's White Talc Mountains, published in May 2018) had documented political rivalries between the IS-K, Taliban and al Qaeda in different parts of Afghanistan:

"In January 2015, the leadership of the Islamic State of Iraq and Al-Shams (ISIS) declared the creation of the Khorasan wilayat or governorate – "Khorasan" being a historical term for a region encompassing Afghanistan, Pakistan and parts of other countries. The group's creation was important for the Islamic State. It marked the first official ISIS affiliate outside of the Arab world, had an important religious dimension, and allowed ISIS to challenge their rival Al Qaeda on the territory where they have their primary base, in the Afghanistan-Pakistan border regions. Indeed, ISKP's initial attacks were against the Taliban, Al Qaeda's ally and protector. ISKP quickly grew into a significant force after it was established. Government offensives in Pakistan's tribal areas helped push militants, including foreign fighters, into Afghanistan, swelling the ranks of the movement, which quickly became active in a dozen provinces around the country (including a number of Northern provinces beyond their original Pashtun power base). In July 2015, the Islamic Movement of Uzbekistan (IMU), a significant foreign-led militant group based in Badakhshan province in northern Afghanistan, also pledged bayat [allegiance] to ISIS. In Nangarhar, the fractured nature in many areas of both tribal society, and of the pre-2015 insurgency, made particularly fertile ground for an ISKP coup......
In April 2017, the largest non-nuclear weapon in the United States arsenal,

the 'Mother of All Bombs', crashed into a hillside in the district of Achin in eastern Afghanistan, targeting a network of tunnels held by the Afghan affiliate of the Islamic State (known as Islamic State–Khorasan Province, or ISKP)."[5]

The absence of chemical attacks outside of Mosul after the city became cut-off from the rest of the 'caliphate' earlier this year indicates that the group has not established alternative production facilities. But US intelligence believes that a new chemical weapons cell has been set up in the Euphrates River Valley. In late July 2015, the Islamic State fired several mortar bombs at Kurdish People's Protection Units (YPG) positions near the city of Hasakah in northeastern Syria. A statement released by the YPG after the attack described how the explosions had released "a yellow gas with a strong smell of onions," and that "the ground immediately around the impact sites was stained with an olive-green liquid that turned to a golden yellow after exposure to sunshine". As events currently unfolding in Afghanistan show, however, when it comes to many of the thousands of Afghan interpreters who over the past 20 years have risked their lives helping allied forces, that promise is an entirely hollow one.1 Experts and writers, Joana Cook and Gina Vale in their research paper (From Daesh to 'Diaspora': Tracing the Women and Minors of Islamic State. ICSR King's College London 2018), have discussed the evolution and strength of the ISIS terrorist group in Iraq and Syria:

"The self-proclaimed Islamic State (IS) has been described as a hybrid terrorist organisation and conventional army, a religious, millenarian group, an insurgency, and a pseudo-state, amongst others. It produced and disseminated propaganda at an unprecedented rate, and reached a wider global audience than any past terrorist organisation in history. As it increasingly seized territory and resources, at its peak in late 2014 it was believed the group controlled over 100,000 km of land and the 11 million resident's therein. IS and those inspired by the group have thus far carried out over 4,300 attacks across at least 29 countries, demonstrating the group remains a significant and shared global concern. Perhaps most notable is the diversity of those who formed its ranks that distinguished it from any terror group in history–as demonstrated in our original dataset at least 41,490 citizens from 80 countries travelled to Syria and Iraq, a quarter of which were women and minors. These figures for affiliates peaked at 2,000 per month in 2014, before receding to just 50 per month in 2016. More than 7,366 of these have now returned to their country of departure. The collapse of IS' so-called 'caliphate' (the territory held and administered by

IS between 2014 and 2017) marked a turning point in the organisation infamous for its brutality and terror, but the future shape and trajectory of the organisation remains unknown. Yet, the group's original vision, and the meticulous and systematic manner in which it was carried out, suggests that its goals extended beyond the 'state' it had built, and considered how to carry its ideology and organisation forward in the face of the imminent loss of territory"[6]

The ISIS carried out deadliest attacks with chemical agents in Syria that needed significant knowledge and the specialized resources. In October 2017, Columb Strack in his paper revealed that the ISIS was the first terrorist group that developed chemical weapons, and the group was the first non-state actor to develop a banned chemical warfare agent and combined it with a projectile delivery system. "However, it appears to have been forced to abandon its chemical weapons production after the loss of Mosul in June 2017. The US left Afghanistan to terrorist Taliban. Taliban, the IS-K and Lashkar-e-Taiba are now torturing women and children and looting mineral resources of the country to make money and retrieve modern weapons. They collect taxes, promoting smuggling of narco drugs and sophisticated weapons"[7] Expert and writer, Oved Lobel in his article (The Taliban are losing the fight against Islamic State, published in Asia Times, on 6 December 2021) has described brutality of Taliban and the IS-K in Jalalabad:

"In response, the Taliban has been conducting a scorched-earth campaign of indiscriminate violence, detaining and disappearing around 1,500 people in Nangarhar province alone. Recently, the Taliban deployed more than 1,000 additional fighters to Nangarhar province and escalated their brutality. Hundreds of suspected IS-K operatives were murdered and many bodies, some beheaded, were dumped in the streets or strung up in public as a warning. So brutal is this Taliban war with IS-K that the hospital in Jalalabad, Nangarhar's provincial capital, treated more casualties in November than it treated during the war between the Taliban, NATO and the Afghan government. Given that many of those being disappeared and murdered are not IS-K operatives, the Taliban's campaign may only serve to increase IS-K recruitment, and there's little evidence that it's having any impact on the group's operations. Indeed, IS-K gives as good as it gets, most recently beheading several Taliban fighters in Kandahar, which, together with the mosque bombing in October, indicates that even the Taliban's stronghold is vulnerable. Taliban intelligence officials in Kabul secretly admit that one area of Nangarhar has become a 'no-go zone' for them and is 'one hundred percent' controlled by IS-K".[8]

BBC (20 August 2021) reported the Taliban door-to-door manhunt across the country: "The hardliner Islamist group has tried to reassure Afghans since seizing power in a lightning offensive, promising there would be "no revenge". But there were growing fears of a gap between what they said and what they did. The warning the group were targeting "collaborators" came in a confidential document by the RHIPTO Norwegian Centre for Global Analyses, which provides intelligence to the UN: "There are a high number of individuals that are currently being targeted by the Taliban and the threat is crystal clear," Christian Nellemann, who heads the group behind the report, told the BBC. "It is in writing that, unless they give themselves in, the Taliban will arrest and prosecute, interrogate and punish family members on behalf of those individuals." He warned that anyone on the Taliban's blacklist was in severe danger, and that there could be mass executions.[9] BBC noted. Writer and expert, Anna Powles in her article (Afghan debacle exposes moral hazard of outsourcing war: Afghan security contractors left behind as US and NATO forces withdrawal could pay the ultimate price for their services, Asia Times, 26 August 2021) has noted that Afghanistan has been a gravy train for the global private security industry for the past two decades:

"Under the Trump administration, private security companies with Pentagon contracts numbered nearly 6,000, costing US$2.3 billion in 2019. When the US military withdrawal began, these private contractors dropped to about 1,400 by July 2021. Until now, however, private security firms were such a critical element of the war effort that their departure was considered a key factor in the collapse of the Afghan army. The appeal of these private security contractors lies in their arms-length advantage they are relatively disposable and carry little political cost. This allows the industry to operate opaquely, with little oversight and even less accountability. In the case of the Australian embassy guards, it would appear their direct employers have done little to secure their safety. How, then, can these companies and the governments that employ them be held accountable? However, ICoC Executive Director Jamie Williamson has said: The situation in Afghanistan is shining a spotlight on the duty of care clients of private security companies have towards local staff and their families ... We expect to see both our government and corporate members ensure the safety and well-being of all private security personnel working on government and other contracts, whatever their nationality"[10].

The New York Times report on Taliban's Suicide Brigade commenced a new debate in international press that Afghanistan has endorsed suicide terrorism as an official policy. Writers Thomas Gibbons-Neff, Sharif Hassan and Ruhullah Khapalwak, on November 3, 2021, noted that the new Taliban government in 2021 brought together families of Afghan and Pakistani suicide bombers in a hotel and praised their suicide mission, and quoted Haqqani that their sacrifices were for religion, for the country and for Islam. "Deputy Minister of information and culture and spokesperson of the Taliban Zabiullah Mujahid said that the battalion would be part of their special forces and would be active under the Defence Ministry." Thomas Gibbons-Neff, Sharif Hassan and Ruhullah Khapalwak noted. They also argued: "the defence Ministry of IEA had said that they are working on building a 100,000-member army that will be fully equipped. IS-KP wrote last year in an editorial in the weekly newspaper al Nabha that the Taliban were merely proxies for the United States. The editorial also criticised the "new Taliban" for wearing an "Islamic guise" to undermine IS-KP in the region. A special suicide battalion named Lashkar-e Mansur will be deployed to Afghanistan's borders," the Hama Press local news agency quoted the governor as saying. According to the report, suicide bombers from this battalion took part in terror attacks against the ousted government's forces and members of the US-led international coalition".[11]

Nuclear trafficking in South Asia was a key concern while the nuclear black marketing networks of Pakistani generals and some mafia scientists were uncovered in Libya to Syria, Malaysia and Afghanistan. Recent media reports identified Moldovan criminal groups that attempted to smuggle radioactive materials to Daesh (also known as the Islamic State of Iraq and Syria, or ISIS) in 2015. Cases of nuclear smuggling in Central Asia were made in recent cases. Analyst and expert, Muhammad Wajeeh, a Research Associate at Department of Development Studies, COMSATS Institute of Information Technology, Abbottabad Pakistan in his research paper (Nuclear Terrorism: A Potential Threat to World's Peace and Security-JSSA Vol II, No. 2) has reviewed a consternating threat of nuclear terrorism in South and Central Asia:

"ISIS is believed to have about 90 pounds of low grade uranium (which was seized from Mosul University in Iraq were the invasion of the city in 2014) that can be used in the Dirty Bomb's to create serious panic among the public. In 2015 and 2016, ISIS became the leading high profile jihadist group in Iraq and Syria. Moreover, ISIS carried out attacks in Paris on November 13, 2015, killing 130 civilians and injuring more than 100 people. The ISIS carried out a series of three coordinated suicide. Bombings in Belgium: one at Maalbeek Metro Staon, Brussels and two at Brussels Airport in Zaventem, killing about 32 civilians and injuring 300 people. During the attacks, a G4S guard working on the Belgian nuclear research centre was also murdered and it led the world believing that the ISIS has a paternal plot to attack the nuclear facility either to steal the radioactive material for dirty bomb or to release the radioactive material and waste into the atmosphere. These attacks also raised the issue of nuclear security were a discovery made by the Belgian authorities that the ISIS has kept an eye on the local nuclear scientists and their families. Moreover, two Belgian nuclear power plant workers at Deol having knowledge of the nuclear sites joined ISIS and could provide assistance to exploit them for terrorist purposes. On March 30, al-Furat, the media wing of ISIS, threatened attacks on Germany and Britain on the eve of Washington Nuclear Security Summit 2016".[12]

The United States manages 3,750 nuclear warheads, while a press release from the State Department confirmed 2,000 warheads to be dismantled. President Biden announced that under the AUKUS agreement, Australia would retrieve nuclear powered submarines while President Putin exhibited his disagreement on the deteriorating regime of arms control but reduced the number of warheads deployed on Russia's ballistic missiles to meet the New START limit. Since January 2022, North Koreans carried out four missile tests, two of what they claim to be a hypersonic missile system, along with tests of ballistic missiles fired from a train and short-range, solid-fuelled ballistic missiles. Nuclear weapons experts and analysts, Hans M. Kristensen and Matt Korda (2021) have noted that 'Russia's nuclear modernization program was motivated in part by Moscow's strong desire to maintain overall parity with the United States'. On 28 July, the United States and Russia restarted bilateral Strategic Stability Dialogue. The Biden administration upheaved prospect of restricting military manoeuvres and missile deployments in Eastern Europe insomuch as Russia corresponds at the fore of dialogue on its military deployment in Ukraine, but the hostile attitude of the Biden administration further caused scepticism when the country's leadership unnecessarily demonstrated superiority and military strength. In January 2022, People's Republic of China, France, Russian, the United Kingdom and the United States in a joint statement declared the avoidance of nuclear war. Experts and writers, Keir A. Lieber and Daryl G. Press in their research paper (Why States Won't Give Nuclear Weapons to Terrorists. International Security, Vol. 38, No. 1, Summer 2013), have warned that transferring weapons to terrorists make sense only if a state fears retaliation. They also noted that giving nuclear capability to a terrorist group with which the state enjoys close relations and substantial trust could allow the state to conduct the attack while avoiding devastating punishment:

"The calculated, "back-door" approach of transferring weapons to terrorists makes sense only if a state fears retaliation. The core of the nuclear attack-by-proxy argument is that a state otherwise deterred by the threat of retaliation might conduct an attack if it could do so surreptitiously by passing nuclear weapons to terrorists. Giving nuclear capability to a terrorist group with which the state enjoys close relations and substantial trust could allow the state to conduct the attack while avoiding devastating punishment. Some analysts are sceptical about such sponsored nuclear terrorism, arguing that a state may not be willing to deplete its small nuclear arsenal or stock of precious nuclear materials. More important, a state sponsor would fear that a terrorist organization might use the weapons or materials in ways the state never intended, provoking retaliation that would destroy the regime. Nuclear weapons are the most powerful weapons a state can acquire, and handing that power to an actor over which the state has less than complete control would be an enormous, epochal decision—one unlikely to be taken by regimes that are typically obsessed with power and their own survival. Perhaps the most important reason to doubt the nuclear-attack-by-proxy scenario is the likelihood that the ultimate source of the weapon might be discovered".[13]

Central Asian terrorist groups based in Afghanistan are seeking nuclear and biological weapons to use against regional state, or they may well use against Russian armed forces. High-level radioactive material stolen from one place can end up in a dirty bomb in another. Even those states that do not engage in international counterterrorism campaigns or possess radioactive materials can be targeted or affected by nuclear terrorism. The UN Security Council has specifically addressed the threat of weapons of mass destruction and chemical, biological, radiological and nuclear terrorism on a number of occasions. In resolution 1373 (2001), the Council recognized the connection between international terrorism and, inter alia, the illegal movement of such materials. As President Putin warned if NATO member state or the United States interfered in Ukraine, his country would go nuclear. This warning of Russian Federation added in the pain of the United Nation. Experts and writers, Edward Lemon, Vera Mironova and William Tobey in their paper (Nuclear, Chemical and Biological Terrorism in Central Asia and Russia: Al Qaeda, the ISIS Affiliated Groups and Security of Sensitive Biological Weapons Facilities) have argued that the fate of defeated Central Asian fighters from the Islamic State and other violent extremist groups will obviously play a critical role in their ability to spread an IS-related CBRN threat:

"The fate of defeated Central Asian fighters from the Islamic State and other violent extremist groups will obviously play a critical role in their ability to spread an IS-related CBRN threat. From 2014 to 2017, the Islamic State produced and used chemical weapons in 37 separate attacks, but there is only one recorded incident of an IS chemical-weapons capability being transferred outside of Iraq or Syria, and it was to Australia, with no public evidence of participation by Central Asians. IS also shrivelled the home of a Belgian nuclear official, although the purpose of that action remains obscure. In 2015, the IS publication Dabiq alluded to an interest in nuclear terrorism. The article with murky intent and provenance warned: "Let me throw a hypothetical operation onto the table. The Islamic State has billions of dollars in the bank, so they call on their wila'yah in Pakistan to purchase a nuclear device through weapons dealers with links to corrupt officials in the region. The weapon is then transported overland until it makes it to Libya, where the mujahedeen move it south to Nigeria." No concrete plots or preparations by ISIS to obtain nuclear weapons or material, however, have been discovered and publicly disclosed. Moreover, even in 2015 when IS controlled far more people, resources and territory than they do today, David Albright and Sarah Burkhard concluded that "Daesh's public boasts and fantasies about its easy pathways to nuclear weapons should be dismissed."[14]

The statement of nuclear powers confirmed their commitment to work with all states to create a security environment more conducive. "We intend to continue seeking bilateral and multilateral diplomatic approaches to avoid military confrontations, strengthen stability and predictability, increase mutual understanding and confidence, and prevent an arms race that would benefit none and endanger all. We are resolved to pursue constructive dialogue with mutual respect and acknowledgment of each other's security interests and concerns". The statement noted. The US assertion that Moscow might create an environment of a false flag operation in Eastern Ukraine as a pretext for invading all or part of the country was repudiated by the Russian military. "Russia is laying the groundwork to have the option of fabricating a pretext for invasion, including through sabotage activities and information operations, by accusing Ukraine of preparing an imminent attack against Russian forces, according to an email of the state department sent to the country's bureaucrats and technocrats. In November 2021, President

Biden and Chinese President held their first face-to-face conversation on managing great power competition and averting a new Cold War but both sides failed to produce a diplomatic breakthrough. Experts and writers, Alexandra Rimpler Sschmid, Ralf Trapp Sarah Leonard, Christian Kaunert, Yves Dubucq, Claude Lefebvre, and Hanna Mohn in their paper (EU preparedness and responses to Chemical, Biological, Radiological and Nuclear (CBRN) threats. Directorate General for External Policies, Policy Department 2021, European Parliament Coordinator: Policy Department for External Relations Directorate General for External Policies of the Union) have highlighted arrival of foreign terrorist fighters from Syria and Iraq and their use of chemical weapons against European states:

"Against that backdrop, concerns grew in the EU that foreign terrorist fighters returning from the Syrian conflict might use chemical weapons against European states. In the wake of the terrorist attacks in Paris in November 2015, which did not involve CBRN weapons but were conducted by several terrorists with links to Syria, the French Prime Minister at the time, Manuel Valls, declared the following: "We must not rule anything out. I say it with all the precautions needed. But we know and bear in mind that there is also a risk of chemical or bacteriological weapons". In its 2016 European Union Terrorism Situation and Trend (TE-SAT) report, the EU Agency for Law Enforcement Cooperation (Europol) noted that "[the] phenomenon of individuals travelling for terrorist purposes to conflict zones increases the risk that expertise in the use of chemical weapons can be transferred to the European Union by returning foreign terrorist fighters'. In addition, Europol has highlighted that CBRN-related topics have regularly been included in online terrorist propaganda. Of particular interest is also the agency's observation that there has been a significant increase in the number of tutorials for conducting small-scale CBRN attacks which have been shared on the internet. Such tutorials usually recommend the use of toxic industrial chemicals since those are available in the EU due to their dual-use nature.[15]

Chapter 7

The Taliban Financial Resources: Drug Trafficking, Hawala, Illegal Mining, and Military Strength

Dr. Sanchita Bhattacharya

Introduction

The Taliban ruled Afghanistan from 1996 until late 2001, when they were ousted by US-led coalition forces. In spite of the 20-year conflict that followed and the deaths of tens of thousands of Taliban fighters, the group's territorial control and military strength kept on increasing, till they made the 'comeback' in August, 2021 (Dawood Azami, 2021). After the 2001 dismissal, the Taliban gradually regrouped and began an insurgency that by 2005 was challenging US and international military forces, along with the new Afghan government and its nascent security forces. Post 2009-2011 surge, US force levels diminished as Afghan forces took charge of the nationwide security. In spite of gaining political legitimacy, deep and abiding divisions among Afghan political elites, along with extensive corruption, damaged the government's authority and in a way reinforced the Taliban militia, which kept on gaining victory in battlefields while expanding its domain. In February 2020, the US-Taliban agreement, signed in Doha, the Taliban agreed to take unspecified action to prevent other groups (including Al Qaeda) from using Afghan soil to threaten the United States and its allies, in return for the full removal of international forces from Afghanistan by May 2021.

In 2021, American President Joseph Biden deferred the withdrawal date by several months; but, two weeks before that withdrawal was to conclude, the Taliban arrived at Kabul on August 15, 2021, the finale of a rapid nationwide military advance that shocked the entire world (Thomas, 2021). The Taliban came out of the shadow after 20 years, more organized, more streamlined and more lethal. Since recapture of power, the Taliban have taken actions evocative of their ruthless rule of the 1990s. They have cracked down on protesters, supposedly imprisoned and beaten journalists, media workers, and also restored their notorious Ministry for the Promotion of Virtue and Prevention of Vice, which under preceding Taliban rule imposed bans on behaviour considered un-Islamic (Maizland, 2021). By mid-2021 they had an estimated 70,000-100,000 fighters, up from around 30,000 a decade ago, according to the US. Continuing such a level of insurgency has required a great deal of funding from sources both inside and outside of Afghanistan (Azami, 2021).

Many view the Taliban as 'experts' in managing illicit industries given that they have derived revenue from all sorts of illegal pursuits, ranging from abduction and smuggling goods to extortion, and especially drug trafficking. As of September 2021, it is estimated that the annual income for the Taliban ranged from USD 300 to USD 1.6 billion, with a large portion of annual revenue coming from opium poppy cultivation, and additional supplemental financial needs met through mining and donations (Maizland, 2021).

Narco-Money

Perhaps nowhere in the world has a country and the international community confronted an illicit drug economy as intensely ingrained as in Afghanistan. Opium remains as a major source of funding for the Taliban, and the finance placed around it, together with farming, manufacture and trafficking of opiate- products for profitable markets in foreign countries. In the year 2020, opium poppy was cultivated on some 224,000 hectares in Afghanistan, one of the highest levels of cultivation in the country. With its extensive territorial control and reach all over the country, the Taliban has taxed cultivation, processing, and smuggling of drugs; and units and members of the Taliban have been profoundly involved in all these elements. Often, the Taliban allowed its fighters to disengage from fighting in order to amass the drug harvest. The Taliban also collected taxes from independent drug traders and various criminal groups, while overpowering others (Felbab-Brown, 2021).

The Taliban also depend on farmers who cultivate poppy, generally located in the southern provinces of Kandahar, Helmand, Uruzgan and Zabul to grow opium poppies, while offering these farmers a decent amount of financial reward for doing so. One of the reasons for continued plantation of poppies in Afghanistan is due to the fact that the sums paid by Taliban to the farmers were usually much higher than what they would make through alternate income programs developed by the international community meant to combat Afghanistan's illicit drug trade. The Taliban also use threats and viciousness to confirm that farmers grow their crops. They profit not only from drug sales, but also by extracting income from various taxes imposed on drugs throughout key trade routes, many of which are located in areas under their control. Moreover, the Taliban also use their trademark threats and violence to guarantee that farmers grow poppies. They profit not only from drug sales, but also by extracting revenue from various taxes forced on drugs throughout important trade routes, many of which are located in areas under their control (Dominguez, 2016).

In Afghanistan's poppy-rich regions of south and southwest, known links exist between Taliban and the drug traffickers who work along the Pakistan border. The fact that the Taliban profit from opium is regularly stated in media reports, academic studies, and comments by the US government officials, yet there is little tangible detail available to the public and policymakers on how the insurgents interact with drug traders and profit from opium (Peters, 2009). However, estimates of the Taliban's annual earnings from the illicit drug economy range from USD 100 million-USD 400 million (Azami, 2021). Afghanistan is the world's largest producer of opium and in 2021, before the Taliban takeover, produced more than 6,000 tons of opium, which a report from the UN Office on Drugs and Crime said could potentially yield 320 tons of pure heroin. Afghanistan produces more opium than all opium-producing countries combined and last year was the sixth straight year of record opium harvests (The Hindu, 2022). The opium-based economy has crippled the agricultural sector of Afghanistan. Poppy cultivation not only depletes minerals and nutrients, essential for the fertility of soil, but also takes the large chunk of agricultural land, which can be rightly used for the cultivation of other crops, such as wheat, barley, rice, corn, cotton etc.

Taxes

Interestingly, Taliban had a Taliban Financial Commission for issuing systematic diktats to traders and transporters to pay taxes while travelling in areas that were controlled by them (before the takeover) (ANI, 2021). The Taliban also has a disturbing sense of entitlement. The militia designed a tax system in the areas under its control, including companies, shopkeepers, trucks using motorways and international aid projects. They also collected a 10 per cent "Ushr" Islamic tax and a 2.5 percent "Zakat" – the Islamic annual tax on wealth. In 2020, a classified NATO report published by Radio Free Europe/Radio Liberty cited a senior Taliban figure, Mullah Yaqoob, as estimating the group took around £117 million in taxes (Aboudouh, 2021). The Taliban validates its charity taxes as one of the five pillars of Islam that are considered obligations for all Muslims. But critics are of the opinion that, Taliban is yet to regulate its rules on collecting tithes and charity taxes. Unfortunately, farmers in the central Afghan province have stated that Taliban gunmen stormed their homes at night to demand that they pay tithes and charity taxes. Those without money to make the payments say the Taliban has grabbed their livestock instead, making their families even more reliant on humanitarian aid (Synovitz, 2021). Over the past two decades an extensive variety of businesses in Afghanistan have confirmed that the Taliban asked for more than it is said and meant by the terms zakat and ushr. In the former government the application of such rules was voluntary/optional. Nevertheless, in the zones where the Taliban had more influence than the government these taxes were a must (Jurist, 2021).

Hawala

The hawala is an informal system of transferring money, including across borders, through a link of money brokers known as "hawaladars". Hawala revolves around the honour system. The sender gives money to a shopkeeper in one country, who calls a shopkeeper in another country so that the receiver can collect an equivalent amount there through a codeword provided by the first shopkeeper. Interestingly, international campaigns against terrorism financing have struggled with hawala for two reasons. First, its independence from the global financial system prevents anti-money laundering software from keeping an eye over hawala transferences. Second, hawala still is popular with majority of Muslim countries in Africa and Asia because it permits them to circumvent the fees of wire transfers while sending payments, adding another layer of complexity to distinguishing valid transactions from the criminal ones (Bodetti, 2016).

Some estimates proposed that 90 percent of Afghanistan's financial dealings ran through hawala, with over 900 providers operating across the country (Reliefweb, 2021). The fall of the Ghani government means the Taliban now collects all taxes and controls customs and border crossings. It controls the central bank and commercial banks. It is expected to impose taxes and extract its share from the massive illegal Hawala transfer network that serves as Afghanistan's de facto banking system (Sundaram, 2021).

Unfortunately, it is well known that after decades of war and the Taliban's prior five-year rule (1996-2001), Afghanistan's formal financial system was almost non-existent. In its place, it relied (and still relies) heavily on hawala, a centuries-old informal money exchange system that provides for both domestic and international transfers. But, regulators around the world hate the system, because of its opacity and its role in helping to fund terrorism. The Taliban is unlikely to meaningfully enforce United Nations sanctions against itself or crackdown against the hawala industry in the same way as the previous government (Zerden, 2021). Money laundering activity associated with hawala will definitely rise under Afghanistan's Taliban regime. Banks can do their part by understanding how their clientele and entities could be unprotected to larger risk during the ongoing time of ambiguity and reporting on doubtful or outlier activity (Ferro, 2021).

Illegal Mining

Afghanistan is abundant in minerals and precious stones, much of it under-exploited as a result of the years of conflict and turmoil. Prior to the collapse of the previous Afghan government, it was reported that officials had control of 281 of the 709 identified mining zones. Of the residual mines, 280 were under direct Taliban control, with 148 reportedly under the control of local warlords. In all, income from illegal mining operations were estimated in 2020 to finance the insurgency at approximately USD 464 million (Teston, et. al., 2021). The Taliban basically now controls one of the largest reserves of natural resources that the world very much needs. These comprise materials such as copper, iron, gold, and lithium. This gives the Taliban considerable leverage when dealing with external interests and possibly gives them political capital with which to negotiate (Ferro, 2021). The Taliban derived income from mining directly under their control and are measured to stem further incomes from at least some of the mining areas controlled by the warlords. No information exists to specify how many actual mines are operating in each zone not under government control, nor is there any reliable method to device quantities being extracted from individual mines on a daily basis (Seal, 2021).

The mining industry in Afghanistan is worth an estimated USD 1 billion annually, according to Afghan government officials. Unfortunately, most of the mining is small scale and much of it is done illegally. The Taliban have taken control of mining sites and extorted money from ongoing legal and illegal mining operations (Azami, 2021). Simply by putting roadblocks on roads connecting these mining sites with towns, the Taliban has easily taken control of the mining locations. In fact, most trucks leaving these sites are forced to dump half of their cargo at gunpoint. Without any official check, extortion from legal as well as illegal mining operations has increased manifold over the years (ANI, 2021). The Taliban were also collecting revenue from the trucks carrying minerals at various mining sites. A fee of about USD 330 was the standard for the large tractor-trailers that haul the heaviest loads – between 40 and 50 tons (Global Witness, 2018).

Taliban are also involved in mining locations, used for exporting minerals. For instance, Talc has been extracted by local residents and mine operators and exported to Pakistan, from where it is further exported to countries of France, Italy, Japan and Saudi Arabia. Mine operators in Sherzad district of Nangarhar province, reportedly pay USD 10 to local officials per ton of talc and USD 12 to the Taliban. Any private company operating a talc mine had to pay "rent" to the Taliban. Moreover, there are reports of substantial smuggling of marble, particularly from Helmand province, where marble is the second largest source of revenue for the Taliban after narcotics (Global Witness, 2018). The key to rising revenues for Taliban has been profits from mining, growing from USD 35 million in 2016 to USD 464 million in 2020. China and the United Arab Emirates were the biggest buyers of the materials from mines (Bezhan, 2020).

Foreign Donation

The Taliban has few sympathizers in other countries as well, who provide the militia with financial support. Several Afghan and US officials have long accused certain countries of giving monetary assistance to the Taliban (Azami, 2021). Taliban leaders have also profited significantly from donations, including from what the UN describes as a "network of nongovernmental charitable foundations" and from affluent supporters. Separately, US officials have said for years the Taliban have gotten money, weapons and training from Russia (Seldin, 2021). As revelations emerged in 2020 of Russia allegedly funding bounties to kill US soldiers in Afghanistan, one part of that reporting defined the usage of hawala to move money for Taliban-linked militants (Zerden, 2021). However, private citizens from Pakistan and several Gulf countries including Saudi Arabia, the United Arab Emirates and Qatar are considered to be the largest individual contributors. Even though impossible to quantify precisely, these sources of funding are thought to offer a significant proportion of the Taliban's revenue. According to experts it could be as much as USD 500 million a year. These links are long-standing (Azami, 2021). Neighbouring Iran has also confirmed about its contacts with the Taliban but maintains that they are for safeguarding the safety of Iranian citizens in Afghanistan and encouraging peace talks. But US officials have accused Tehran of providing a variety of assistance to the Taliban, an allegation it denies. According to a November 2019 report, the US Defense Intelligence Agency (DIA) said Iran provides political, financial, training, and material support to the Taliban (Bezhan, 2020).

Pakistan's Support

Pakistan's ties to the Taliban date back to the 1990s, when it provided arms, training, and intelligence to the militants. Islamabad was one of only three countries to recognize and acknowledge the Taliban regime as the official government of Afghanistan. After the regime's fall in 2001, many Taliban leaders took shelter inside Pakistan, especially in North Waziristan and South Waziristan, and also in Baluchistan (nearing Afghan border). Observers say Pakistan sees the Taliban as an insurance policy for attainment of its long-standing calculated goals in Afghanistan, i.e., installation of a pro-Pakistan government in Kabul and preventing the influence of India, which has close ties to Kabul (Bezhan, 2020). If there was any doubt about the intention and the nexus between the Taliban and Pakistan one just needs to see the days after the fall of Kabul. The then Prime Minister of Pakistan Imran Khan's declaration that the Taliban insurgence in Afghanistan is a holy war against the occupation by foreign forces, shows Pakistan's support of a terrorist organization that they have received billions of dollars in assistance to destroy (ANI, 2021).

It is common knowledge that Pakistan has long protected the top Taliban leadership and has supported the insurgents to regroup as it fought with the US troops. So much so that the former US President Donald Trump had accused Pakistan of seriously undermining the US efforts in Afghanistan. "The United States has foolishly given Pakistan more than 33 billion dollars in aid over the last 15 years, and they have given us nothing but lies & deceit, thinking of our leaders as fools. They give safe haven to the terrorists we hunt in Afghanistan, with little help. No more!" Trump had said in a 2018 tweet (News18, 2021). Many experts are of the opinion that the Pakistani security establishment continues to provide monetary and logistical support to the Taliban, together with providing sanctuary to Taliban militants, in an effort to counter India's influence in Afghanistan. However, as expected Islamabad dismisses these charges (Maizland, 2021).

More disturbingly, the Taliban use the other side of the Durand Line to gather money from Pakistani citizens. They are openly collecting donations, adding that the removal of foreign troops will have a severe impact on the north western and western provinces of Pakistan, as the areas are home to tens of thousands of Afghan Taliban supporters (Khan, 2021). Taliban militia stay with coal miners in the mountains nearing Quetta, Balochistan and come to Friday market to solicit 5,000-10,000 Pakistani rupees (USD 50 to USD 70) from local shop owners. Taliban usually travel on motorbikes and ask larger stores for contributions. The riders say that they belong to the Taliban movement and that they are fighting in Allah's path. Taliban openly hold fundraising campaigns in several places of Baluchistan: Pashtun Abad, Quetta, Farooqia Town, Kuchlak Bypass, Ishaq Abad etc." (Noorzai, 2021). Local sources reported that mining companies in Baluchistan were involved in quarrying precious minerals and marble that was later refined in Karachi, Sindh and sold as products of Pakistan. Taxation and revenues from mining contracts were reportedly supervised by the Taliban's "Dabaro Comisyoon" (Stones and Mines Commission) (United Nations Security Council, 2020). Apart from common people, the influential religious leaders and clerics also gather financial help for the Taliban. One such person is, Maulvi Allah Dad, a powerful cleric of Baluchistan. Reportedly, he is proud to have spent years contributing to the Afghan Taliban's war chest. Dad runs a large mosque in Baluchistan's northern city of Zhob. As an elder leader of a faction of the Islamist group Jamiat Ulema-e Islam, he exercises substantial influence over the predominantly Pashtun region where he has defended numerous combatant Afghan Islamist factions since the 1980s. According to Dad, clerics across Baluchistan help with fundraising during Ramzan, when Muslims offer charitable donations. "We typically raise between 200,000 and 300,000 rupees ($2,000 to 3,000) every year", he stated. Dad is not the only cleric involved in fundraising. He said there are at least 15 donation collection centers for the Taliban in the city of Quetta alone (Kakar, 2017).

Conclusions

Whether we like it or not, the Taliban are here to stay in Afghanistan. As the US and erstwhile Afghan government never took a workable approach, the domestic situation of Afghanistan was never resuscitated from a complete breakdown. Resultantly, the Taliban could again be in the forefront, with their own sets of dictums and substantial support from the Afghan people. The stories of corruption and financial swindles committed by the local Afghan warlords and the maintenance of their respective territories worked against the imposed system of democracy in Afghanistan. These warlords could neither establish a workable democracy at the basic societal level, nor could they completely terminate the Taliban's influence over common Afghan people. The Taliban with its new found power will prove more lethal and organized in future. It is extremely important to note that the force is no longer a group of religiously motivated and extremist militia, rather it has attained a shape of organized and politically motivated syndicate. Since their takeover, and in their media statements, the Taliban have demonstrated a 'new' side to their political philosophy. The group's political office in Doha (Qatar), established in 2013, may have provided the group with the experience, training and the chance to be involved in the art of political negotiation and diplomacy (Yousaf and Jabarkhail, 2021). The various sources of 'income' as explained above are channels of sustenance for Taliban and their ideology. The Taliban no doubt would exploit the resources to recruit the foot soldiers, purchase arms and ammunition from various illegal sources, fill its own coffer, and be financially independent to rule a ravaged country on their own terms.

Chapter 8

Under the Hood–Learning and Innovation in the Islamic State's Suicide Vehicle Industry

Ellen Tveteraas

Abstract

This article explores how the Islamic State learned from its suicide bombings, a tactic that in theory undermines the in-group stability associated with organizational learning. Using interviews from Mosul and Baghdad together with internal documents from the Division of Soldiers it provides a case study of the learning and production process underlying innovations in suicide vehicle designs between 2014 and 2017. It examines how the group acquired, distributed, interpreted, implemented, and stored information from suicide vehicle operations in its military-industrial complex, and details how the group learned by maximizing continuity among personnel in support, coordinating, and production roles. In the summer of 2014, the Islamic State launched an offensive in Iraq that enabled the group to establish a territorial presence in several of the country's provinces, most notably Nineveh and its urban capital, Mosul.[1] This was the beginning of the group's three-year war against the Iraqi government where it sought to expand and defend its newly consolidated Islamic State. During the conflict, the group began to employ battlefield tactics in open confrontation with military forces to a greater extent than its Iraqi predecessors, al-Qaeda in Iraq (AQI) and the Islamic State in Iraq (ISI), had done against the U.S. between 2003 and 2010.[2] At the same, time the Islamic State also kept tactics that had become signatures in these groups' violent repertoires, most notably suicide bombings.

The Islamic State used suicide bombings more in Iraq in its first year than AQI and ISI combined between 2003 and 2010.[3] It also made greater use of suicide vehicles, introducing some of the most novel changes to the devices since Hezbollah put drivers in truck bombs in its attack against the U.S. and French marine barracks in Beirut in 1983.[4] Its main suicide bombing innovation was both low-tech and simple – it began adding armor on the outside of vehicles to prevent premature detonation in direct confrontation with military forces, in essence adapting an inherited technique to new operational realities.[5] Innovation is usually a concept reserved for radical departures from current methods, but it is also used to capture incremental modifications of existing technologies and procedures.[6] While Hezbollah's first suicide vehicle bomb in 1983 can be characterized as a radical innovation, the Islamic State's suicide vehicle modifications are better described as incremental, aimed at producing gradual improvements rather than novelty-induced shock.[7] Changes were made in response to new operational circumstances and evolving military countermeasures, and were the outcome of a learning process wherein the group acquired, analyzed, and applied knowledge to adjust equipment, aiming to gain the upper hand from government forces.[8]

But how did the Islamic State learn from its suicide bombings? After all, a tactic where the death of the perpetrator is a necessary condition for the success of the mission is not exactly conducive to learning.[9] Although several studies have outlined why the Islamic State developed these vehicles, only a few have sought to explore how they did it.[10] This reflects a trend in the terrorism literature more broadly, namely that "while many studies on terrorism acknowledge that successful terrorist organizations must learn, very few show how they learn."[11] Using interviews from Mosul and Baghdad and documents from the military branch of the Islamic State, this case study explores the learning process and structures underlying incremental innovations in suicide vehicle designs in Iraq between 2014 and 2017.[12] It is structured around Huber's model of organizational learning, examining how the group aquired, distributed, interpreted, implemented, and stored knowledge relevant to suicide vehicle development.

Whereas source availability makes it difficult to trace a particular learning process to a particular innovation outcome, it is nevertheless possible to outline general processes that were likely involved in a range of adjustments of both vehicles and related infrastructure. By so doing, the article finds that the Islamic State learned by ensuring continuity in support, coordinating, and production roles while making suicide bombers as peripheral as possible to everything but pressing the detonator. While this is commensurate with literature on learning in terrorist and insurgency groups, the sources used in this study grant a unique level of detail on how this division of labour was designed, achieved and maintained. By outlining this in-depth, it increases our understanding of learning in the Islamic State, especially of how the group was able to innovate under conditions of high membership attrition.

The first reports of up-armored suicide vehicles in Iraq emerged around Baghdad in October 2014, with the Islamic State employing Humvees left behind by the Iraqi army following the fall of Mosul in June that same year.[13] Because they were a limited resource and had utility in other aspects of battle, these cars proved impractical to use for suicide bombings in high numbers. Combining the benefits of the Humvee with the requirement for mass production, the group gradually developed a reproducible and bulletproof design based on civilian vehicles.[14] Personnel would cover all or parts of cars with thick iron plates, slanting it in front to increase the effective thickness of the metal and heightening the odds of small arms and heavy munitions ricocheting off.[15] They also added metal grids to increase the distance between exploding munitions and the car.[16] In rural operations, the group would paint the armor beige to blend in with desert terrain and make the discovery by reconnaissance units more difficult.[17] In urban operation the armor would be painted in more radiant colors to mimic civilian vehicles.[18] The added armor initially caught the Iraqi military off-guard, and to effectively stop some of these new contraptions they had to procure Kornet missiles at around $250 000 apiece.[19]

While a relatively minor change to design, it facilitated a radical departure from how suicide vehicles had been used in Iraq and abroad before 2014. Following the U.S. invasion in 2003, the asymmetry in both technology and manpower between Islamist insurgents and U.S. forces made suicide vehicles an attractive instrument for inflicting damage without having more than one person face the enemy directly. The vehicles used by both AQI and ISI were therefore intended to be as inconspicuous as possible to maximize the likelihood of reaching the desired target undetected.[20] This emphasis on stealth characterized the majority of suicide bombing campaigns from the 1980s onwards, regardless of delivery mechanism.[21] It was characteristic of Palestinian groups' use of explosive belts in Israel, the Kurdistan Worker Party's use of similar contraptions in Turkey, the Tamil Tigers' use of belts, vehicles, and boats in assassinations and guerilla assaults in Sri Lanka, the Taliban's use of suicide vehicles in Afghanistan, and the use of suicide bombing by al-Qaeda cells internationally.[22]

While the Islamic State kept using inconspicuous suicide vehicles in clandestine operations, it also designed a new type with an emphasis on repelling, rather than avoiding, incoming fire. This expanded the tactical functions of suicide vehicles. In addition to their utility in guerrilla assaults and as symbolic acts of terrorism, they could now be integrated into battlefield operations to weaken enemy defence positions in advance of ground-troop assaults, in some ways paralleling the use of traditional artillery.[23] This capability became particularly pertinent following the fall of Mosul in June 2014, when the Islamic State obtained enough arms to equip nearly 50,000 soldiers from Iraqi military stocks and sought to further expand the state.[24] As the tide of battle turned against the Islamic State around 2016, the vehicles also proved useful as a stalling mechanism to delay government forces. Historically, the closest functional equivalents among non-state actors are perhaps the Tamil Tigers' integration of suicide attackers in some ground offensives and the Viet Cong's occasional use of sapper units in advance of ground forces.[25] However, neither used suicide attackers for this purpose as systematically as the Islamic State, nor modified the associated equipment to the same extent. Whereas the ultimate success of the Islamic State's suicide vehicle innovations can be debated considering the fall of Mosul in 2017, they reflect both adaptability and an aptitude for learning worth exploring in depth.

Learning in Terrorist and Insurgent Organizations

Regardless of whether an organization is legal or illegal, learning is important for both short-term performance and long-term success.[26] Researchers have defined organizational learning in several ways, but most articulate it as experience-driven knowledge change.[27] By seeing knowledge as expressed in behaviour, learning is observed as improvements in either practices or performance.[28] However, experience can be partially internalized, poorly interpreted, and is subject to a range of cognitive biases that can lead organizations to either fail to make changes or to make the wrong ones. As noted by Michael Kenney, "experience is often dimly perceived. Participants may not understand what happened, why it happened, and whether what happened is beneficial or harmful to the organization."[29] To take this into account, scholars have adopted a process view, defining learning as organizations broadening their range of potential behaviours.[30] Whether and to what extent the potential is actualized depends on how groups process experience-based information; how it is acquired, distributed, interpreted, and stored in the organization.

Terrorist and insurgent groups' ability to learn is often indicated by their ability to adapt to changing operational circumstances.[31] Adaptability can manifest in a range of behaviours, with the most studied being innovation and contagion. The literature on contagion has found that both violent and nonviolent political movements have a propensity to mimic tactics that are perceived to have been successful elsewhere.[32] The likelihood of occurrence increases with the strength of the bond between the original user and aspiring adopter, with direct organizational ties being most conducive for exchange.[33] The literature on innovation has been more focused on identifying motives, conditions, and group characteristics that differentiate innovative from conservative groups.[34] Jackson identified eleven factors intended to predict the occurrence of innovative behaviour, encompassing group characteristics, the nature of the technology, and the modalities of the struggle.[35] Similarly, seeing innovation as a physical manifestation of creativity, Gill and others explored factors that can predict the transition from one to another.[36]

While indicators of adaptability are a focus in the literature, the underlying learning- and creative processes have been less explored. This might be due to the fact that empirical insight on this subject is rare, or, as suggested by Gill et al., that studies on the topic are less interesting for counter-terrorism efforts.[37] A notable exception is Kenney, who examined the learning process underlying competitive adaption in al-Qaeda.[38] One of his key contributions was to highlight that a group's ability to adapt depends on whether the knowledge required to do so is codified or tacit. Codified knowledge has an agreed-upon language that lends itself to oral and written communication.[39] In this context learning is a rather straightforward process: know-what, like technical instructions, can be transferred via manuals, while know-how, how to carry out instructions, might require the addition of time and practice.[40] Tacit knowledge is unarticulated and manifests in a sense of effortlessness when executing a complex task, social traits like charm or trustworthiness, or – in an organizational setting – in ease of cooperation and coordination.[41] This cannot be acquired from papers but requires interpersonal interaction and time to develop, with common transfer mechanisms being mentorships and apprenticeships.[42]

For insurgent and terrorist groups, acquiring both types of knowledge is restricted by the organizational imperative for secrecy, especially in contexts where the state has high levels of control.[43] Moreover, while groups have developed several ways to acquire codified knowledge clandestinely, utilizing it to develop a capability or improve performance often requires knowledge on coordination.[44] Being a tacit skill, not only does this require time to develop in groups, but it also takes a degree of membership stability, neither of which are typically associated with organizations of the terrorist or insurgent variety.[45] This is arguably particularly acute in organizations that opt to employ suicide bombings. While it might have advantages from a tactical point of view, from an organizational perspective the intentional blowing up of operatives risks undermining the organizational stability required to improve performance. Despite the level of membership turnover suggesting that systematic learning in rebel and terrorist organizations is difficult, it sometimes has the opposite or little effect.[46] The main reason for this is that insurgency groups are not homogenous decision-making actors, but separate between leadership and foot-soldiers in a way that allows the former to persist and learn from the demise of the latter.[47] While this division is well known, the finer details of how groups organize and process information to learn and innovate under high levels of membership attrition are not. The following section provides a detailed account of how this was done in the case of the Islamic State's suicide vehicle industry.

Gaining Insight into the Islamic State's Suicide Vehicle Industry

Learning and innovation in the Islamic State's military effort took place within the Division of Soldiers (*Diwan al-jund*), the Islamic State equivalent of a Ministry of Defense. Its main responsibilities were managing wars, training and deploying soldiers, protecting the borders of the caliphate, and planning the overall conflict.[48] To this end, the Division was comprised of a number of sub-departments and committees, with bureaus responsible for leadership, administration, logistics, management of special skills, and human resources.[49] The Division was a trans-national body with a particular presence in Syria and Iraq. While this article focuses on Iraq, the place where the group used suicide bombings most prolifically, the involvement of the Division in Syria and evidence of exchange across the border, suggests that the learning process was similar in both places and informed by knowledge gained in both countries.[50]

To obtain insights into the procedures and activities of the Division, the study uses internal Islamic State documents and propaganda material in combination with information from thirteen interviews conducted in Mosul and Baghdad between March and August 2021. Due to the ethical and security challenges associated with interviewing Islamic State members inside Iraq, interviews were conducted with members of the Iraqi military and civilians who have all directly engaged with aspects of the group's operations. These were carried out with the help of a local research assistant due to travel restrictions imposed by COVID-19.[51] Participants were selected during a three-month preparation period where we worked to identify people with relevant expertise and more than a decade of experience in their fields. Consent was acquired in this period, which gave participants several weeks to determine whether they wished to take part in the study.[52] Those who agreed to take part included engineers tasked with raiding Islamic State explosives facilities, army personnel tasked with countering and dismantling up-armored suicide vehicles, and intelligence officials tracking Islamic State networks. It also included people involved in a metal works facility incorporated by the Islamic State and doctors in and outside of areas under Islamic State control.[53] All requested full anonymity due to the security situation in Iraq. While participants had in-depth knowledge on aspects of the Islamic State's organization and capabilities, they were not members. A key challenge in interpreting the interviews was therefore to separate hearsay from reliable information and empirically grounded knowledge from prejudice. This was done by matching the information given by a participant against his experience and knowledge in that field and by triangulating the information against documentary sources and interviews conducted on similar topics in the same environment.

The study also uses primary sources from the Islamic State collected and archived by scholars and analysts in the last decade. Work led by Aaron Zelin and Aymenn Tamimi have made accessible several hundred Islamic State administrative documents, publications, and propaganda material. Moreover, documents from the Division of Soldiers hosted at George Washington University (GWU) have recently enabled scholars to outline the group's military organization in more detail.[54] Much of the GWU archive is restricted, but the author received access while working on this article. While these documents provide insights into the group's activities, they have to be interpreted with caution. Documents from armed groups in conflict environments are likely to be imperfectly sampled, selectively preserved, and in an imperfect state. Islamic State documents are no exception, and archives constitute a nonrandom collection of papers made available to the public after several rounds of selection. Similarly, material from the Islamic State news services and propaganda apparatus are the result of the group seeking to project a particular image and is prone to suffer from both misrepresentation and omissions as a result.[55]

This combination of sources nevertheless gives valuable and unique insights into both the structure of the organization and the nature of its activities. That said, the below analysis should be regarded as an outline of the learning process in the Division of Soldiers under ideal conditions by actors looking from the outside in and documents displaying the group at its most organized. Findings likely coexisted with a degree of improvization, miscommunication, and system breakdowns that are not captured in the sources used for this paper.[56]

The Learning and Production Process Underlying Innovations in Suicide Vehicles in the Islamic State

How did the Division of Soldiers overcome the learning impediment associated with the systematic use of suicide bombings to produce incremental innovations in suicide vehicle designs? The process can be usefully analyzed in terms of Huber's model of organizational learning.[57] Huber divides learning into four constructs based on recurring themes in the literature on organizational learning and knowledge management: (1) knowledge acquisition, (2) information distribution, (3) information interpretation, and (4) integrating lessons in organizational memory. Learning can be defined as the sum of these activities, but as Huber was primarily interested in understanding processes and the range of new potential behaviours they aspire, his model does not include a construct for observable outcomes. Outcomes are therefore analyzed in an implementation section. Implementation is defined as the organization using interpreted information to realize one or several new potential behaviours, and is placed between information interpretation and embedding lessons in organizational memory.

The breadth of Huber's model and its focus on knowledge management makes it apt for examining how the Islamic State learnt under conditions of membership turnover, but its broad scope comes at the cost of examining its constitutive constructs in detail.[58] For example, the information interpretation section assumes the pursuit of SVBIED innovation was grounded in instrumental considerations. While this was a important aspect, it does not consider the historical, social, cultural, and emotive antecedents that made SVBIEDs appear in the Islamic State repertoire in the first place. This has inspired books of its own but is outside the scope of this article as it does not examine why SVBIEDs became an attractive option, but rather how SVBIED innovation was achieved once it already featured on the "menu of tactics".[59] With that caveat in mind, the below contains a step-by-step analysis of how the Islamic State developed and produced their suicide vehicles while blowing up their members with remarkable zeal.

Knowledge Acquisition

Most activities undertaken by the Islamic State were grounds for acquiring new knowledge, and suicide attacks were no exception.[60] However, suicide bombings were particularly challenging in this regard as few bombers survived long enough to learn from their mission, much less to author post-action reports to inform future deliberations of superior officers. On an individual level, perpetrators could only gain knowledge and communicate lessons if they failed. According to doctors in both Baghdad and Mosul, failure did happen, and if the perpetrator was lucky enough to return to a hospital under Islamic State control, the organization often granted them the opportunity to try again.[61] While some had to be persuaded, others appeared much keener on a second attempt and tried until they got it right, despite – or perhaps due to – debilitating injuries in the first attempt.[62] In any case, returning suicide bombers were the exception, most were either successful, killed, or arrested, rendering them unavailable for debriefs.[63] To ensure the group could conduct a series of suicide bombings while also acquiring feedback, the organization built a division of labor during operations that separated operative, supporting, and coordinating functions, leaving the bomber to play a bit part in his own demise. This created continuity in supporting and coordinating roles, enabling the group to communicate and make improvements to different aspects of its operations over time, despite experiencing continuous losses in the execution phase.

Suicide operatives were the purview of the special skills bureau, with prospective bombers organized in a section called the Martyrdom Operatives Battalion (*Katibat al-Istishadiin*).[64] Members of the suicide battalion would normally arrive at the area of operation shortly before the execution of an attack and spend the preparation period in isolation with clerics to build the mental fortitude required to execute this type of mission.[65] The battalion had no shortage of volunteers and, following the group's acquisition of territory, its size far outgrew the tactical demand for suicide operations.[66] The Islamic State was not the first group to find itself in this situation. Around 2006, an ISI document shows that it too had more suicide bombers than the group was able to deploy.[67] However, while ISI was unable to utilize aspiring bombers for logistical reasons, the Islamic State was arguably unwilling to waste them. Winter's analysis of suicide attack use in 2015-16, suggests that the group appeared reluctant to use bombers in campaigns where it did not feel it could win.[68] While this changed during the Battle of Mosul in 2016–17, it corresponded with the impression of several interviewees, one of whom remarked, "The Islamic State does not use suicide bombers unnecessarily, they are cheap, but they are also indispensable."[69]

The most important support functions for suicide operations were filled by intelligence and logistics personnel, responsible for providing mission-critical information and supplying equipment. Like the suicide bomber, the suicide vehicle and explosives would arrive shortly before the start of an operation, typically around one day in advance.[70] These were manufactured in a decentralized production chain overseen by a sub-division of the logistics bureau called the Committee for Development and Manufacturing (*Hay'at al-tatwir wa al-tasnia'*). This process is outlined in detail in the implementation section. The suicide vehicles could either be assembled near the attack site or completed in a factory and transported to areas of operation, depending on the type of vehicle and extent of Islamic State territorial control.[71] Transportation of components was usually overseen by the intelligence department.[72] If planning a series of attacks in one location, the leadership could order factories to be opened near the area of operation to reduce the risk associated with moving equipment around.[73]

In addition to transportation, intelligence personnel were charged with collecting the information required for the suicide bomber to reach the target. Depending on the nature of the target, type of government presence, and nature of the operation, these reports could be prepared for hours or months with the use of anything from drones, to civilians, to intelligence operatives themselves scoping the area of interest.[74] For example, a plan to drive a covert suicide vehicle near a government installation inside Baghdad would likely be based on long-term surveillance by members of the intelligence department looking for routines, opportunities, and obstacles.[75] In active battlefields, reports would more likely stem from army battalion personnel on the ground or live drone imagery.[76] Operatives in these settings could also be guided to the target by personnel with strong local knowledge, senior members in radio contact, maps on iPads, and – eventually – drones.[77] With both the car and intelligence in hand, the suicide bomber would depart and attempt to carry out the mission.

The task of acquiring attack performance information was given to a person described as an attack coordinator.[78] The coordinator – or someone reporting to this function – would ideally be in direct contact with the suicide bomber from ignition to detonation. Coordinators were described as relatively senior Islamic State members that were tied to an operation room. The configuration and function of operation rooms varied, with some being mission and campaign specific, comprised of a small group of leaders, including from the intelligence section and relevant battalions in the province of operation.[79] Some had more overarching strategic functions, but these were likely inhabited by leaders with responsibilities on the Division level.[80]

Information Distribution

Following the execution of one or several suicide operations, information on performance and outcome would be communicated by the attack coordinator up the chain of command, where it would be assessed and used for planning future operations in conjunction with other sources of information.[81] The distribution of some feedback would stop at the provincial level and inform leadership deliberations in a local battalion but information considered to have wider strategic implications would likely reach the higher levels of Division leadership.[82] Interviewees noted that operational feedback would most commonly be circulated in chats on social media, using apps like WhatsApp and Telegram.[83] While sensible from a time-saving perspective and in clandestine operations where leaving a paper trail is particularly disadvantageous, these informal means of exchange are somewhat surprising knowing what we do about the Islamic State's penchant for paperwork.[84] Documents from the drone unit known as the Al-Bara' bin Malik Brigade, for example, indicate that evaluations of drone training operations were communicated in written reports.[85] While none of the archives consulted for this paper had similar documents for suicide missions, it is not impossible that they existed.

Information Interpretation

Upon receiving feedback from the attack, the leadership at the relevant level would use the information to imagine potential device changes and select which modifications the group should attempt to realize in light of operational needs. Because of the decentralized nature of the Islamic State's military and production complex, systematic changes to technology, equipment, and infrastructure based on operational feedback would likely be decided by Division-level leadership.[86] Here, responsibilities included planning operations and coordinating the group's five main armies.[87] This encompassed deciding what targets to pursue, instructing intelligence operatives to monitor particular areas, and – relevant to innovation in suicide vehicle equipment – ordering the manufacturing of necessary materials.[88] As this article does not have sources privy to the discussions in Division leadership, it is difficult to pin-point suicide vehicle outcomes from decisions made at that level with any degree of certainty. However, two decisions strongly indicate top-level involvement due to the scale and systematic nature of their implications. The first was the decision to develop up-armored suicide vehicle production infrastructure following experimentation with Humvees against military targets around Baghdad in 2014.[89] The second was the expansion of up-armored suicide vehicle production infrastructure in Mosul around 2016, after it had proven useful to stall military onslaught in other Iraqi cities.[90] Because these crossed provincial boundaries in scope and in personnel implications, it is unlikely that they could have been made without involvement by leaders responsible for coordinating between armies in different localities.

Although the efficacy of both decisions can be debated, interview participants tasked with countering the consequences considered Islamic State leaders highly competent at interpreting incoming information. As noted by one intelligence officer, "I think they learned something from every operation. They learned from their mistakes very quickly, both in terms of how they made the explosives, where they made it, and how they execute the operation."[91] Whereas international interest in the conflict gave interviewees incentives to exaggerate the ability of their opponents, the group did have a distinct advantage when it came to extracting relevant and actionable lessons from attack information. The individuals who came to inhabit leadership positions in the Islamic State after 2013 all had several years of fighting experience combined with periods of apprenticeships where they learned from senior fighters in U.S.-run prisons.[92] Beyond the top echelon, this also had a favourable effect on the types of people that came to inhabit positions of mid-level leadership. As argued by Vera Mironova about jihadi groups in Iraq and Syria, Three groups that had, from the very beginning, enjoyed the luxury of having experienced leaders were ISIS, Jabhat al-Nusra, and Ahrar al-Sham. (…) Because of their own previous fighting experience, they knew the exact qualities a fighter and leader needed. In other words, they knew what to look for when making a promotion or recruitment decision.[93] In this way, experience at the top positively impacted the quality of people lower in the hierarchy. This arguably improved the overall analytic ability of the group and enhanced the odds of interpreting information in a way that enhanced, rather than deteriorated, performance and capabilities. However, this quality was not a static feature of the leadership throughout the conflict but worsened over time due to in-group dynamics as the tide of battle turned against the group.[94]

Implementation

While the leadership decided which changes to equipment the group should attempt to realize in line with operational needs, the actual modifications were developed and produced elsewhere. Following the interpretation of operational feedback, leadership at either the central or provincial level would issue orders about desired equipment modifications to sub-divisions in the Division of Soldier's logistics section.[95] These sub-divisions would oversee a production process drawing on civilian and military expertise to meet requirements. As already mentioned in the discussion on knowledge acquisition, the most involved sub-division in suicide vehicle development was the Committee for Development and Manufacturing (CDM). The CDM was responsible for production infrastructure, development and production of weapons, as well as quality control across Islamic State-run workshops.[96] By 2015, documents indicate that the CDM was divided based on divisions and sectors, meaning they were present in different provinces and had a degree of subject specialization.[97]

Interviews suggest some equipment orders would be aspirational, prompting a relatively centralized experimental and development process within the CDM, while others would be more easily achievable and integrated into a preexisting production chain. Most changes to suicide vehicle design fell in the latter category, with the CDM's role being coordinating a network of evolving production infrastructure. Experimental work, on the other hand, centered around particular facilities. In Iraq, much of the experimental work took place in the laboratories of the University of Mosul, described by one engineer as an "ISIS research center".[98] Before it was bombed in 2016, the group made particular use of the departments of engineering and chemistry, as well as the workshops of the technical institute.[99] They also incorporated some of the staff from these departments in their work.[100] While some capabilities were realized, like the group's weaponization of drones, use of chlorine gas, and new IED linking methods, others never left the drawing table.[101] An example of the latter was experimentation with remote-controlled vehicle bombs in Iraq, Libya, and Syria.[102] While it appears in one Islamic State video from Mosul, and a document from the Research and Development Section of the Aleppo Province outlines rudimentary lessons from the manufacturing process, the contraption was hardly used and never put into mass-production.[103]

As a rule, members with responsibilities in the CDM or its associate facilities were not involved in planning or executing operations but received orders from leadership in their province and supplied equipment to battalions in the field.[104] Like the division between operative, support, and coordinating functions during operations, this created continuity in key roles and enabled the group to make improvements to equipment and infrastructure over time despite experiencing continuous losses in other parts of the organization. The group's ability to maintain the separation varied based on context. While it was rarely an issue in the production of up-armored suicide vehicles, as the factories required to prepare and assemble these were too large to establish outside of areas of Islamic State control, the operative and production roles would sometimes be merged in government-controlled areas.[105] This was likely because the tradeoff between cell size and detection risk was more pressing in that context. That said, production staff in Islamic State-controlled areas were not outside of government reach, with both factories and research facilities being targets of airstrikes.[106]

Production Infrastructure and Expertise

So, what types of facilities and people were used in the production of suicide vehicles under the CDM? In areas of Islamic State control, suicide vehicle manufacturing was typically divided based on the component being produced, with different types of workers involved in each stage and the CDM engaged in a coordinating capacity.[107] Because ironwork required special machinery that was neither widely available nor easily moved, the decision to add armour increased the decentralization of production. In Mosul, for example, this led the group to make particular use of facilities and technical equipment in the eastern industrial zone.[108] The CDM would also take-over local metalwork businesses, with some owners being incorporated into the production chain and others dispossessed and replaced.[109] These locations could be staffed by civilians, some of whom gained employment through family members and similar informal avenues, while others responded to more traditional work-adds.[110] One ironworker described his employment in the following way:

One day, one of my Islamic State relatives offered me to work with them because I didn't have a job. I accepted to work with them, but I didn't belong to the organization. I was in charge of 10 workers, the business was booming and never stopped. There were delegates from within the Islamic State in the Military Development and Manufacturing Authority who visited the site and supplied us with iron. (...) It was a very normal factory. We received raw materials, work orders, and measurements, and we told them what we needed.[111]

The production of explosives was also overseen by the CDM but appears to have been a separate process confined to separate locations, usually staffed by Islamic State members belonging to explosives manufacturing battalions.[112] Military engineers tasked with raiding explosives factories described encountering two main types, one run by personnel focusing on vehicle-based bombs (*Tafkhikh*) and another focused on smaller IEDs (*Tafjir*).[113] While the former required space and was usually located on the outskirts of cities, the latter could be established inside government-controlled territory. The composition of the explosives used in *Tafkhikh* factories varied based on vehicle type and available material, with common components being TNT, ammonium nitrate, gasoline, oxygen bottles, and rocket propellants.[114] Engineers estimated that the ammonium nitrate, gasoline, TNT combination would typically cost between 15-20 dollars per kilogram to manufacture.[115] In some cases, they would also use C4, but this was more common in suicide belts, vests, and motorcycles, instruments that would be the purview of *Tafjir* personnel focusing on smaller IEDs.[116] Doctors in both Mosul and Baghdad noted that the damage of suicide bombs gradually increased after 2013, with the Islamic State making greater use of shrapnel and producing explosions that were more powerful than both ISI and al-Qaeda.[117]

Ensuring that factories under CDM supervision had the necessary material for production was the responsibility of another logistics sub-division called the General Supply Committee (*Hay'at tajhiz al-'am*). The Supply Committee oversaw warehouse management and procured materials for the group's military industry, ranging from explosive precursors to electronic components. Soon after taking over Mosul, the group leveraged cross-border networks, partially built before 2014, to import materials *en masse*.[118] In line with findings by conflict Armament Research (CAR), Islamic State documents and interviewees indicated that much of the material found in the group's warehouses came from Turkey, through Syria.[119] Army engineers noted that while explosives like TNT could be manufactured domestically but required importing raw materials from abroad, there were no signs of domestic C4 production, meaning this would have to be imported ready-made.[120] Some materials used in suicide vehicles, such as rocket propellants, could be found in the equipment left behind by the Iraqi army in 2014. Yet other components, like oxygen bottles, iron plating, and the vehicle itself, would be available in and around the Islamic State-controlled provinces.

Implementation of leadership orders in explosives battalions drew on technical expertise obtained from a range of sources, with the most important being people with experience in the field obtained prior to joining the organization. Having been in a state of insurgency for more than ten years, Iraq had much to offer on this front. All military interviewees mentioned former Ba'athist army engineers as the most competent explosive experts in the Islamic State. "In some cases, like the drone manufacturing process, the group would hire foreign experts," stated one interviewee, "However, when it came to experts on booby traps and mines, Iraqis, especially those who worked in the former Iraqi Army Military Engineering Division, were the best."[121] That being said, researchers have suggested that the influence of Ba'athists on the Islamic State organization is exaggerated.[122] It is entirely possible that these played a less important role than the interviewees indicated, and that other experts mentioned, especially foreign fighters from Azerbaijan, Afghanistan, and Europe, were more significant.[123] In either case, the geographical scope of production between 2014 and 2017 required distributing technical know-how to members in different areas to implement leadership orders. Engineers reported encountering suicide vehicle factories in Mosul, Ramadi, Fallujah, Tal Afar, and Tikrit.[124] Their list was not exhaustive, but these were all areas where the group faced military onslaught and had a sufficient level of control to set up the type of factory required for production.

Theoretical and practical knowledge was distributed in several ways, both in-person and remotely. Most members received lessons on explosive manufacturing during basic training, but only a few would receive more advanced instructions.[125] Candidates for the latter would often be identified based on exam results in the subject.[126] These individuals generally had some prior education, mainly in the sciences, although this was described as non-essential.[127] More specialized teaching was described as structured lessons with both theoretical and practical exercises, which corresponds with examination papers on the construction of improvised explosive devices found by CAR throughout the eastern sector of Mosul.[128]

While some instruction took place in person, instruction videos and manuals were also shared online. Interview participants involved in raiding explosive factories reported finding both electronic training material and handwritten notes, and intelligence officials described amassing repositories of manuals in both physical and e-book formats in Arabic, Russian, English, and French.[129] Several participants noted that trainers would often avoid travel due to security risks, so in-person training conducted by explosive experts in one province would be recorded and distributed to personnel in other provinces.[130] This was primarily shared through closed channels on social media, although some instructions were also made publicly available on channels like YouTube.[131] Training also happened "on the job" with factories described as hierarchical systems where more senior members guided less experienced and skilled workers.[132]

Evaluating the Islamic State's explosives competence, statements by interviewees were characterized by the same tension found in discussions on terrorist group expertise more generally – alternating between describing them as highly competent and completely clueless.[133] The contradictory assertions can in part be accounted for by the fact that different phases of the manufacturing process required different levels of technical knowledge. Some participants noted that the group forbade unqualified personnel from participating in production, but engineers described that what constituted necessary qualifications varied greatly based on task.[134] Assembling explosive devices did not require particularly high levels of skill, and members of the group with basic training – even children – would be capable of doing it given instructions.[135] Working with electric components was among the more difficult tasks which required advanced training, although this depended on the sophistication of the method.[136] This range in technical knowledge combined with on-the-job training likely contributed to a fair share of factory accidents described by doctors interviewed for this paper.[137]

Integrating Lessons in Organizational Memory

Organizational memory captures how knowledge is stored for future use in both documentary form and the memories of individual group members.[138] As just discussed, the Islamic State made use of both documents and videos to store knowledge on production and manufacturing related to suicide vehicles and explosives manufacturing. The group also developed standard production procedures to ensure interoperability between provinces. In the CDM, standardization was the responsibility of a committee called the Central Organization for Standardization and Quality Control (*Al-jihaz al-markazi la al-taqaiis wa al-saitara al-nua'ia*) (COSQC). While it is unclear when the COSQC started operating, a document found by CAR, dated 31 August 2016, instructed all production facilities to produce only to the standards specified by the branch.[139] Another COSQC document contained technical standards, measurements, and acceptable ranges for mortar manufacturing.[140] Mortar components measured by CAR and compared to standard procedures in production facilities indicate that instructions were followed.

To what extent suicide vehicle manufacturing was codified in standard procedures is not entirely clear. On the one hand, the range of car types used in operations, which varied from SUVs to 4×4 vehicles and tankers, required a degree of improvisation that made standardization impractical.[141] On the other, the group did on occasion mass-produce designs based on particular vehicle types. The most striking example was during the Battle of Mosul when the group used so many Kia SUVs, Kaaman noted it was "as if IS had seized all the vehicles in a car dealership within the city."[142] This is not unlikely, with interviewees stating that the group had seized control of businesses relevant to its military industry and that it faced no shortage of civilian cars locally.[143] That said, the ironworker interviewed in Mosul reported regularly receiving measurements for iron plates, suggesting that these generally varied.[144] Some intelligence officials and engineers reported having seen standardized production schemas for the initial stage of explosives manufacturing, but others said it was largely random.[145] Detonation mechanisms appear to have been the most uniformly produced component, with Kaaman observing a higher degree of standardization between 2014–2017 compared to what groups used in Iraq between 2007–2012.[146]

While suicide vehicle production might have seen some standardization at the component level, it did not reach the level seen in the group's mortar production. Moreover, the standards the group did have faltered when it was under high levels of pressure. Toward the end of the Battle of Mosul in 2017 when the Islamic State lost territorial hold of the city, army personnel and doctors reported observing a wider variety of devices and a higher proportion of injuries consummate with low-tech improvisation.[147] This local deterioration in ability was likely due to the destruction of production facilities, supply chains being cut, and high levels of membership attrition. The latter is considered the biggest threat to the human aspect of organizational memory, with high personnel turnover potentially leading to the loss of both know-how and more tacit forms of knowledge.[148] The group's division between coordination, production and high-risk operative roles prevented this for as long as the organization could maintain territorial safe havens. However, the containment of personnel loss to expendable functions became harder when areas under Islamic State control came under direct military onslaught. When this happened, the group literally imploded locally, with scores of people blowing themselves up with a starkly diminishing rate of return to the battle effort. That said, lessons related to the use and production of suicide vehicles from the battle in Mosul were implemented in Syria, suggesting that the know-how was processed and stored in the organization but that the provinces in Iraq were increasingly unable to act on it.[149]

Conclusion

How did the Islamic State learn from its suicide bombings? Using Huber's model to analyze the learning process and structures underlying incremental innovations in its suicide vehicle industry, this article shows it did so by minimizing membership attrition in roles critical to processing information and implementing changes to vehicle components. This not only required a separation between leadership and foot-soldiers, but between each function relevant to planning, preparing, and executing operations. Given their certain death, suicide bombers were made as peripheral as possible to everything but driving the car and pressing the detonator. Personnel in supporting, production, and coordinating functions, in contrast, were specialized and shielded from military confrontations to ensure continuity in roles needed for information acquirement, distribution, interpretation, and implementation – in short, those necessary for learning and production.

Exploring the structures and learning processes underlying incremental innovations in suicide vehicle design gives rise to several questions that would be interesting to explore in more depth. While the certainty of losing the suicide bomber made the separation described above paramount for learning from suicide operations, the ever-present possibility of losing operatives in conventional attacks arguably makes it sensible in most situations. Do organizational demands associated with systematic use of suicide bombing shape organizational structures in a way that makes groups that employ them better at learning from other types of operations as well? Or is it the case that groups that opt to employ suicide bombings systematically already have the appropriate divisions in place because operating in a high-repression environment or executing other types of high-risk operations have sparked a similar division of labor?

The Islamic State grew out of a movement that had structures separating bombers from other functions and had members that were already socialized into seeing suicide bombers as a public good.[150] Suicide bombings come at a greater cost to young and small groups, as well as groups whose members are not socialized to accept the tactic, as they are less equipped to contain the effect of personnel loss to expendable individuals and sections of the group.[151] The Islamic State was never forced to contend with this issue because the social and ideological controversies had been overcome by al-Qaeda throughout the 1990s and 2000s and the structures to absorb martyrs and support mass-use had been developed by AQI and ISI in Iraq between 2003 and 2010.[152] Knowing how to execute and learn from such operations without creating an organizational imbalance, and with an experienced leadership to translate lessons into modifications based on operational needs, the group's suicide bombing complex hit the ground running, resulting in the most novel changes to suicide vehicles since they were first employed.

The complexity of the structures underlying these innovations is cause for reflection about how learning might manifest differently in territorial and clandestine groups. Groups that operate under high levels of government pressure often divide roles in a way conducive to acquiring, distributing, and interpreting knowledge in the organization much like the Islamic State.[153] However, in lieu of a territory, it seems more likely that innovations in clandestine context would be confined to changes in practice rather than technology and equipment. To a certain extent, this would be a practical matter related to infrastructure and availability of materials, but not all innovations require the military-industrial complex underlying suicide vehicle development. Equally important to the Islamic State was continuity among its group of experts and a stable level of communication between organizational branches, neither of which are typically associated with a clandestine mode of existence.[154]

That said, there might also be a difference between a group's ability to conduct one-off innovations rather than systematic improvements over time. The past holds many examples of clandestine groups that have conducted technological experiments and developed proofs of concepts in areas of government control.[155] However, systematic changes based on operational feedback in the manner seen in the Islamic State are increasingly rare. This is arguably because the required continuity in key production functions is unfeasible given government countermeasures in modern high repressions states.[156] Should we, therefore, expect groups in high-repression environments to employ technological innovations developed in environments more hospitable to violent learning? This is not the current tendency, at least not in Europe and the U.S., but whether this is a short- or long-term trend remains to be seen.[157]

Although these and other questions abound, the paper at hand had a much more limited scope, seeking simply to unpack the learning processes and structures underlying Islamic State innovations in suicide vehicle design and to detail how the group learned under conditions of high membership attrition. High levels of compartmentalization and specialization in the Islamic State's military-industrial complex was key to this. While the paper is too narrow to contribute to broader theorizing on learning and innovation, it might prompt further exploration into whether these are necessary conditions for terrorist group learning to manifest in incremental technological innovations over time.

Acknowledgements: I would like to thank Dara T. A., as well as Hugo Kaaman and Vera Mironova, for their invaluable support in different stages of the data collection process. I am very grateful to Stathis Kalyvas and the participants of the T. E. Lawrence Program on the Study of Conflict at the University of Oxford, who all provided much needed feedback on an early draft of this article. I also benefitted greatly from the comments by Truls Hallberg Tønnessen, Petter Nesser, Mikael Hiberg Naghizadeh, Clara Voyvodic Casabo, Giuseppe Spatafora, and the two anonymous reviewers. Your constructive and helpful comments made this article significantly better. Finally, I would like to thank Sean Patrick Hughes and Anthony Long, whose coffee in Derry made the writing process thoroughly enjoyable. Disclosure statement; No potential conflict of interest was reported by the author(s). Ethics statement: This article includes human research participants and was approved by the Social Sciences and Humanities Inter-Divisional Research Ethics Committee (IDREC) at the University of Oxford, Ref No: R68407. Additional information. Funding: This study was funded by The Norwegian Defence Research Establishment. Under the Hood – Learning and Innovation in the Islamic State's Suicide Vehicle Industry Ellen Tveteraas: Department of Politics and International Relations, University of Oxford, Oxfordshire, United Kingdom. Journal information. Print ISSN: 1057-610X Online ISSN: 1521-0731. 2 issues per year. Abstracted/Indexed: America: History & Life; American Bibliography of Slavic and Eastern European Studies (ABSEES); CSA; EBSCOhost Online Research Databases; Elsevier Scopus; Expanded Academic ASAP (Gale Group); H.W. Wilson Indexes; Historical Abstracts; International Bibliography of the Social Sciences (IBSS); International Political Science Abstracts; ISI: Current Contents - Social & Behavioral Sciences and Social Science Citation Index; Lancaster Index to Defence & International Security Literature; National Criminal Justice Reference Service Abstracts (NCJRS); OCLC; PAIS International; Periodical Abstracts Research (PerAbs); ProQuest Research Library; PsycFirst; PsycINFO/ Psychological Abstracts; Research in Higher Education Abstracts; Sage Abstracts; SwetsWise All Titles; Thomson Reuters© Current Contents: Social & Behavioral Sciences; Thomson Reuters© Social Science Citation Index; and Ulrichs Periodicals Directory. Taylor & Francis make every effort to ensure the accuracy of all the information (the "Content") contained in our publications. However, Taylor & Francis, our agents (including the editor, any member of the editorial team or

Studies in Conflict and Terrorism aims to cast new light on the origins and implications of conflict in the 21st Century and to illuminate new approaches and solutions to countering the growth and escalation of contemporary sub-state violence. The journal is specifically oriented to both practitioner and scholarly audiences and is thus meant to bridge the divide between theory and practice. Studies in Conflict and Terrorism thus seeks to publish theoretical and empirical studies that contribute to a better understanding of the causes of terrorism and insurgency as well as the measures required to achieve their resolution. The journal addresses security challenges fuelled by religious and nationalist strife, moribund peace processes, and disputes over natural resources, and transnational organized crime. In a world of diverse and changing threats, enigmatic adversaries, and continued uncertainty, the editor's goal is to provide fresh insight, thoughtful analysis, and authoritative prescriptions to the most pressing concerns that affecting global security in the 21st century.

Chapter 9

Armed Governance: The Case of the CIA-Supported Afghan Militias

Antonio De Lauri and Astri Suhrke

Abstract

This article examines the genealogy and behaviour of the CIA militias in Afghanistan against the backdrop of persistent armed governance whereby a plurality of actors competes over control and rule. The non-accountable use of force by militias and their volatile alliances increase the extent of armed governance, exacerbating issues of human rights abuses and undermining the possibility of future claims for justice. We discuss the effects of recurrent political violence on the peace talks and the implications for a sustainable peace, the need to include a solution for the role of militias in a peace agreement, and the necessity of ending impunity.

Keywords: Afghanistan armed governance CIA Afghan militias' peace talks' accountability

Armed governance as a modality of rule, violent competition, and control has characterized the modern history of Afghanistan. A plurality of actors participates in determining such a modality of governance, including militias supported by foreign states. Since 2001, Afghan paramilitary forces that work with the United States Central Intelligence Agency (CIA), assisting the US war on terrorism in Afghanistan and the border region with Pakistan, have become an important but nontransparent element in the country's structure of armed governance. This article examines the nature and behaviour of the CIA militias in Afghanistan in light of broader questions of non-accountable use of force by quasi-official militias supported by foreign powers, and the strategic, legal, policy, and moral issues this entails. With US military withdrawals from Afghanistan on the near horizon, this article also considers the further question of how these militias can be integrated into a final peace agreement and related principal-agent concerns. Whose interests do the militias represent? Can control relationships, currently tied to the CIA, be reconfigured and institutionalized through a peace agreement? Is dissolution of the militias possible and practicable, or will they attain a measure of autonomy? Whichever development eventuates, it seems that the militias–whether with a continued CIA sponsorship or not–are by now so well established that they will remain an important agent of violence in the configuration of armed governance in Afghanistan.

Afghanistan did not always attract the same attention in the global media and academic circles as it has since 2001 in the aftermath of September 11, yet there has been a certain consistency in the economic and political interests of external actors in Afghanistan at least from the nineteenth century onward, from the Anglo-Afghan wars in the late nineteenth century to the Soviet invasion and eventually the US-led operation Enduring Freedom in recent history. By early 2020, the agreement between the US and the Taliban involving US military withdrawals and Taliban commitments not to support international terrorism seemed to open up a more peaceful future for the country. However, among the many important issues that remain to be settled is the role of Afghan militias in the possible continuation of what we will call 'armed governance' in the country.

Militias and irregular forces are not a new phenomenon in Afghanistan; they have contributed significantly to the military history of the country and affected the process of state formation. When Afghans expelled the British in the late nineteenth century, the use of rural militias in rebellions (over which the Afghan dynastic elite had little control) proved crucial. This has historically created an ambivalent dynamic; Afghan rulers typically encouraged armed resistance to expel foreign invaders when useful but were reluctant to confirm the power of local militias after the war ended, even though local agents of violence could be useful to mediate and extend state interests.[1] In the contemporary version of this dynamic, the influence of major international actors such as the US, Saudi Arabia, and Pakistan combined with militia power to fuel the development of a consolidated form of armed governance, that is, a modality of rule, violent competition, and control characterized by the dominant position of multiple state and nonstate military actors.[2]

The succession of conflicts and the transformation of the social fabric over the past four decades of violence and instability have reconfigured the political landscape of Afghanistan, changed political structures and forms of leadership, and significantly empowered local military commanders. The so-called years of *jihad* (1980s–1990s) saw an increase in the power of religious leaders such as the *mullahs* and *mawlawi*, due in part to the growing influence they had on customary assemblies, such as *jirgas* or *shuras*, at a time when the authority of local leaders, such as *khan, malik*, and *mir*, was significantly declining. As commanders, warlords,[3] provincial politicians, and religious figures gained power, armed groups and militias supported by foreign states developed in tandem. Militias came to define political and security transitions in the country with growing intensity since at least the early 1980s.[4] After 2001, the militias were further developed and semi-institutionalized with massive support from the US.

The CIA-supported militias are a less well-known but particularly troublesome version of this development. The present units originated in the 2001 invasion of the country, when US military forces and the CIA organized Afghan militias to fight Islamist militants. Almost two decades later, the CIA is still running local militias in operations against the Taliban and other Islamist militants. Throughout the country, the militias reportedly have committed serious human rights abuses, including numerous extrajudicial killings of civilians. CIA sponsorship ensures that their operations are clouded in secrecy. There is virtually no public oversight of their activities or accountability for grave human rights violations.

A brief genealogy of the CIA's Afghan army

Although the interest shown by Western intelligence in the work of militias and paramilitary forces in the region goes back to the creation of Pakistan in 1947, the concrete engagement of the US with Muslim guerrillas began in early 1979 with the kidnapping and murder of the American ambassador in Kabul, Adolph Dubs.[5] Partly guided by a 'messianic impulse'[6] and partly by specific political and economic interests, the CIA played a key role during the Soviet–Afghan war in the 1980s in American efforts to assist Afghan rebels who invoked the duty of holy warriors (*mujahedin*) to fight the Soviet forces and the Afghan communist government. An integral part of CIA operations was the great increase in the production of opium and heroin. Trucks and mules supplied by the agency to transport arms into the country were used on the way out to supply opium to heroin laboratories along the Afghan–Pakistan border.[7]

The rapid collapse of the government forces following Soviet military withdrawal in 1989 brought the *mujahedin* to power in 1992. Soon, however, the *mujahedin* began to fight among themselves, leading to the rise of the faction calling itself *Taliban* (students), which found logistic and political support in Pakistan.[8] At this point, the CIA, which had scaled back its presence in Afghanistan when the *mujahedin* took power, re-engaged in the country. Claiming that the Taliban in the 1990s was supporting international terrorism by allowing the militant Islamist movement al-Qaeda ('the Cell') to operate from Afghanistan, the agency clandestinely supported rival Afghan *mujahedin* factions that were fighting the Taliban. Thus, when al-Qaeda attacked the US mainland in 2001, the CIA already had a long history and a well-established infrastructure in Afghanistan. This enabled the agency to rapidly spring into action after September 11. Operatives equipped with cell phones and large bundles of dollar bills entered the country on a mission to mobilize Afghan militias.

In accounts by US military historians, the use of Afghan militias in 2001 to rapidly defeat the Taliban regime and scatter Osama bin Laden's al-Qaeda fighters was a major success story.[9] Although bin Laden himself evaded capture for many years, US Special Forces and the CIA operatives paid local Afghans to form militias to work with the US-led coalition. They found ready recruits among ex-militia leaders and other strongmen who had opposed the Taliban, switched sides, or returned from exile in Pakistan and Iran. Many had latent networks of supporters that were easily mobilized. The militias also enabled the US to run search-and-destroy operations in the eastern and southeastern parts of the country in 2002–2003 with only a few American boots on the ground.

While useful to US and coalition forces, the well-paid and well-equipped militias formed a complex, decentralized structure of military power that posed serious problems for the liberal 'nation-building' agenda of the international operation. By 2003, the militias were slated for demobilization; its members were to be disarmed and either returned to civilian life or reintegrated in a new, regular Afghan national army. However, the large United Nations (UN) program launched for this purpose had only limited success. One reason was the unwieldy structure of the international operation in Afghanistan, which made it difficult to get consensus on most policies. In this case, the US military did not fully support the demobilization program, claiming the militias were necessary in the continuing war against the Taliban. Another major hurdle was the opposition of many militia leaders themselves, who, in a worst-case scenario, could turn their forces against the international operation. This nightmare scenario haunted Western diplomats and UN officials who had a mandate to promote peace and stability in the war-torn country and made them reluctant to pressure the militia leaders. Finally, as in any disarmament program of this kind, the opportunities for cheating by falsifying numbers and hiding the best weapons were numerous.[10] The program's modest results clearly demonstrated that, once built up, militias are hard to build down.

After 2006, when the Taliban had manifestly revived and the insurgency intensified, the US government formally reversed its policy toward militias: local militias should no longer be disbanded but instead supported as a key component in a new counterinsurgency strategy.[11] US Special Forces initially organized new militias at the local level, presenting them in public as village defense units. Some central government figures, including President Hamid Karzai, were at first reluctant to endorse this practice as policy, fearing an erosion of centralized control and the sovereignty of the Afghan government. Yet the government's heavy military and economic dependence on the US gave it limited room for opposing the latter's initiatives, particularly those advanced by the US military command in Afghanistan. Many Afghans also stood to gain economically and politically from the build-up of new military units. Officials in the Ministry of Interior supported the move to place the units under its control. Appearing under various names, the program was eventually called the Afghan Local Police, which had units in many parts of the country.[12]

Some militias were not placed under the Ministry of Interior, however, but were run separately by US Special Forces and CIA operatives. While the Special Forces command (later the Joint Special Operations Command) and the CIA apparently developed a rivalry over controlling the Afghan militias, the competition was muted by the Pentagon's practice of lending active-duty members of the Special Forces to the CIA through its so-called Omega Program.[13] The CIA itself had few paramilitary officers. In 2017, its Special Activities Division with a global field of mission was reported to have only a few hundred.[14] Rostering Special Forces from the military as its own enabled the CIA to vastly expand its covert missions. By 2010, as Bob Woodward claimed in a much-cited passage from his book on the Obama administration, the CIA had an army of 3,000 Afghans called Counterterrorist Pursuit Teams, institutionalized with the acronym CTPT.[15] As discussed more fully below, they were paid and trained by the CIA and the Special Forces and protected by the ring of secrecy surrounding their sponsoring agent. As such, they were distinct from the militias established under the formal Afghan Local Police program. Yet the formal public program to employ militias as a fighting force also served to facilitate and legitimize the proliferation of militias that formed the CIA's Afghan 'army.'

This army was not designed for classic counterinsurgency operations and definitely not for 'winning hearts and minds.' Their mission was to hunt and kill 'terrorists.' This became even clearer after the major withdrawal of US and coalition forces in 2014. Initial speculation that withdrawal would spell reduced US support for the Afghan militias proved wrong. The CIA and its Afghan army instead became more strategically important as a means to pursue the war covertly, with attendant low political visibility in the US. In 2015, the CIA helped its Afghan counterpart, the National Directorate of Security (NDS), to establish new Afghan paramilitary units to fight militants, allegedly aligned with the Islamic State, who reportedly were active in the northeastern part of the country. The new NDS units added significantly to the total number of irregular forces supported by the CIA.[16] Two years later, in 2017, then-CIA Director Mike Pompeo publicly announced a policy change to use the militias more intensely. The CIA would expand its operations in Afghanistan, targeting Taliban as well as al-Qaeda. Small teams of CIA-rostered officers would spread out alongside Afghan units in a campaign that Pompeo promised would be 'aggressive,' 'unforgiving,' and 'relentless.'[17]

The CIA's army: who are its members and how do they operate?

Little is publicly known about the CIA's Afghan 'army.' Nevertheless, investigative journalists, concerned analysts, and human rights activists have pieced together the covert program's basic outlines. The 'army' has two types of components. One is a set of older units whose relations with the CIA go back to the offensive operations carried out during and immediately after the 2001 invasion. They work closely with the agency. The most well-known and powerful of these is the Khost Protection Force (KPF), which operates out of the CIA's Camp Chapman in the northeastern province of Khost.[18] Significantly, the KPF is an illegal armed group in the sense that its existence has no basis in Afghan law and no formal place in the state security apparatus or its budget, as the UN has emphasized.[19]

A second type of unit is the formally designated Special Forces of the Afghan intelligence agency, the NDS. There are four main units, numbered from 01 through 04, each with its own regional area of operation: NDS-01 operates in the Central Region, NDS-02 in the Eastern Region, NDS-

03 in the Southern Region, and NDS-04 in the Northern Region.[20] This is the only transparent and publicly known part of their organization. The NDS Special Forces exist in a regulation twilight zone. The NDS is heavily funded by the CIA, and its Special Forces have a close working relationship with CIA operatives: according to most reports, they are trained and paid directly by the CIA. As a result, information about their size, operations, funding, and command structure is not publicly disclosed.[21] In the temperate language of the United Nations Assistance Mission in Afghanistan (UNAMA), the operations of NDS Special Forces, like those of the KPF, 'appear to be coordinated with international military actors, that is, outside the normal governmental chain of command.'[22] In UNAMA reports, the term 'military *actors*' commonly refers to the CIA, as distinct from the term 'US military *forces*' (our italics). Afghan institutional control over the NDS Special Forces also appears to be tenuous. The UN mission concluded in 2018 that 'these forces appear to operate outside of the regular NDS chain of command, resulting in a lack of clear oversight and accountability.'[23]

There is no public disclosure of the size of the CIA-supported units, but they probably have more than doubled since the estimate of 3,000 given by Woodward in 2010. A journalist maintained in 2017 that NDS-02 alone had 1,200 men.[24] Among the older units, the KPF was said to have 4,000 members in 2015.[25] Three years later, in 2018, estimates of the KPF size were 'anywhere from 3,000 to over 10,000.'[26] Other than that, all we know is that the CIA-sponsored forces are uniformed and well equipped, sometimes work with men who speak American English during raids, use American phrases, and have been able to call in air strikes, most of which are executed by the American military.[27] The paramilitary forces are also very well paid, which may be a principal reason why highly skilled and capable Afghans would want to join the units.[28]

The secrecy of the CIA program greatly compounds the difficulties of ascertaining facts about civilian casualties and related violence involving progovernment forces. These problems notwithstanding, the UN, human rights organizations, and investigative analysts have documented a pattern of abuse and possible war crimes of the kind that are emblematic of paramilitary forces operating with impunity, unconstrained by political or judicial accountability. Whether the military effects of these units are large or small, the political effects are certainly even greater, since they have long-term impacts on local governance.[29] The paramilitary units are mainly used in night operations against residential areas harboring suspected militants in so-called search operations. The operations typically lead to high civilian casualties. UNAMA, which has reported on civilian casualties in Afghanistan annually since 2009, now singles out the operations of paramilitaries associated with the CIA as a matter of grave concern. The UN mission report in 2019 cited 'continuing reports of the KPF carrying out human rights abuses, intentionally killing civilians, illegally detaining individuals, and intentionally damaging and burning civilian property during search operations and night raids.'[30] The UN used similar language to describe the CIA-supported Special Forces of the Afghan intelligence agency, the NDS, in both its 2017 and 2018 reports.[31]

Relative to the total number of civilian casualties recorded – around 11,000 killed and injured in 2018 – those caused by the CIA's Afghan 'army' are small. Even so, the UN singles out the rise in casualties from covert pro-government forces as a matter of 'deep concern.'[32] In 2018, the civilian toll of the dead and injured from what the UN categorizes as 'search operations' was 353 – a stunning 185% increase over the previous year. These numbers are likely even higher, since the UN mission includes only data on incidents that it can document with reasonable certainty and thus tends to err on the conservative side. Most of the search operations are executed by the CIA-sponsored paramilitaries. According to UN figures for 2018, the NDS Special Forces and the KPF caused almost as many civilian deaths as the total number attributed to all Afghan national security forces in that year.[33] Moreover, the paramilitaries were much more likely than the regular Afghan forces to kill civilians rather than to injure them. The high ratio of deaths to injuries, the UN report concludes, suggests a pattern of intentional killing and excessive use of force. The sharp increase in civilian deaths from search operations reflects Mike Pompeo's promise in 2017 that the CIA would launch an 'aggressive,' 'unforgiving,' and 'relentless' campaign. The increase was also in line with the general escalation of violence in 2018, as all parties appeared to intensify their efforts to gain advantages on the ground that could translate into political bargaining power during peace negotiations that seemed to be on the horizon.

Nonaccountable use of force

The two main techniques for targeted killing are kill-or-capture raids and air strikes from drones. These modalities of political violence continue the reproduction of armed governance whereby the individuals targeted are alleged terrorists, active insurgents and others considered part of their networks. In Afghanistan, US military intelligence units with assistance from coalition forces deployed under NATO command regularly compiled long kill-or-capture lists, known in NATO under the mystifying name of Joint Prioritized Effects List.[34] As in other theaters of the US global 'war on terror,' the CIA has also been actively engaged in kill-or-capture missions in Afghanistan, sometimes in cooperation with the regular military forces and the Special Forces under the Joint Special Operations Command (JSOC). While more is known about the frequency and criteria for individual targeted operations by the US regular armed forces, the lists used by the CIA are secret. The agency will neither confirm nor deny their existence.[35]

In terms of international law, targeted killings are deeply problematic, especially when carried out by an intelligence agency. As Philip Alston, UN Special Rapporteur on extrajudicial, summary or arbitrary executions (2004–2010) notes, the practice (1) represents a significant regression in the evolution of both international law and US domestic law; (2) provides legitimacy to the position held by some officials, commentators, and scholars who believe that the US should officially adopt a policy of extraterritorial targeted killings that would go well beyond what is currently allowed by international law; and (3) supports the notion that intelligence agencies can legitimately expand their activities from traditional intelligence-gathering to killing and still enjoy the same de facto immunity from the constraints of international law.[36]

Overall, as the UN mission reports repeatedly note, the CIA-sponsored program and activities of its Afghan army are shielded from public oversight and accountability. Afghan authorities appear to be uninformed or unwilling to divulge anything about the program's structure, funding, or operations. It is telling that UN officials investigating reports of abuse and intentional killings of civilians by NDS Special Forces were unable to obtain any information from Afghan officials, including in the NDS itself.[37] In legal terms, the CIA has long enjoyed a privileged position in Afghanistan by being outside the jurisdiction of Afghan laws and decrees that regulate the operations of international military forces. For instance, prior to 2014, Afghan restrictions on certain coalition practices that disproportionately harmed Afghan civilians, notably night raids, did not apply to the CIA and its operatives because these do not constitute 'military *forces.*' The 2014 Bilateral Security Agreement that governs military relations between the US and Afghanistan maintains this distinction. The agreement explicitly prohibits US *forces* from entering Afghan homes except when necessary for immediate self-defence, forbids them to arrest or detain Afghans, and bars them from operating detention facilities in Afghanistan. Again, the restrictions do not apply to the CIA because, in formal terms, the agency does not have military *forces*. Extending the provision to the CIA would signal that it was carrying out such activities in Afghanistan and thus conflict with its principal function of undertaking covert missions.

The Afghan government, being heavily dependent on US support, has accepted the US position. At the time of the Bilateral Security Agreement discussions, President Karzai faced critics at home who favoured an expansive CIA role in the country, including the Afghan intelligence community and local beneficiaries of CIA largesse. There were also broader considerations that graphically illustrated some of the scholarly literature on the outsourcing of violence to militias in civil war.[38] From a short-term tactical perspective, it was argued that exempting the CIA from the constraints that applied to the regular forces was an advantage; its 'army' could wage a truly 'aggressive', 'unforgiving', and 'relentless' campaign against the Taliban and other militants. For both the Afghan and US governments, these considerations came to outweigh the recognized costs: grave human rights violations, potential breaches of international law, and the alienation of the Afghan people, whose support was necessary to stabilize the government.

In the US, only the House and Senate Intelligence Committees have an oversight function relative to the CIA. Their ability to obtain information from the agency is limited, as the Senate Select Committee on Intelligence experienced when investigating alleged CIA use of torture in 2001–2006 worldwide. Congressional willingness to release findings to the public is also constrained, as evidenced in the heavily redacted summary that the Select Committee released in 2014. In Afghanistan, the UN, human rights organizations, journalists, and families of victims of abuse or killings have no access to CIA representatives. Unlike in the US military, there is no spokesperson or liaison office to contact when missions go astray, individuals are executed, innocent civilians are killed, or property destroyed. Identifying alleged perpetrators can be difficult. When US military Special Forces participate in an operation and are rostered as CIA officers, US military spokesmen can plausibly deny involvement by the military. To the casual observer, Americans are indistinguishable in the field. To local Afghans, they are all 'foreigners with beards on motorcycles.' The identity of their Afghan teams is not always clear to the villagers either.

Despite numerous reports that CIA-sponsored paramilitaries have committed serious human rights abuses and possible war crimes, very few cases have been investigated and even fewer prosecuted. The exceptional cases reflect a system of politicized justice based on proximity to centers of political power rather than the rule of law. Two reported cases illustrate the system. In 2009, a Kandahar-based strike force that was linked to the CIA killed a local police chief for having had the temerity to arrest one of its members. The de facto execution of a highly placed official prompted the Afghan government to arrest and convict 38 members of the strike force of murder. A second reported case took place in 2015, when a KPF unit killed a young boy who was related to a local leader and former *mujahedin* commander. The family was able to use its political connections to secure an investigation, and a court convicted two KPF soldiers to ten years in prison. Compensation for civilian deaths caused by the KPF can also be obtained if villagers complain to local authorities who have lines of communication to the force or if they collectively protest, for example, by blocking roads.[39] More commonly, it seems, villagers lodge protests with the local authorities who are most accessible to them at the district or provincial level. Sometimes investigations are promised, but usually nothing further happens. In 2018, a member of the Afghan Independent Human Rights Commission said that, in 13 years of working in the eastern region, she could recall no case of being able to access paramilitary forces operating in the region to question them about reports of abuse.[40]

US-supported militias and Afghan armed governance

Setting up foreign-supported militias always creates a dynamic of escalation in the implementation of security and control, thus generating spirals of violence. This in turn produces a type of political capital that defines both the dimensions and structure of violence. Such political capital constitutes the lifeblood of armed governance. One consequence of protracted situations of armed governance, as in Afghanistan, is the blurring of the categories of war, soldiers, combatants, and military, on the one hand, and of those of peace, criminals, security, and police, on the other. As Ian Shaw and Majed Akhter maintain, the figure of the terrorist is quite emblematic in this regard, since it increasingly straddles these two classifications: the terrorist is not simply an 'enemy combatant' and not merely a 'criminal'[41] but, rather, the manifestation of a violent, competing political project.

In discussing what they define as the 'dronification of state violence,' Shaw and Akhter argue that a major feature defining today's covert drone war is that it targets individuals allegedly linked to globalized, transnational networks instead of nation-states and their military forces. Through this mechanism of individualization, the discrete battlefield is converted into a boundless battle space, thus challenging the foundations of international law. The target of state-supported violence is shifting in scale from conquering territory to destroying individual human bodies. The CIA has played a central role in the genesis of this new cartography of violence. Shaw and Akhter define the dronification of state violence as: '(a) the relocation of sovereign power from the uniformed military to the CIA and Special Forces; (b) the technopolitical transformations performed by the Predator drone; (c) the bureaucratization of the kill chain; and (d) the individualization of the target.'[42]

Both dronification and the use of local militias are key aspects of armed governance in Afghanistan and have been implemented as strategic patterns of CIA operations. As such, they take place within a larger landscape of armed governance where both the CIA and the regular US forces rely on armed drones in the air and a wide range of US-funded 'regular' militias on the ground – including the massive Afghan Local Police (funded with almost 500 million dollars in 2010–2015) and the Critical Infrastructure Police. These forces were militias in all but name, established as part of the US counterinsurgency strategy promoted from 2009 onward. Over the years, some of these militias allegedly protected local populations, others preyed upon them, and some have done both.[43] A critical point, however, is that the more institutionalized militias like the Afghan Local Police are more open to public scrutiny of their practices than the CIA-sponsored militias.

Regardless of their sponsorship, the outcomes of externally supported militias programs are volatile, reflecting common dynamics of principal–agent relationships. When the goals of militias and their supporters are incongruent, for instance, external support can be appropriated in ways that contradict the intended (or at least declared) outcomes and strategic interests of the foreign supporter. These goals are shaped in the context of an armed governance in which short-term victories on the battlefield generally overshadow longer-term political objectives. Moreover, militias often use external resources to serve their own local agendas. In Kunduz, for example, Pashtuns have been particularly affected by the predatory behavior of US-backed Tajik, Uzbek, and Turkmen militias. Thus, the US support for the militias led to incentives among Pashtuns that fueled rather than countered the insurgency.[44]

CIA militias and peace talks

In the context of peace talks, CIA-supported militias represent a wild card. The direct talks between the US government and the Taliban that started in Qatar in July 2018 led to an agreement signed on February 29 (fittingly a leap year date), 2020, which provided for the withdrawal of all military forces of the US and its allies over a fourteen-month period, and a commitment by the Taliban not to permit international 'terrorist' groups to operate from Afghanistan. The agreement covered withdrawal of foreign private security forces but, unsurprisingly, said nothing about the CIA's role. The agreement stipulated that intra-Afghan negotiations would follow to discuss a cease-fire and 'the future political roadmap of Afghanistan.'[45] A comprehensive peace agreement negotiated by the Afghan parties was expected to include the legal framework for political, social, economic, and other human rights, possible constitutional revisions, and provisions for accessing political power, possible power-sharing formulas, and the structure of the post-war armed forces, including the CIA-sponsored militias. If an Afghan agreement were modelled on the peace accords promoted by the UN since the early 1990 s, the CIA's Afghan 'army' would have to be disbanded. Almost all internal war settlements during the past three decades have provided for partial demobilization and restructuring of armed forces – including paramilitary forces and militias. The 2001 Bonn Agreement for Afghanistan likewise allowed an opening for security sector reform. The 2003 UN program for disarmament, demobilization, and reintegration (DDR) covered some 80,000 armed fighters in military organizations that mostly were structured like militias.

The case for including a similar program in a peace agreement is compelling. Militias that operate outside the control of the central state and the chain of command of its armed forces will undermine the process of state formation and the prospects for a sustainable peace, as the experience of the massive international operation during the past eighteen years demonstrates. The continued de facto fragmentation of military power was one of the main reasons for the lack of major progress after 2001 to rebuild and strengthen the central Afghan state. Foreign-financed militias have been the scourge of Afghan history in the modern era as well as earlier centuries. Shielded from accountability by powerful foreign protectors and freed from the need to secure local support, they can run a prolonged, under-the-radar, dirty war, as the record of the CIA's Afghan army illustrates. While the case for disbanding the militias is strong, it is not easily realized. For a start, an apparent precondition would be a basic legal framework for dealing

147

with the Afghan military forces on all sides of the conflict. Hard trade-offs and compromises between deeply antagonistic adversaries will likely be necessary. Implementation poses a separate set of issues. Efforts to disarm and integrate militias after 2001 were short-lived, as noted, reflecting the pressures of renewed war and vested interests in a fragmented military power, as well as the demanding and long-term task of building a regular national army. This time around, two decades of CIA support for local militias and paramilitaries has left a deeply problematic legacy.

Even if the US withdraws its regular forces from Afghanistan, Washington may well be interested in keeping 'intelligence assets' for counterterrorist purposes.[46] Such a presence would require some local infrastructure of support. To this end, the CIA could easily maintain some of its local units, and – given Afghanistan's forbidding geography and complex social environment – probably mount operations on a fairly significant scale. Zalmay Khalilzad, the chief US negotiator with the Taliban has mentioned the militias as one of several items to be included in a general peace agreement.[47] Pompeo, previously the CIA director and currently US Secretary of State, had not said anything about them by late 2019. After the Taliban-US agreement was signed in 2020, analysts in Washington suggested that the Taliban would make it a priority to take over the NDS and end its relationship with the CIA.[48] This would mean the militias could also be taken over by the Taliban (e.g., to fight rival militant factions), or the militias might break away to find new sponsors or operate autonomously.

If violence continues in the future, militias will be in much demand in the political market place. The well-trained and well-equipped CIA militias would be particularly valuable. Whatever their allegiance to the CIA in the past, Afghan history is famously replete with tales of rapidly shifting allegiances and a pragmatic approach to alliances. The CIA paramilitaries constitute a formidable set of actors in their own right. Given their highly paid and privileged status, they are unlikely to welcome a drastic reduction in pay that would accompany integration into the regular armed forces or demobilization. If cut loose by the CIA, they may be reborn as private armies or 'security guards' in the service of powerful individuals or operate autonomously to prey on civilians and commercial sources.[49] Either possibility is in line with patterns of armed governance and collective violence in modern Afghan history.

Peace talks must always face the possibility of recurrent political violence. The CIA's particular capacity to carry out state violence in the form of political destabilization, drone strikes, and targeted killings may erode the potential of the peace process in Afghanistan from within. The signs of agreement between the US and Taliban to withdraw US and NATO forces in return for a guarantee that Afghan territory would not be used for launching attacks outside the country would not translate into concrete steps toward a comprehensive peace agreement without a dialogue between Afghan parties and a permanent cease-fire. It is particularly in relation to these two last elements that the CIA-supported militias could play a negative role by jeopardizing the future of a lasting peace.

Policy implications

In contexts of armed governance, such as today's Afghanistan, state and nonstate actors alike can avoid accountability for human rights violations. Evasion of political accountability can take a variety of forms, including interference with the monitoring activities of nongovernmental organizations (NGOs) and the media, the use of alternative types of repression such as disappearance or encounter killings, or the delegation of repression to other states, as with the policy of rendition, or to other actors like militias.[50] If policy is positioned in an explicitly normative frame of reference, efforts to end impunity for serious cases of such violations and possible war crimes take priority. Vigorous investigation and prosecution of possible war crimes committed by militias will likely also strengthen rather than weaken the prospects for a peace settlement acceptable to the US and the Afghan governments. As military experts on counterinsurgency have long recognized, tactical victories gained by the unrestrained and unaccountable use of force against civilians undermine the overall strategic objective of winning the support of the population.

Ending impunity means addressing the accountability issue in both its legal and moral dimensions. Legal accountability requires US and Afghan authorities to urgently investigate and prosecute alleged human rights abuse and war crimes that are reported and in part carefully documented by the UN and the Afghan and international human rights communities. The Afghan government can investigate and take further legal action under Afghan laws against members of the illegal armed groups, notably the CIA-sponsored KPF. Afghan military authorities or special commissions can investigate and take further action against the paramilitaries with formal institutional links to the Afghan government, namely the NDS Special Forces. Absent a political agreement for a durable cease-fire or peace, structural reforms of the CIA's Afghan 'army,' including disbanding the illegal armed groups or integrating elements in the regular forces, are not likely to find much support in US or Afghan government circles. A consistent judicial offensive against impunity would be a shade easier.

Steps to end impunity conform to broadly accepted norms and could invoke precedents. As discussed above, even CIA-supported illegal armed groups were not always protected from the legal consequences of their actions. Egregious attacks on a high-profile civilian (a Kandahar police chief) and a victim whose family was politically well connected (the family of the Khost boy) brought prosecutions and convictions. In addition, at least one widely reported case of serious abuse committed by US Special Forces (or CIA operatives) and their Afghan partners against civilians has been investigated by ad hoc Afghan commissions and a mixed US-Afghan commission.[51] Nevertheless, a more vigorous campaign against impunity would require a great deal of active US engagement – certainly much more than US civilian and military authorities have demonstrated to date.[52] More fundamentally, efforts to end the impunity of the CIA's army require a focus on the CIA itself. As the primary reference in a principal–agent relationship with the militias and the paramilitaries, the CIA ultimately bears responsibility for their actions – at least in a moral-political sense if not in strictly legal terms.[53] That responsibility, in short, is to ensure that its Afghan army acts in line with Afghan law and relevant international humanitarian and human rights law. Responsibility also rests with the US government and the wider American public, which allow the CIA to operate armed groups that have no legal standing in the country where they operate, to support the paramilitary forces of its local intelligence partner, and to run operations shielded from transparency and public accountability.

Disclosure statement: *No potential conflict of interest was reported by the author(s). Additional information. Notes on contributors. Antonio De Lauri is Senior Researcher and Coordinator at the Chr. Michelsen Institute. He is the co-director of the Norwegian Centre for Humanitarian Studies and the founding Editor-in-Chief of Public Anthropologist. Astri Suhrke is a political scientist and Senior Researcher Emerita at the Chr. Michelsen Institute. She has published widely on the social, political, and humanitarian consequences of violent conflict, and strategies of response. Armed governance: the case of the CIA-supported Afghan militias. Antonio De Lauri & Astri Suhrke. Antonio De Lauri & Astri Suhrke (2021) Armed governance: the case of the CIA-supported Afghan militias, Small Wars & Insurgencies, 32:3, 490-508, DOI:10.1080/09592318.2020.1777618To link to this article: https://doi.org/10.1080/095923 18.2020.1777618.© 2020 The Author(s). Published by Informa. UK Limited, trading as Taylor & Francis Group. CONTACT Antonio De Lauri antonio.delauri@cmi.no*

Chr. Michelsen Institute, Norway SMALL WARS & INSURGENCIES 2021, VOL. 32, NO. 3, 490–508. https://doi.org/10.1080/09592318.2020.1777618. © 2020 The Author(s). Published by Informa UK Limited, trading as Taylor & Francis Group.
Small Wars & Insurgencies provides an international and interdisciplinary forum for the academic and scholarly discussion of the historical, political, social, economic and psychological aspects of insurgency, counter-insurgency, limited war and irregular warfare. Peer-reviewed and long-established, Small Wars & Insurgencies invites papers concerned with, but not limited to, the following areas: •insurgencies and guerrilla conflicts past and present.• counterinsurgencies including national doctrines. Terrorist movements and ideologies. •irregular warfare and the debates on its historiography. Peacekeeping and "humanitarian intervention". Journal information. Print ISSN: 0959-2318 Online ISSN: 1743-9558. 8 issues per year. Indexed/abstracted in: Periodicals Content Index. Taylor & Francis make every effort to ensure the accuracy of all the information (the «Content») contained in our publications. However, Taylor & Francis, our agents (including the editor, any member of the editorial team or editorial board, and any guest editors), and our licensors, make no representations or warranties whatsoever as to the accuracy, completeness, or suitability for any purpose of the Content. Any opinions and views expressed in this publication are the opinions and views of the authors, and are not the views of or endorsed by Taylor & Francis. The accuracy of the Content should not be relied upon and should be independently verified with primary sources of information. Taylor & Francis shall not be liable for any losses, actions, claims, proceedings, demands, costs, expenses, damages, and other liabilities whatsoever or howsoever caused arising directly or indirectly in connection with, in relation to, or arising out of the use of the Content. Essential reading, Small Wars & Insurgencies facilitates the discussion of historians, political scientists and students of International Relations and Security Studies on theoretical and practical issues related to the past, present and future of this critical area of both international and domestic politics. The journal is historically focused and is keen to see contributions from scholars using primary and archival sources, as well as interviews. It also welcomes contributions investigating media, literary and cinema representations of insurgencies, counter-insurgencies and irregular warfare. Most issues include an authoritative review section, and the journal's policy is to have 2–3 special issues each year devoted to specific themes and issues, often edited by guest editors.

Postscript

On 19 October 2021, Taliban's acting Interior Minister, Sirajuddin Haqqani (listed as a global terrorist by the United States), hosted a ceremony in Kabul to honour suicide bombers responsible for the killings of innocent Afghans. He praised the families of 1,500 suicide bombers in Afghanistan and fixed monthly salary for them. On October 2021, ISIS suicide bombers attacked the Fathemyah mosque in Kandahar, killing at least 33 people and injuring 74 others. Another attack in 2022, in which an ISIS-K suicide bomber hit a mosque in Kunduz, killing at least 100 people. However, BBC in its news story (Iraq bombing: IS says it was behind deadly suicide attacks in Baghdad-22 January 2021) reported attacks of IS-K in Afghanistan. Suicide tactics of ISIS and IS-K in Iraq and Afghanistan are identical but recent development in using Armoured Suicide Vehicles (ASV) in Iraq made a huge difference. Professor in Department of International Development, London School of Economics and Political Science, Florian Weigand in his paper (Afghanistan's Taliban-Legitimate Jihadists or Coercive Extremists? Journal of Intervention and Statebuilding-2017) has noted that Taliban and other extremist groups were growing again across Afghanistan and they describe themselves as jihadists-fought against the US and NATO forces:

"The Taliban are usually depicted as ideological fighters – religious extremists who want to introduce harsh rules in Afghanistan, including the prohibition of music and the suppression of women. Their mode of governance stands in stark contrast to Western ideals, with the fall of the Taliban government in 2001 being portrayed as a victory against terrorism and human rights abuses. However, the influence of the Taliban and other armed opposition groups is steadily growing again throughout Afghanistan. They describe themselves as 'jihadists' that fight against the government and its foreign supporters. According to a report for the United States (US) Congress, not even 60% of the country's districts were under Afghan government control or influence in 2017 (SIGAR 2017, 87). At the same time the US is welcoming direct peace talks with the Taliban (ToloNews, February 24, 2016). This development raises the question as to what the affected people – rather than the foreign interveners – think about the Taliban. The 'armed opposition' or 'insurgency' groups in Afghanistan today are commonly associated with the label 'Taliban'. Indeed, after successfully turning an insurgency into a government in 1996 and being toppled again in 2001, the Taliban have returned to insurgency strategies to subvert the current government and its foreign allies. However, armed opposition today is a complex phenomenon, consisting of various groups and factions that change alliances fairly readily".[1]

The G7 Foreign Ministers in their press release gave a joint statement on the increasing restrictions imposed on women and girls in Afghanistan by the Taliban terrorist group. On 13 May 2022, statement by the Foreign Ministers of G7 countries and the High Representative of the European Union argued: "We, the G7 Foreign Ministers of Canada, France, Germany, Italy, Japan, the United Kingdom, the United States of America, and the High Representative of the European Union, express our strongest opposition and deplore the increasing restrictions imposed on the rights and freedoms of women and girls in Afghanistan by the Taliban....With these moves, the Taliban are further isolating themselves from the international community. Echoing our joint statement, together with Norway, from March 24, we call on the Taliban to urgently take steps to lift restrictions on women and girls, respect their human rights, and meet the expectations of Afghans and the world to permit their full, equal, and meaningful participation in work, education and public life, as well as freedom of movement and freedom of speech, which is crucial for long-term peace, stability and development of the country".[2]

Following the Taliban takeover, millions of dollars lost, spiked prices, and cash shortages triggered by former donor countries, especially the United States, have deprived much of the population of access to food, water, shelter, and health care, said Halima Kazem-Stojanovic, a core faculty member of SJSU's Human Rights Institute and a scholar on Afghanistan. "They are caught between Taliban abuses and actions by the international community that are pushing Afghans further into desperation every day." Human Rights watch in its report (Unlawful Killings, Enforced Disappearances, Violations of Laws of War, events of 2021) has highlighted human rights violations of Taliban and their affiliated groups in Afghanistan: "The United Nations reported that Taliban forces were responsible for nearly 40 percent of civilian deaths and injuries in the first six months of 2021, although many incidents were unclaimed. Women and children comprised nearly half of all civilian casualties. Attacks by the ISKP included assassinations and a number of deadly bombings....Both the Taliban and ISKP carried out targeted killings of civilians, including government employees, journalists, and religious leaders. On January 17, 2021, unidentified gunmen fatally shot two women judges who worked for Afghanistan's high court and wounded their driver. ISKP claimed responsibility for killing nine polio vaccinators in Nangarhar between March and June. On June 9, gunmen killed 10 humanitarian deminers in Baghlan; ISKP claimed responsibility. In August, an ISKP suicide bombing at Kabul's airport killed 170 civilians, including many Afghans trying to flee the country".[3]

The question of Central Asian jihadists is being discussed in every forum in Russia and South Asia where most experts have focussed on extremist joining the IS-K to get military training and weapons in Afghanistan. Jabhat Fateh al-Sham, Lashkar-e-Taiba, Jaesh Muhammad and Katbat Imam Bukhari have already received hundreds of young fighter from Central Asia-planning to declare jihad against Russia, Tajikistan and Uzbekistan. Taliban have extended hands of cooperation to these terrorist organizations in their war against humanity. Moreover, jihadists from Central Asia often look differently than other jihadists in Pakistan but their ideology is jihad against infidels. In all of the Central Asian states, an influx of jihadists posing a huge challenge in terms of demobilization and reintegration. Taliban jihadist ideology has destroyed Afghanistan as they continue to train more suicide bombers and deploy them on China and Tajik borders. Taliban are supporting Uyghur jihadists, who exploited martyrdom exclusively against the Chinese authorities. Experts and scholars, Edward Lemon, Vera Mironova and William Tobey in their research paper (Jihadists from Ex-Soviet Central Asia: Where Are They? Why Did They Radicalize? What Next? December 07, 2018, Russia Matters and the U.S.-Russia Initiative to Prevent Nuclear Terrorism) has documented existence of terrorist groups suchlike Jamaat Ansurallah, Jundullah, Islamic Jihad Union and the ISIS Khorasan in Afghanistan:

"Among the world's existing conflict zones, it is indeed Afghanistan—with its geographical proximity and linguistic affinities with Central Asia—that appears to be a logical destination for ex-fighters and new recruits alike. Three radical groups operating there have roots in post-Soviet Central Asia: the Tajik group Jamaat Ansurallah, which pledged allegiance to IS in 2017 after having once been affiliated with al-Qaeda, which, in turn, had been strong in Afghanistan prior to 9/11; Uzbekistan's IMU, often referred to by Afghan officials as Jundallah; and its splinter group, the Islamic Jihad Union, or IJU, which has a base in Sar-e Pul, less than 100 miles from the border with Turkmenistan, albeit with an estimated 25 fighters. All these organizations, however, have been weakened by years of war, and it has been the Islamic State-Khorasan Province (ISKP) that has been most active in trying to recruit fighters from Central Asia. The group declared its existence as an affiliate of IS in January 2015. Like IS-K, it has developed a sophisticated media presence matching the Taliban's and it has targeted Central Asian recruits directly: In March 2018, for example, the group released a video in which Uzbek fighters called on militants in Syria and Iraq to join it. ISKP's messaging, like IS's, stresses the purity of its Salafi ideology and the obligation of believers to engage in jihad and romanticizes life as a fighter. ISKP propaganda also projects a transnational cause centered on apocalyptic narratives from the Prophet Muhammed about jihadis from Khorasan winning a decisive victory near the end of times. ("Khorasan" is a Persian word referring to the territory of modern-day Afghanistan and parts of Central Asia.) For recruits from Central Asia, the ISKP's promises of expansion into the region may be more appealing than the Taliban's nationalist vision, which focuses strictly on Afghanistan and has ruled out northern expansion."[4]

In 2018, terrorist attacks spotlighted Tajikistan's Achilles heel of the internal security dynamics on Asian and European forums that jihadists returned from Iraq and Syria may possibly escalate sectarian and ethnic conflict in the country. The Islamic State of Khorasan claimed credit for the killing of four Western cyclists who were run over by a car, then shot and stabbed to death. These attacks alerted Uzbekistan and Kazakhstan that terrorists might carry out attacks in these two Central Asian states. Recent turmoil in Kazakhstan further added pain to the neck of these states. Kazakhstan, Kyrgyzstan, Tajikistan, Turkmenistan and Uzbekistan have become noteworthy players on the field of international terrorism by purveying young Muslim fighters to the infrastructure of the Islamic State of Khorasan. Afghanistan based Central Asian terrorist groups have also trained thousands fighters and now trying to declare jihad. For now, the flow of foreign fighters to Afghanistan seems insignificant. This flow has been facilitated by the United States, UK, and EU. The US army transported thousands of terrorists from Iraq and Syria to Afghanistan in 2021. According to the UN report (October 2018), the ISKP attacks caused huge fatalities in Afghanistan. A recent U.N report revealed presence of all but 10,000 foreign fighters in Afghanistan associated with al Qaeda, the Turkestan Islamic Party, the Katibat Imam al-Bukhari, the Katibat al-Tawhid wal-Jihad, the Islamic Jihad Union and Jamaat Ansarullah. Expert and writer, Dr. William B. Farrell in his PhD thesis (Fragmentation, Frustrated Revolt, and Off-Shore Opportunity: A Comparative Examination of

Jihadi Mobilization in Central Asia and the South Caucasus-15 November 2019) has noted some aspects of Islamic movements in Central Asia and Afghanistan. He also highlighted participation of these groups in civil wars in Syria, and Iraq:

"Mobilization of citizens of Central Asia and the South Caucasus has not been confined to organizations that have been implicated in documented attacks within the region; nor primarily to Central Asian organizations that were displaced or formed in Afghanistan and Pakistan. In fact, with estimates of Central Asian and South Caucasian foreign fighter recruitment to Syria and Iraq ranging from approximately 2,200 to 5,000 individuals at the high point between 2014 and 2016 and recruitment to Afghanistan and Pakistan of Central Asians reaching an estimated high range of 2,500 to 7,000 prior to 2015 (BAAD, 2018), the emphasis for mobilization disproportionately leans towards external engagement. While the jihadi organizational focus in the Caucasus had already been northerly oriented, two simultaneous dynamics caused a further shift in engagement that affected those mobilized from the South Caucasus. First, there was notable, and at times brutal, state consolidation of authority in the North Caucasus, particularly under the leadership of Ramzan Kadyrov in Chechnya. Additionally, ongoing Russian political pressure and implicit threats towards Georgia and Azerbaijan to prevent jihadis sheltering and recruiting in their countries, resulted in erosion of fruitful operating theatres within Chechnya and Dagestan placing pressure on jihadi organizations. Second, the war in Syria emerged as a more compelling jihadi theatre for fighters".[5]

The Taliban cannot be trusted to keep their promise to China not to harbour Islamist militants seeking separatism in its Xinjiang region, Afghanistan's Ambassador to China told Reuters. The withdrawal of U.S. forces from Afghanistan, and a surge in fighting as Taliban insurgents gained territory, raised concerns for China, which worried that more instability in the region will disrupt its Belt and Road plan for infrastructure and energy links to the west and embolden separatists to destabilise its far western Xinjiang region. Instead of backing one Afghan side against another, as the United States and the Soviet Union have done in the past, China has adopted an "Afghan-led, Afghan-owned" approach, in line with its principle of non-intervention. "The Chinese position is they want to mediate, "Ambassador Qaem said, adding that the U.S.-backed Afghan government welcomed China's involvement and he understood why it wanted to stick to the middle ground. The United Nations said in one of its reports that the East Turkestan Islamic Movement (ETIM), a militant group affiliated with al

Qaeda that China said wanted to set up a separate state in Xinjiang. "As the Taliban gain inroads, China wants to maintain contact and ensure that it is not in the Taliban' bad books, just in case they come to power," said Yang Chaohui, a lecturer at the School of International Studies at Peking University. "China would normally be wary of any grouping that operates on the basis of religious extremism, but it has no intention of fighting the Taliban, because it knows it has no chance of succeeding in what the United States and Soviet Union have both failed to do," Yang said.

The Taliban can offer bases to Central Asian jihadists on Afghan territory to blend in with Uzbek, Tajik and Turkmen tribes in the northern Badakhshan, Kunduz, Jowzjan and Takhar provinces. Iranian Foreign Minister Mohammad Javad Zarif warned that the Taliban has to "change based on democratic ways." Addressing the Raisina 2021 conference virtually, Zarif stated: "If they (Taliban) want to go back to their 90s ideology, it will be impossible, as there is a new and different Afghanistan today." Zarif's remarks come a day after US President Joe Biden and NATO Secretary-General Jens Stoltenberg announced a full withdrawal of all foreign troops starting 01 May 2021. Zarif stated that the US withdrawal from Afghanistan was a positive move. He also called on the Taliban to reduce violence as the US prepares to leave Afghanistan. "The Taliban should not use this opportunity to increase their violence. They should understand that the people of Afghanistan have had enough violence," Zarif said. "It is important for all Afghans to agree on what they want and then work on the details on how to create it. Regional countries should help Afghanistan create that picture, a democratic government, balanced ethnic representation, and a strong economy," he added. "The role of Civil Society in Afghanistan today is not comparable to 2001 or the 1990s. While there are problems that remain in the country, we need to preserve what has been achieved in Afghanistan and ensure its continuity," Zarif noted. Taliban-backed Uzbek, Uyghur and Tajik jihadi groups are overwhelmed by the IS-K's sophisticated operational abilities and its high potential to conduct targeted strikes on the Taliban's vulnerable points.

Special Eurasia, a geopolitical and Intelligence analysis platform whose purpose is to inform the Italian and foreign audience on local, regional, and international dynamics in Eurasia in its report (Geographical report-November 04, 2021 Monitoring Jihadist Propaganda and Terrorism projects) has noted activities of Central Asia terrorist groups in Afghanistan: "Over the quarter-century of the jihadi relationship, they have experienced ups and downs associated with violating the bay'at and joining some IMU militants led by Usmon Ghazi to the Islamic State (ISIS). After Usmon Ghazi's faction changed its jihadi banner and openly made bay'at to the Islamic State leader Abu Bakr al-Baghdadi in August 2015, the Taliban brutally punished the Uzbek jihadists. As punishment for this betrayal, in November 2015, the Taliban killed Usmon Ghazi and about a hundred Central Asian defectors at a base in Zabul Province. The second time Central Asian jihadists were hit hard by the Afghan Taliban in the Darzab district of Jawzjan province was in 2018 when the Taliban defeated the Qari Hikmatullah's network, which was the main pillar of IS-K in the northern Afghan province of Jawzjan. Qari Hekmatullah, a former Uzbek Taliban commander, joined his forces with IS-K and came to lead the group's north territorial project for an extended period of time. He also served as the IS-K's senior foreign fighter facilitator in northern Afghanistan, poaching Central Asia fighters and the Tehrik-i-Taliban Pakistan's (TTP) militants".[6]

The Islamic State of Khorasan is the strangest non-state actor in Afghanistan that poses a serious security threat to Taliban and Pakistan. The IS-K has deep roots in South Asia with its branches in Pakistan, India, and some Southeast Asian states. Well-organized and well-established organization with over 250,000 trained fighters that can anytime challenge authority of the failed state in Afghanistan. There are countless books and journals in markets and libraries that highlight infrastructure of the IS-K with different perspectives and view its operational mechanism and suicide technique with different glasses. My glasses are not as different from them as I have written books on the suicide operation of the ISIS and IS-K, and contributed article to the newspapers and journals. The IS-K threat to the existence of Taliban is intensified by the day as the group consecutively targeted government installations and public place. Expert and analyst, Mohamed Mokhtar Qandi in his paper (Challenges to Taliban Rule and Potential Impacts for the Region: Internal and external factors are weakening the Taliban, making the group's long term stability increasingly unlikely. Fikra Forum. The Washington Institute for Near East Policy-09 February 2022) has noted the intensifying threat of ISIS and IS-K in Afghanistan, and asserted that the ISIS seeks to be an alternative to the Taliban movement:

"ISIS views the Taliban movement as a major strategic foe in South Asia. From the outset, members of Khorasan Province began questioning the Taliban's legitimacy in jihadi circles, which helped ISIS win new followers who splintered from the movement. Furthermore, ISIS may be attractive to those seeking revenge on the movement. In some cases, ISIS has attracted former Afghan intelligence members as well as younger middle-class youth who may become increasingly disaffected with the Taliban. There is also the dispute between the Taliban and the Salafist current inside Afghanistan that is not affiliated with Khorasan Province. The Taliban's harassment of these Salafists may push them to join the ranks of ISIS, or at least provide a haven for its members. Since the Taliban came to power by force, their lack of legitimacy can quickly lead to a decline in their popular support vis-à-vis ISIS, especially if they fail to meet the needs of the people and improve the economic situation. Despite the power that the Islamic State demonstrated in Khorasan, it is unlikely that the movement will be able to plan or launch attacks on distant targets. However, if ISIS-Khorasan succeeds in controlling more territories in Afghanistan and recruiting elements who resent Taliban, it will be tantamount to reviving the organization in the Middle East. On the one hand, the organization will intensify its propaganda and its claims that it is the sole carrier of the banner of jihad and hence, must be supported in establishing the Islamic caliphate as a global project. This will provide the organization with many opportunities to set up training camps for its elements and export them to the Middle East where they previously experienced a harsh defeat".[7]

With the establishment of the ISIS-K in Jalalabad province of Afghanistan in 2015, six commanders of the Tehrik-e-Taliban Pakistan immediately joined the group. Mr. Hafiz Saeed Khan became the top commander of the group, and started terrorist attacks against the Afghan government forces and civilian population in Kunar and Jalalabad provinces. The sardonicism, that Afghan parliamentarians, Ministers and military commanders purchased weapons for the ISIS-K group, lurked its fighters and suicide bombers in their houses and offices, and transported them to the centre-stage. The role of Afghan police was underwhelming as well. They all received millions dollars and appreciation certificates. The Jalalabad governor Mr. Gulab Mengal was dancing to the CIA and MI6 tangos, protected the ISIS-K fighters in governor house, financed and armed their leadership. Former Foreign Minister Hanif Atmar purveyed millions of dollars in helicopters to the ISIS centres in Paktika province. Reporting on the group's early expansion efforts indicated that IS-K, at its height, had controlled eight districts across southern Nangarhar province with the military and financial assistance of war criminals governor Gulab Mengal and Hanif Atmar.

The US State Department in November 2021 blacklisted and imposed sanctions on three leaders of the Islamic State Khorasan Province. The

State Department in a statement said the decision is taken to ensure Afghanistan cannot again become a platform for international terrorism. According to the statement, three key members of Daesh were blacklisted as "Specially Designated Global Terrorists." The Amir of IS-K was also included among those blacklisted, the statement read. "Sanaullah Ghafari, also known as Shahab al-Muhajir, was ISIS-K's current overall emir. He was appointed by the ISIS core to lead ISIS-K in June 2020. Mr. Ghafari was responsible for approving all ISIS-K operations throughout Afghanistan and arranging funding to conduct operations," the statement reads. The IS-K spokesperson Sultan Aziz Azam was also blacklisted who, according to the statement, had been acting as Daesh's spokesperson since the group's emergence in Afghanistan. Maulawi Rajab, the leader of Daesh in Kabul province, was also blacklisted. "Rajab was planning ISIS-K's attacks and operations and commands ISIS-K groups conducting attacks in Kabul," the statement reads. Moreover, the IS-K has expanded its media strength and established several media outlets. Expert and analyst, Riccardo Valle (Islamic State Khorasan Province threatens Uzbekistan, Central Asia, and neighbouring countries. Geopolitical Report ISSN 2785-2598 Volume 19 Issue 04. Jihadest Propaganda and Terrorism Project) had noted some important media and propaganda outlets of the Islamic State for furthering its agendas:

"Islamic State has a long history of propaganda that specifically addresses its Uzbek militants. ISKP propaganda in Pashto or Dari language had been regularly translated into the Uzbek language by Xuroson Ovozi (Voice of Khurasan, the Uzbek version of Khurasan Ghag Radio, ISKP Pashto radio channel), which for instance, subtitled several videos from Akhbar Wilayah Khurasan and Khalid Media since at least November 2021. Moreover, since the start of 2022, Uzbek media channels officially published their propaganda output under the al-Azaim Foundation banner. One channel, Aqida Darsliklari, issued eighteen lessons on the Islamic State's creed and method (aqeeda and manhaj), while it also started to publish speeches from former Islamic Movement of Uzbekistan's (IMU) prominent ideology Asadullah Urganchiy. According to an audio file from Mohammed Ali Domla – former Chief Security Officer of the IMU – shared by a pro-ISKP Uzbek channel, the Asadullah Urganchiy was killed by the Taliban in Zabol province in 2015 when the group pledged allegiance to the Islamic State. In February, al-Azaim Foundation also published a book in the Uzbek language titled "Until When the Ignorance?" which specifically addressed Uzbek and Turkmen militants in Afghanistan. The book lashes out against the Taliban, arguing the group is an ally of Russia, Pakistan, and Turkey, planning to eradicate Islam from the entire region and is becoming the "Hayat Tahrir al-Sham of Afghanistan", meaning abandoning jihad in favour of being part of the international community. ISKP also featured propaganda in the Tajik language for Tajik militants, too. Moreover, similar to Uzbek propaganda, Sadoi Khurasan (Voice of Khurasan, the Tajik version of Khurasan Ghag Radio) has produced around 150 audio files since January 2021".[8]

Ariana News reported concerns of the Secretary-General of the Shanghai Cooperation Organization (SCO) Vladimir Norov about the transportation of ISIS militants from the Middle East that posed a threat to regional security. Speaking at a webinar organized by the Islamabad Policy Research Institute, Norov said he was concerned about the deteriorating situation along the border regions of Afghanistan. Norov said: "According to the SCO regional anti-terrorist structure, the numbers of fighters arriving in the north of the country [Afghanistan] are growing." These militants were moved from Syrian and Iraqi conflict zones and posed a threat to the SCO member states, he added. Norov also said that Daesh members useed information and communication technologies in Afghanistan to promote the ideology of terrorism and manage the terror group's sleeper cells. Jumakhon Giyosov, the SCO Director of the Executive Committee of the Regional Anti-Terrorist Structure, also said that growing number of Daesh militants in Afghanistan was a serious threat to the region. "There is an increase in the number of militants arriving in northern Afghanistan, whose leaders are actively interacting with the leaders of the other terrorist organizations," Giyosov said. An Ariana News reporter also reported an increase in military presence after flying over the area in a helicopter. SpecialEurasia, a geopolitical and Intelligence analysis platform whose purpose is to inform the Italian and foreign audience on local, regional, and international dynamics in Eurasia, Dilemma of Central Asian Jihadists between IS-K and Taliban Political tensions and security threats in Tajikistan in its report (Geographical report, 18 May, 2022. Geograpolitika Evrazija projects) has noted the Moscow concerns about the activities of ISIS terrorists in Afghanistan:

"Moscow has been concerned about the situation on the Tajik-Afghan border, which is the focus of Russian attention. In this framework, Moscow and Dushanbe have maintained intensive contacts between defence departments, border services and diplomatic missions seeking cooperation in strengthening the defence capability of Tajikistan and its border service. Furthermore, as noted during the recent meeting between Tajik President

Emomali Rahmon and Russian President Vladimir Putin, Russia is still the leading trade and economic partner of Tajikistan. So, at the beginning of 2022, trade between the countries increased by more than 70%. Dushanbe has also discussed security cooperation with Beijing reaching an agreement with Chinese authorities to build a militarised base in the GBAO thanks to the equipment and machinery imported to Tajikistan from China. Considering the significant role that Gorno-Badakhshan has in Tajik security and economy and the Kremlin and Beijing's political and financial interests in the region, the Tajik Government might use military forces to stabilise the GBAO also in the future exasperating the regional social situation and pushing local young generations towards terrorist organisations such as the Islamic State which recently started propaganda orchestrated to recruit people from Tajikistan, Uzbekistan and Kyrgyzstan."[9]

The presence of the ISIS terrorist group in South East Asian states suchlike Philippines and Indonesia, has generated fear and intimidation. The Philippines has so far controlled ISIS but its recruitment process hasn't halted. In Malaysia, the Eastern Sabah Security Command (ESSCOM) eliminated individuals attempting to create a safe haven in Sabah for Abu Sayyaf members fleeing from the AFP. In Indonesia, national counter terrorism force hasn't achieved their gaol, but trying to dismantle sleeping cells. However, more than 2,000 nationals of South Asian states have joined the ISIS terrorist group in Iraq, Syria and Afghanistan. Citizens of some states have joined Al Nusra terrorist group. These recruitments heighten concerns about the potential threat posed by returnees who may seek to relocate to the region with the fall of ISIL's so-called caliphate. The Daesh-K was founded in 2015 by the US army to counter Taliban in Afghanistan. Immediately, after its establishment, the ISIS-K launched attacks against Shia communities, state and private institutions, and government targets in major cities across Afghanistan and Pakistan. The ISIS-K targeted minorities suchlike Hazara and Sikhs, journalists, aid workers, security personnel and government infrastructure.

BBC reported (11 October 2021) establishment of the Khorasan-K, and its successful attacks in Iraq, Syria and Afghanistan: "Islamic State Khorasan Province - is the regional affiliate of the Islamic State group. It is the most extreme and violent of all the jihadist militant groups in Afghanistan. IS-K was set up in January 2015 at the height of IS's power in Iraq and Syria, before its self-declared caliphate was defeated and dismantled by a US-led coalition. It recruits both Afghan and Pakistani jihadists, especially defecting members of the Afghan Taliban who don't see their own organisation as extreme enough. "Khorasan" refers to a historical region covering parts of modern-day Afghanistan and Pakistan."[10]The power structures, social institutions and local authorities of the Central Asian states are unable to work with radical Islamic groups. The prospect of nuclear terrorism in Central Asia and possibly in Russia, is crystal clear. The risk of a complete nuclear device falling into the hands of terrorists will cause consternation in the region. Nuclear terrorism remains a constant threat to global peace".5 Despite initial scepticism about the group's existence from analysts and government officials alike, IS-K is responsible for attacks against civilians in Afghanistan and Pakistan. Wilayat Khorasan, or ISIS-K, intends to secure Afghanistan to legitimize the Islamic State's caliphate across the 'Khorasan Province' including portions of Central Asia, China, Iran, the Indian Subcontinent, and Southeast Asia.

The Taliban return to the Afghan power game received mixed responses from Tajikistan, Uzbekistan and Kazakhstan and deployed special commandos on their borders with Afghanistan. In response to their military preparations, Taliban deployed suicide brigade on border with Tajikistan. A shift in the strategy of Uzbekistan and Turkmenistan was also seen in their approach towards the Taliban government. However, the IS-K practiced violence and attacked some religious places. Taliban called them Khawarij, but the IS-K leadership decided in Kabul to create law and order crisis for Taliban by targeting Shia Muslim community in different provinces. The IS-K practices Takfiri sect that declare every Muslim infidel. They want to purge the Muslim societies of all the "deviations" and "sins". Afghan newspaper, Haste Subh in its comment (ISKP's Power Exaggeration: The Islamic State in Khurasan Province operates in Afghanistan in the most mysterious way possible-May 22, 2022) has noted Afghanistan's intelligence struggle to find the origin of the IS-K terrorist group:

"The number of ISKP members was also constantly exaggerated, as government security officials were reporting several hundred fighters as thousands of fighters. It was believed that magnifying ISKP would guarantee the US presence and aid. Pakistan, on the other hand, tried to use the expansion of ISKP as a strategic approach to lobby for legitimization of the Taliban. With the Taliban takeover of Afghanistan, ISKP has once again become a propaganda tool in order to legitimize the Taliban and oppress their opponents. Some of the propaganda targeted former Afghan army officers, others targeted non-Pashtun anti-Taliban fighters, and some targeted Taliban insurgents who were eliminated in the name. Bloody attacks on Hazaras and Sufis can also be analysed in this context, another managed attempt to magnify ISKP. The ISKP exists in Afghanistan, but studies show that: first, its actual members are very small; second, there are no prominent figures who have the ability to lead its fighters; third, the group's influence among the Afghan people is far less than significant. The ISKP and the Taliban are both dangerous, but the threat of several hundred ISKP members in Afghanistan is in no way comparable to the threat posed by the 80,000 Taliban to the people of Afghanistan and regional security. Whatever the game players label the insurgent groups, the reality that Taliban has enabled the ground for their emergence and gaining power cannot be out of the discussions and imagination. Throwing every single fragile security related issues to ISIS-K's ground are nothing more than politics being played by the proxy war actors in the region and Taliban is the very right tool to be used".[11]

There are reports from different parts that Taliban were reportedly detaining and beating the civilians. According to local sources, following recent Taliban clashes with the National Resistance Front in Panjshir and Baghlan, the Taliban have shot dead a number of civilians in the province. The Taliban, however, denied the claims. Journalist Sakhi Khalid in his Hasht Subh paper analysis (Taliban Spreads Panic in Central Afghanistan: Arrests, Tortures and Extortions Intensify in Behsud, Maidan Wardak- May 11, 2022) has noted incarceration of civilians by the Taliban in Behsud districts: Taliban have been harassing the residents of Behsud of Maidan Wardak province on charges of vague and baseless pretexts since 2021. Local sources claimed that the Taliban had arrested, tortured and extorted a large sum of money from the residents of Hesa-i-Awal and Markazi Bihsud districts. According to the residents, in most cases, the Taliban detained residents of the two districts of Maidan Wardak on charges of collaborating with Abdul Ghani Alipour, a former local commander.[12] On 16 May, 2022, Afghanistan Times reported Around 30 people who attempted to commit suicide have been brought to the hospital in 2022, the health officials in the western province of Herat said. Homayoun Forutan, head of the Badakhshan Provincial Hospital, added that most of the patients are women. Two have died and others have been rescued. "In total, there have been 29 cases of violence [attempted suicide] in the last three months, of which 27 are women and two are men," he said.[13] Expert and analyst, Javid Ahmad in his commentary (The Taliban's religious roadmap for Afghanistan. Middle East Institute--January 26, 2022) noted challenged of Taliban and their war against the IS-K in Afghanistan:

"On top of that, several other challenges have beset the militant emirate. The evolving power struggle among competing Taliban factions has plagued the Taliban-plus government, which comprises elements of terrorist groups in governing structures. This uneasy coalition includes the Haqqani Network in top government ranks, who remain in bed with jihadists like al-Qaeda. Domestically, tensions between the Haqqanis and the larger southern Taliban factions increasingly resemble two scorpions in a bottle-antagonistic, territorial, and deadly. Meanwhile, the Islamic State-Khorasan Province (ISKP), the terror group's Afghan offshoot, has locked horns with the Taliban in violent competition. While traditional Salafism follows the strict Hanbali version of Sunni Islam (as observed in Saudi Arabia), most Salafists groups in Afghanistan (minus al-Qaeda) arguably dabble between Hanafi and Salafist Islam. Increasingly, this includes the members of ISKP, who, as former or rebranded Taliban, typically follow a textualist version of Hanafi Islam rather than Hanbali Islam. In fact, ISKP members have generally avoided making public pronouncements of their Salafist credentials. Instead, they have set themselves apart by targeting non-Sunni groups they consider apostate, mainly the Shi'a community."[14]

Notes to Chapters

Chapter 1: The Taliban, ISIS-K, Al Qaeda, the Haqqni Network, their Atrocities, Torture and the Degradation of Afghan Nation

1. Yoram Schweitzer and Sari Goldstein Ferber, in their research paper (Al-Qaeda and the Internationalization of Suicide Terrorism. Jaffee Center for Strategic Studies, Tel Aviv University. Memorandum No. 78 November 2005

2. Ellen Tveteraas (Under the Hood–Learning and Innovation in the Islamic State's Suicide Vehicle Industry, Studies in Conflict & Terrorism-2022

3. Michael A. Peters in his research paper (Declinism' and discourses of decline-the end of the war in Afghanistan and the limits of American power, Educational Philosophy and Theory, DOI: 10.1080/00131857.2021.1982694.

4. Afghanistan: Taliban Deprive Women of Livelihoods, Identity: Severe Restrictions, Harassment, Fear in Ghazni Province-18 January, 2022)

5. Kate Clark (Afghanistan's conflict in 2021 (2): Republic collapse and Taliban victory in the long-view of history. Afghanistan Analysts Network--30 Dec 2021.

6. Afghanistan: Taliban Kill, 'Disappear' Ex-Officials: Raids Target Former Police, Intelligence Officers- November 30, 2021

7. Qasim Jan, Yi Xie, Muhammad Habib Qazi, Zahid Javid Choudhary and Baha Ul Haq in their research paper (Examining the role of Pakistan's national curriculum textbook discourses on normalising the Taliban's violence in the USA's Post 9/11 war on terror in South Waziristan, Pakistan. British Journal of Religious Education-2022.

8. Eric Schmitt, "ISIS Branch Poses Biggest Immediate Terrorist Threat to Evacuation in Kabul", November 3, 2021, the New York Times

9. Clayton Sharb, Danika Newlee and the CSIS iDeas Lab in their joint work (Islamic State Khorasan (IS-K). Center for Strategic and International Studies-2018.

10. Mohamed Mokhtar Qandi in his paper (Challenges to Taliban Rule and Potential Impacts for the Region: Internal and external factors are weakening the Taliban, making the group's long term stability increasingly unlikely. Fikra Forum. The Washington Institute for Near East Policy-09 February 2022.

11. Amira Jadoon, Abdul Sayed and Andrew Mines in their research paper (The Islamic State Threat in Taliban Afghanistan: Tracing the Resurgence of Islamic State Khorasan. The Combating Terrorism Center at West Point. January 2022, Volum 15, Issue-1.

12. April 17, ISIS called on all fighters around the world to carry out "big and painful" attacks targeting officials and soldiers". Salam Times

13. Roshni Kapur in his paper (The Persistent ISKP Threat to Afghanistan: On China's Doorstep. Middle East Institute-January 6, 2022

14. Editor of Terrorism Monitor. Jacob Zenn in his article (Islamic State in Khorasan Province's One-Off Attack in Uzbekistan. Volium XX. Issue 9, 06 May 2022.

15. Amy Kazmin in her article (Isis-K insurgency jeopardises Taliban's grip on Afghanistan: New rulers accused of betraying Islam by jihadis intent on creating ideologically pure caliphate-October, 26, 2021.

16. Salman Rafi Sheikh in his article (Eight months on, Taliban's rule is far from stable: Resistance groups are mounting an increasingly potent challenge to the Taliban and may have Pakistan's clandestine support-Asia Times, May 2, 2022.

Chapter 2: Military and Political Confrontations between Taliban and the ISIS-K in Afghanistan

1. Niamatullah Ibrahimi and Shahram Akbarzadeh in their research paper (Intra-Jihadist Conflict and Cooperation: Islamic State–Khorasan Province and the Taliban in Afghanistan, Studies in Conflict and Terrorism, https://doi.org/10.1080/1057610X.2018.1529367.

2. 08 May 2022, Afghanistan Times

3. Taliban Governance: Reinstating the Islamic Emirate of Afghanistan Announcement and International Recognition. European Asylum Support Office: Afghanistan Country focus, Country of Origin Information Report-2022

4. Heather Barr in her recent article (Speak Up on Behalf of Afghan Women: What is happening right now in Afghanistan is the most serious women's rights crisis in the world today. The Diplomat-May 12, 2022

5. DW News, 09.05.2022

6. Ariana News (10 May 2022

7. 12 May 2022, Ariana News

8. Seth G. Jones in his paper (Center for Preventive Action: Countering a Resurgent Terrorist Threat in Afghanistan-14 April 2022

9. Amira Jadoon, Abdul Sayed and Andrew Mines in their recent research paper (The Islamic State Threat in Taliban Afghanistan: Tracing the Resurgence

of Islamic State Khorasan.The Combating Terrorism Centre at West Point, January 2022, Vol 15, ISSUE-1.

10. Niamatullah Ibrahimi and Shahram Akbarzadeh in their research paper (Intra-Jihadist Conflict and Cooperation: Islamic State–Khorasan Province and the Taliban in Afghanistan, Studies in Conflict and Terrorism, DOI:10.10 80/1057610X.2018.1529367.

11. Why the Taliban won't tackle ISIS-K: Afghanistan's new rulers know if they seriously crack down on the terror group their new government could collapse overnight-Asia Times, October 21, 2021.

12. Scott Lucas. ISIS-K violence could force the West into alliance with Taliban: The August 26 attack reconfigured the Afghan mosaic, pushing the US and other countries to recalculate their approach-Asia Times, 01 September 2021.

13. David Fox in his article (Kabul Airport Islamic State bombers kill dozens: Taliban denounce jihadist rival group's attack; Biden vows vengeance; UN Security Council to meet.

14. 22 April 2022, Asharq Al Aausat. Who Is Slaughtering the Hazaras of Afghanistan? Asharq Al Aausat, Camelia Entekhabifard. Editor-in-chief of the Independent Persian. 22 April, 2022.

15. European Foundation for South Asian Studies (EFSAS), Amsterdam-No. 2. The Haqqani Network: A brief profile. February 2022.

16. Seth G. Jones in his research paper. Countering a Resurgent Terrorist Threat in Afghanistan. Centre for Preventive Action, Council on Foreign Relations-12 April 2022.

17. Joshua T. White in his article. Nonstate threats in the Taliban's Afghanistan-01 February, 2022

18. Afghanistan-The Intercept, 14 April 2022

19. Mrityunjoy Kumar Jha (Taliban deploy fresh unit of suicide bombers to take on Pakistani forces on Durand Line. 25-February-2022.

20. The Diplomat--February 09, 2022

21. Marco Nilsson. Motivations for Jihad and Cognitive Dissonance–A Qualitative Analysis of Former Swedish Jihadists, Studies in Conflict & Terrorism. Volume 45, 2022 - Issue 1. 18 Jun 2019.

Chapter 3: Suicide Brigades, ISIS-K Military Strength and Taliban's Misrule in Afghanistan

1. Atal Ahmadzai. Dying to Live: The "Love to Death" Narrative Driving the Taliban's Suicide Bombings.

2. Amira Jadoon, Andrew Mines and Abdul Sayed in their research paper (The evolving Taliban-ISK rivalry, 07 Sep 2021, The Interpreter.

3. Global Witness research report

4. William A. Byrd and Javed Noorani. Industrial-Scale Looting of Afghanistan's Mineral Resources, 2017, the United States Institute of Peace.

5. BBC 11 October 2021

6. Niels Terpstra (2020) Rebel governance, rebel legitimacy, and external intervention: assessing three phases of Taliban rule in Afghanistan, Small Wars & Insurgencies,31:6, 1143-1173, DOI: 10.1080/09592318.2020.1757916-25 May 2020.

7. Asfandyar Mir. The ISIS-K Resurgence-08 October 2021

8. Asia Pacific Group on Money Laundering and Global Centre on Cooperative Security in its report (Financing and Facilitation of Foreign Terrorist Fighters and Returnees in Southeast Asia," Asia Pacific Group on Money Laundering and Global Centre on Cooperative Security, November 2021.

9. Niamatullah Ibrahimi & Shahram Akbarzadeh in their research paper (Intra-Jihadist Conflict and Cooperation: Islamic State–Khorasan Province and the Taliban in Afghanistan, Studies in Conflict & Terrorism, DOI: 10.1080/1057610X.2018.1529367.

10. Sushant Sareen in his paper (The ISKP is Nothing but an Exaggerated Threat. SPECIAL Report. Of Observer Research Foundation: Afghanistan and the New Global (Dis)Order: Great Game and Uncertain Neighbours-December 2021.

11. Aman Bezreh, Chris Hitchcock, Jacob Berntson, Jen Wilton, Jennifer Dathan, Khalil Dewan, Leyla Slama, Michael Hart, Shaza Alsalmoni, Sophie Akram and Tim Hulse. Understanding the Rising Cult of Suicide Bomber. Action on Armed Violence AOAV.

Chapter 4: The Taliban, IS-K, TTP and their War against Hazara Muslims in Afghanistan and Pakistan

1. Atal Ahmadzai and Faten Ghosn. Asia Times. 19 January 2022

2. Editor Iain Overton and Aman Bezreh, Chris Hitchcock, Jacob Berntson, Jen Wilton, Jennifer Dathan, Khalil Dewan, Leyla Slama, Michael Hart, Shaza Alsalmoni, Sophie Akram and Tim Hulse. Understanding the Rising Cult of Suicide Bomber. Action on Armed Violence AOAV.

3. On 15 August 2015, the ISIS-K terrorists attacked Mawdoud Education Center, ToloNews.

4. The deadliest targets of such attacks was a mosque called Imam-e Zaman on 20th of November 2017 which is located in western part of Kabul. According to Media's coverage, the attack on Imam-e-Zaman mosque resulted in 111 civilian casualties". The Hazara Muslims were tortured by nomads, Taliban and extremist mujahedeen. On 18 January 2018, Human Rights Watch (HRW) and Amnesty international reported widespread atrocities against Hazara population in Afghanistan.

5. Mohammad Hussain Hasrat. Over a Century of Persecution: Massive Human Rights Violation against Hazaras in Afghanistan. Concentration on attacks occurred during the National Unity Government. Feb 2019.

6. The Global Centre for the Responsibility to Protect in 01 March 2022

7. Atrocity Alert No. 298: Ukraine, Sudan and Afghanistan-27 April 2022. The Global Centre for the Responsibility to Protect.

8. Peter Mills. Afghanistan-in-Review: Institute for the Study of War. January 3–January 25, 2022

9. Ananya Varma. In Afghanistan, NRFA Continues Training in Panjshir; New Resistance Formed against Taliban

10. 23 August 2021, BBC

11. Nilly Kohzad an Afghan American economist and journalist in her article (What Does the National Resistance Front of Afghanistan Have to Offer? The NRF says it is pushing for a new trajectory in Afghanistan. The Diplomat December 15, 2021

12. The BBC Chief Correspondent, Lyse Doucet. BB, 29 April 2022

13. The USAF, Retired; and CPT Joshua Fruth, US Army Reserves, Maj Gen Buck Elton and Dr. Vanessa Neumann. Evacuation Operations, Great-Power Competition, and External Operations Terror Threats in Post-Drawdown Afghanistan: Mapping out the Path Ahead- Journal of Indo-Pacific Affairs. Published November 01, 2021.

14. Abdul Sayed in his paper. The Evolution and Future of Tehrik-e-Taliban Pakistan. Carnegie Endowment for international peace 21 December, 2021.

15. Ibid

16. Patricia Gossman, Associate Asia Director at Human Rights Watch

17. Ibid

18. The British House of Lords recalled to debate the situation in Afghanistan in 18 August 2021

19. Madiha Afzal in her commentary (Pakistan's ambivalent approach toward a resurgent Tehrik-e-Taliban Pakistan. Madiha Afzal Friday, Brooking, February 11, 2022.

Chapter 5: Al Qaeda, the Haqqni Terrorist Network, Lashkar-e-Taiba, Taliban and the Islamic State of Khorasan's Plundering of Mineral Resources in Afghanistan and their expedition Towards Central Asia.

1. Analyst and expert, Ashok K. Behuria (2007) Fighting the Taliban: Pakistan at war with itself,Australian Journal of International Affairs, 61:4, 529-543, DOI: 10.1080/10357710701684963).

2. Cosmin Timofte in his paper. Unlikely Friends: What role would the USA play in the fight between ISIS K and the Taliban? The Institute of New Europe's Work-29 November 2021.

3. Hassan Abu Haniyeh in his commentary (Daesh's Organisational Structure-3 December 2014, Aljazeera Centre for Studied.

4. Expert and analyst Ellen Tveteraas "Department of Politics and International Relations, University of Oxford, Oxfordshire, United Kingdom" highlighted operational mechanism of the ISIS terrorist group in Iraq, and performance of Martyrdom Operatives Battalion (Katibat al-Istishadiin), and its associates in her paper (Under the Hood–Learning and Innovation in the Islamic State's Suicide Vehicle Industry. Studies in Conflict & Terrorism. 13 February, 2022.

5. Pepe Escobar. Who profits from Kabul suicide bombing? ISIS-Khorasan aims to prove to Afghans and to the outside world that the Taliban cannot secure the capital. 30 August, 2021

6. Michael Rubin in his commentary (Biden ignores Afghanistan at America's peril, The National Interest- April 28, 2022

7. Damon Mehl. Damon Mehl, CTC Sentinel, November 2018, Volume-11, Issue-10

8. Christian Bleuer. Chechens in Afghanistan: A Battlefield Myth That Will Not Die. 27 Jun 2016

9. Michael W. S. Ryan in his research paper (ISIS: The Terrorist Group That Would Be a State. U.S. Naval War College and Pepe Escobar (Who profits from the Kabul suicide bombing? ISIS-Khorasan aims to prove to Afghans and to the outside world that the Taliban cannot secure the capital. Asia Times-27 August 2021.

10. Dr. Sanchita Bhattacharya. The Taliban Financial Resources: Drug Trafficking, Illegal Mining, and Military Strength.

11. Global witness Press Release. 06 June 2016

12. Asad Mirza. For quick revenue, Afghan mining wealth is the best option for Taliban: A decade back some US geologists had calculated the mineral reserves in Afghanistan to be in excess of $1 trillion-14 March 2022.

13. Nik Martin (Afghanistan: Taliban to reap $1 trillion mineral wealth-18 August 2021

14. Tim McDonnell in his article (The Taliban now controls one of the world's biggest lithium deposits: Illegal mining of lapis lazuli, a gem, is a major source of revenue for the Taliban. December 28, 2021.

15. Christopher McIntosh and Ian Storey. 20 November 2019

16. Scholar and Lecturer Department of Social Sciences, Lahore Garrison University Pakistan, Dr. Yunis Khushi. A Critical Analysis of Factors and

Implications of ISIS Recruitments and Concept of Jihad-Bil-Nikah-26 June 2017.

17. Rushni Kapur in her paper (The Persistent ISKP Threat to Afghanistan: On China's Doorstep, Middle East Institute--January 6, 2022

18. Assistant Professor and Research Faculty with Terrorism, Transnational Crime and Corruption Center (TraCCC) and the Schar School of Policy and Government at George Mason University. Dr. Mahmut Cengiz, in his paper (ISIS or al-Qaeda: Which Looms as the Greater Threat to Global Security? Small War Journal 01 October, 2022

Chapter 6: The IS-K, Central Asian Terrorist groups, Taliban and Prospect of Nuclear Terrorism.

1. 29 April 2022. Islamic State in Afghanistan Looks to Recruit Regional Tajiks, Inflict Violence against Tajikistan: ISKP's expanded media campaign seeks to recruit ethnic Tajik and nationals as well as incite militant violence against Tajikistan. Lucas Webber and Riccardo Valle.

2. Thomas Gibbons-Neff and Najim Rahim

3. 23 April 2022, Tehran Times

4. Soufan Centre. IntelBrief. Terrorism Trends in Central Asia. The Soufan Center (TSC) November 26, 2018

5. Global Witness in its research report (At Any Price we Will Take the Mines: The Islamic State, the Taliban and Afghanistan's White Talc Mountains-May 2018.

6. Joana Cook and Gina Vale. From Daesh to 'Diaspora': Tracing the Women and Minors of Islamic State. ICSR King's College London 2018.

7. October 2017, Columb Strack paper

8. Oved Lobel in his article (The Taliban are losing the fight against Islamic State-Asia Times-6 December 2021

9. BBC. 20 August 2021

10. Anna Powles Afghan debacle exposes moral hazard of outsourcing war: Afghan security contractors left behind as US and NATO forces withdrawal could pay the ultimate price for their services, Asia Times-26 August 2021.

11. Thomas Gibbons-Neff, Sharif Hassan and Ruhullah Khapalwak-Nov. 3, 2021

12. Muhammad Wajeeh, a Research Associate at Department of Development Studies, COMSATS Institute of Information Technology, Abbottabad Pakistan in his research paper (Nuclear Terrorism: A Potential Threat to World's Peace and Security- JSSA Vol II, No. 2.

13. Keir A. Lieber and Daryl G. Press in their research paper (Why States Won't Give Nuclear Weapons to Terrorists. International Security, Vol. 38, No. 1 (Summer 2013), doi:10.1162/ISEC_a_00127.

14. Edward Lemon, Vera Mironova and William Tobey in their paper (Nuclear, Chemical and Biological Terrorism in Central Asia and Russia: Al Qaeda, the ISIS Affiliated Groups and Security of Sensitive Biological Weapons Facilities'

15. Alexandra Rimpler Sschmid, Ralf Trapp Sarah Leonard, Christian Kaunert, Yves DUBUCQ, Claude Lefebvre, and Hanna Mohn in their paper (EU preparedness and responses to Chemical, Biological, Radiological and Nuclear (CBRN) threats. Directorate General for External Policies, Policy Department 2021. European Parliament Coordinator: Policy Department for External Relations Directorate General for External Policies of the Union

Chapter 7: The Taliban Financial Resources: Drug Trafficking, Illegal Mining, and Military Strength. Dr. Sanchita Bhattacharya

Aboudouh, Ahmed (2021), "Where do the Taliban get their money and weapons from?", https://www.independent.co.uk/asia/south-asia/taliban-where-weapons-money-funds-b1911655.html

ANI (2021), "Taliban money trail: How funding continued over 20 years", https://www.aninews.in/news/world/asia/taliban-money-trail-how-funding-continued-over-20-years20210909075548/

Azami, Dawood (2021), "Afghanistan: How do the Taliban make money?" BBC News, https://www.bbc.com/news/world-46554097

Bezhan, Frud (2020), "Exclusive: Taliban's Expanding 'Financial Power' Could Make It 'Impervious' To Pressure, Confidential Report Warns", https://www.rferl.org/a/exclusive-taliban-s-expanding-financial-power-could-make-it-impervious-to-pressure-secret-nato-report-warns/30842570.html

Bodetti, Austin (2016), "From WhatsApp to Hawala, How the Taliban Moves Money Around", https://www.vice.com/en/article/bmv3g3/from-whatsapp-to-hawala-how-the-taliban-moves-money-around

Dominguez, Gabriel (2016), "How the Taliban get their money", https://www.dw.com/en/how-the-taliban-get-their-money/a-18995315

Felbab-Brown, Vanda (2021), "Pipe dreams: The Taliban and drugs from the 1990s into its new regime", https://www.brookings.edu/articles/pipe-dreams-the-taliban-and-drugs-from-the-1990s-into-its-new-regime/#footref-39

Ferro, Brian (2021), "What the Taliban Resurgence Means for Money Laundering", https://feedzai.com/blog/what-the-taliban-resurgence-means-for-money-laundering/

Global Witness (2018), "At any price we will take the mines", file:///C:/Users/lenovo/Downloads/AfghanistanTalcInvestigation_May2018.pdf

Jurist (2021), "Afghanistan dispatches: 'The Taliban Ministry of Agriculture is setting new rules to collect Islamic taxes'", https://www.jurist.org/news/2021/10/afghanistan-dispatches-the-taliban-ministry-of-agriculture-is-setting-new-rules-to-collect-islamic-taxes/

Kakar, Boriwal and Abubakar Siddique (2017), "Pakistani Clerics Raise Funds for Afghan Taliban's War", https://gandhara.rferl.org/a/pakistan-balochistan-fundrasing-for-the-taliban/28529570.html

Khan, S. (2021), "Pakistan: Taliban donations, recruitment on the rise", https://www.dw.com/en/pakistan-taliban-donations-recruitment-on-the-rise/a-57703423

Maizland, Lindsey. (2021), "What is the Taliban?" Council on Foreign Relations, https://www.cfr.org/backgrounder/taliban-afghanistan.

News18 (2021), "Opium Trade, Extortion. How Taliban earns over $1 Billion Yearly and What Keeps It going", https://www.news18.com/news/explainers/explained-opium-trade-extortion-how-taliban-earns-over-1-billion-yearly-and-what-keeps-it-going-4091171.html

Noorzai, Roshan (2021), "Taliban Donations Soar in Pakistan Ahead of US Pullout from Afghanistan", VOA, https://www.voanews.com/a/extremism-watch_taliban-donations-soar-pakistan-ahead-us-pullout-afghanistan/6207199.html

Peters, Gretchen (2009), "How Opium Profits the Taliban", United States Institute of Peace, https://www.usip.org/sites/default/files/resources/taliban_opium_1.pdf.

Reliefweb (2021), "Remittances to Afghanistan are lifelines: They are needed more than ever in a time of crisis", https://reliefweb.int/report/afghanistan/blog-remittances-afghanistan-are-lifelines-they-are-needed-more-ever-time-crisis

Seal, Rajashree (2021), "Where Does the Taliban Get its Money From and How Wealthy is it?", https://www.india.com/news/world/where-does-the-taliban-get-its-money-from-and-how-wealthy-is-it-taliban-funds-opium-illegal-mining-donations-kabul-afghanistan-takeover-4898570/

Seldin, Jeff (2021), "Where Are the Taliban Getting Their Money?" https://www.voanews.com/a/us-afghanistan-troop-withdrawal_where-are-taliban-getting-their-money/6209559.html

Sundaram, Rajesh (2021), "Despite billions of dollars frozen, here's how the Taliban will run Afghanistan", https://www.businesstoday.in/latest/world/story/despite-billions-of-dollars-frozen-heres-how-the-taliban-will-run-afghanistan-304674-2021-08-19

Synovitz, Ron (2021), "Taliban Imposing 'Charity' Taxes on Farmers Who Need Aid", https://gandhara.rferl.org/a/taliban-charity-tax-afghan-farmers/31535773.html

The Hindu (2022), "Taliban announce ban on poppy production in Afghanistan", The Hindu, https://www.thehindu.com/news/international/taliban-announce-ban-on-poppy-production-in-afghanistan/article65286898.ece

Thomas, Clayton (2021), "Taliban Government in Afghanistan: Background and Issues for Congress", CRS Report, https://crsreports.congress.gov/product/pdf/R/R46955

United Nations Security Council (2020), "Letter dated 19 May 2020 from the Chair of the Security Council Committee established pursuant to resolution 1988 (2011) addressed to the President of the Security Council", https://www.securitycouncilreport.org/atf/cf/%7B65BFCF9B-6D27-4E9C-8CD3-CF6E4FF96FF9%7D/s_2020_415_e.pdf

Yousaf, Farooq and Moheb Jabarkhail (2021), "US withdrawal and the Taliban regime in Afghanistan: Future Policy Directions", https://reliefweb.int/sites/reliefweb.int/files/resources/PB_5_2021_US-withdrawal-and-the-Taliban-regime-in-Afghanistan.pdf

Zerden, Alex (2021), "Reassessing Counter Terrorism Financing in a Taliban-Controlled Afghanistan", https://www.justsecurity.org/78221/reassessing-counter-terrorism-financing-in-a-taliban-controlled-afghanistan/

Chapter 8: Under the Hood–Learning and Innovation in the Islamic State's Suicide Vehicle Industry. Ellen Tveteraas

1   Suadad Al-Salhy and Tim Arango, 'Sunni Militants Drive Iraqi Army Out of Mosul', 10 June 2014, https://www.nytimes.com/2014/06/11/world/middleeast/militants-in-mosul.html.

2   Craig Whiteside, Ian Rice, and Daniele Raineri, 'Black Ops: Islamic State and Innovation in Irregular Warfare', Studies in Conflict and Terrorism, 2019, 1–28, https://doi.org/10.1080/1057610X.2019.1628623; Craig Whiteside et al., 'The ISIS Files The Department of Soldiers' (Washington D.C.: George Washington University, April 2021), https://isisfiles.gwu.edu/downloads/q237hr95t?locale=en.

3   According to the Global Terrorism Database (GTD), AQI and ISI conducted 108 suicide bombings between 2003 and 2010, while the Islamic State conducted 392 between 2014 and 2015 alone. If we include all groups in Iraq, the GTD registered 776 instances of suicide bombings between 2003 and 2010. In contrast, the Islamic State alone conducted 1023 attacks between 2014 and 2017. These estimates should be considered approximations. As noted by Charlie Winter, the limited presence of reporters, and military rather than terrorist nature of some of the group's attacks could mean that the GTD could be undercounting. Global Terrorism Database, 'National Consortium

for the Study of Terrorism and Responses to Terrorism (START)', [Data File]. Retrieved from https://www.Start.Umd.Edu/Gtd, 2018; Charlie Winter, 'War by Suicide: A Statistical Analysis of the Islamic State's Martyrdom Industry', ICCT Research Paper (Online) 8, no. 3 (2017): 1–34, https://doi.org/10.19165/2017.1.03.

4   Mike Davis, Buda's Wagon. (Place of publication not identified: Verso, 2017), 78–89.

5   Hugo Kaaman, 'The History and Adaptability of the Islamic State Car Bomb', Hugo Kaaman - Open Source Research on SVBIEDs (blog), 14 February 2017, https://hugokaaman.com/2017/02/14/the-history-and-adaptability-of-the-islamic-state-car-bomb/.

6   Dolnik, Understanding Terrorist Innovation: Technology, Tactics and Global Trends; Gill et al., 'Malevolent Creativity in Terrorist Organizations', 1 June 2013; Gill, 'Tactical Innovation and the Provisional Irish Republican Army', 2017; Bloom, 'Constructing Expertise: Terrorist Recruitment and "Talent Spotting" in the PIRA, Al Qaeda, and ISIS'; DeVore, Stähli, and Franke, 'Dynamics of Insurgent Innovation: How Hezbollah and Other Non-State Actors Develop New Capabilities'.

7   Paul Gill et al., 'Malevolent Creativity in Terrorist Organizations', The Journal of Creative Behavior 47, no. 2 (1 June 2013): 125–51, https://doi.org/10.1002/jocb.28.

8   Michael Kenney, From Pablo to Osama: Trafficking and Terrorist Networks, Government Bureaucracies, and Competitive Adaptation (University Park, Pa.: Pennsylvania State University Press, 2007), 13.

9   Diego Gambetta, Making Sense of Suicide Missions (Oxford: Oxford University Press, 2005).

10   Craig Whiteside and Vera Mironova, 'Adaptation and Innovation with an Urban Twist: Changes to Suicide Tactics in the Battle for Mosul', Military Review 97, no. 6 (2017): 78; Hugo Kaaman, 'Car Bombs as Weapons of War: ISIS'S Development of SVBIEDS, 2014-19', Middle East Institute, 2019.

11   Gill et al., 'Malevolent Creativity in Terrorist Organizations', 1 June 2013, 128.

12   The timeframe was selected because the Islamic State had a relatively stable level of organisation in Iraq. Before 2014 it operated clandestinely and following the fall of Mosul in 2017 the Iraq provinces underwent a re-organisation aimed at clandestine survival. Whiteside et al., 'The ISIS Files The Department of Soldiers', 8; Daniel Milton, 'Structure of a State - Captured Documents and the Islamic State's Organizational Structure' (West Point: Combating Terrorism Center, June 2021), 33, https://ctc.usma.edu/wp-content/uploads/2021/06/Structure-of-a-State.pdf.

13   The Islamic State did something similar in Syria a year earlier, using a BMP-1 reenforced with steel pipes in a coordinated attack on the Menagh air

base. In that case the Free Syrian Army (FSA) faction called the Northern Storm Brigade modified the vehicle and the Islamic State supplied a driver. Kaaman, Hugo, 'The First SVBIED Attack Using a Modified BMP-1 Armored Personnel Carrier in the Syrian Civil War. Jabhat al-Nusra Used It to Attack a Loyalist Checkpoint in Daraa al-Balad on June 27, 2013 – h/t @E_of_Justice', Twitter (blog), 18 September 2020, https://twitter.com/HKaaman/status/1306 984555434438657?s=20. Max Fisher, 'ISIS Just Pulled off Its First Carbombing with a Stolen American Humvee', Vox, 27 October 2014, https://www.vox. com/2014/10/27/7078635/isis-carbomb-stolen-american-humvee-iraq.

14 For more comprehensible overviews of the different modifications, see: Kaaman, 'Car Bombs as Weapons of War: ISIS'S Development of SVBIEDS, 2014-19'; Kaaman, 'The History and Adaptability of the Islamic State Car Bomb'.

15 Kaaman, 'The History and Adaptability of the Islamic State Car Bomb'.

16 Kaaman.

17 Wilayat Slah al-Din, Who Never Escape From War, 2016, https://jihadology. net/2016/06/08/new-video-message-from-the-islamic-state-but-god-will-perfect-his-light-wilayat-%e1%b9%a3ala%e1%b8%a5-al-din/; Wilāyat al-Ānbār, Determination of the Brave #3 (Anbar, 2017), https://jihadology. net/2017/12/24/new-video-message-from-the-islamic-state-determination-of-the-brave-3-wilayat-al-anbar/; Wilayat Slah al-Din, Holding Wounds of Their Nation #9, 2015, https://jihadology.net/2015/12/08/new-video-message-from-the-islamic-state-holding-wounds-of-their-nation-9-wilayat-%e1%b9%a3ala%e1%b8%a5-al-din/.

18 Wilayat Slah al-Din, Who Never Escape From War; Wilāyat al-Ānbār, Determination of the Brave #3; Wilayat Slah al-Din, Holding Wounds of Their Nation #9.

19 Interview with BTU1, August 2021; Tamer El-Ghobashy and Ali A Nabhan, 'Iraq's Vital Weapon Against ISIS in Mosul; $250,000 Kornet Missiles Target Toughest Islamic State Truck Bombs', Wall Street Journal (Online), 4 November 2016, 1836035993, ABI/INFORM Global; Global Newsstream, https://www. proquest.com/newspapers/iraqs-vital-weapon-against-isis-mosul-250-000/ docview/1836035993/se-2?accountid=13042.

20 Gambetta, Making Sense of Suicide Missions.

21 A history of the use and spread of suicide bombing is beyond the scope of this article, but can be found in the following works: Mia Bloom, Dying to Kill (New York: Columbia University Press, 2005); Gambetta, Making Sense of Suicide Missions; Robert A. Pape, Dying to Win, Epub (New York: Random House, 2006); Assaf Moghadam, The Globalization of Martyrdom: Al Qaeda, Salafi Jihad, and the Diffusion of Suicide Attacks (Baltimore: Johns Hopkins University Press, 2008).

22   Ami Pedahzur, Root Causes of Suicide Terrorism: Globalization of Martyrdom, Cass Series on Political Violence (London: Routledge, 2006), 1–12.

23   Kaaman, 'The History and Adaptability of the Islamic State Car Bomb'.

24   UNSC, 'The Islamic State in Iraq and the Levant and the Al-Nusrah Front for the People of the Levant: Report and Recommendations Submitted Pursuant to Resolution 2170 (2014)' (The United Nation, 14 November 2014), 15.

25   C. Christine Fair, 'Sri Lanka', in Urban Battle Fields of South Asia, 1st ed., Lessons Learned from Sri Lanka, India, and Pakistan (RAND Corporation, 2004), 11–68, http://www.jstor.org/stable/10.7249/mg210a.10; Stephen Hopgood, 'Tamil Tigers, 1987–2002', in Making Sense of Suicide Missions (Oxford: Oxford University Press, 2005), 46; Pedahzur, Root Causes of Suicide Terrorism: Globalization of Martyrdom, 115–18.

26   Linda Argote and Ella Miron-Spektor, 'Organizational Learning: From Experience to Knowledge', Organization Science (Providence, R.I.) 22, no. 5 (2011): 1123, https://doi.org/10.1287/orsc.1100.0621.

27   Argote and Miron-Spektor, 1124.

28   George P Huber, 'Organizational Learning: The Contributing Processes and the Literatures', Organization Science (Providence, R.I.) 2, no. 1 (1991): 89, https://doi.org/10.1287/orsc.2.1.88.

29   Kenney, From Pablo to Osama: Trafficking and Terrorist Networks, Government Bureaucracies, and Competitive Adaptation, 5.

30   Huber, 'Organizational Learning: The Contributing Processes and the Literatures'.

31   Brian A. Jackson et al., Aptitude for Destruction, Volume 1, 1st ed. (RAND Corporation, 2005), http://www.jstor.org/stable/10.7249/mg331nij; Brian A. Jackson et al., Aptitude for Destruction, Volume 2, 1st ed. (RAND Corporation, 2005), http://www.jstor.org/stable/10.7249/mg332nij; Kenney, From Pablo to Osama: Trafficking and Terrorist Networks, Government Bureaucracies, and Competitive Adaptation; Paul Gill, 'Tactical Innovation and the Provisional Irish Republican Army', Studies in Conflict & Terrorism 40, no. 7 (3 July 2017): 573–85, https://doi.org/10.1080/1057610X.2016.1237221.

32   Charles Tilly, From Mobilization to Revolution (Reading, Mass.: Addison-Wesley, 1978); Manus Midlarsky, Martha Crenshaw, and Fumihiko Yoshida, 'Why Violence Spreads: The Contagion of International Terrorism', International Studies Quarterly 24, no. 2 (1980): 262, https://doi.org/10.2307/2600202; Sarah A. Soule, 'The Diffusion of an Unsuccessful Innovation', The Annals of the American Academy of Political and Social Science 566 (1999): 120–31; Sidney Tarrow, The New Transnational Activism, Cambridge Studies in Contentious Politics (Cambridge: Cambridge University Press, 2005); Michael Horowitz, 'Nonstate Actors and the Diffusion of Innovations: The

Case of Suicide Terrorism', International Organization 64, no. 1 (January 2010): 33, https://doi.org/10.1017/S0020818309990233.

33 Sidney Tarrow, 'Dynamics of Diffusion: Mechanisms, Institutions, and Scale Shift', in The Diffusion of Social Movements: Actors, Mechanisms, and Political Effects, ed. Kenneth M. Roberts, Rebecca Kolins Givan, and Sarah A. Soule (Cambridge: Cambridge University Press, 2010), 204–20, https://doi.org/10.1017/CBO9780511761638.012; Kristin M. Bakke, 'Copying and Learning from Outsiders? Assessing Diffusion from Transnational Insurgents in the Chechen Wars', in Transnational Dynamics of Civil War, ed. Jeffrey T. Checkel (Cambridge: Cambridge University Press, 2013), 31–62, https://doi.org/10.1017/CBO9781139179089.005.

34 Dolnik, Understanding Terrorist Innovation: Technology, Tactics and Global Trends; Mauro Lubrano, 'Navigating Terrorist Innovation: A Proposal for a Conceptual Framework on How Terrorists Innovate', Terrorism and Political Violence, 5 April 2021, 1–16, https://doi.org/10.1080/09546553.2021.1903440.

35 Brian A Jackson, 'Technology Acquisition by Terrorist Groups: Threat Assessment Informed by Lessons from Private Sector Technology Adoption', Studies in Conflict and Terrorism 24, no. 3 (2001): 183–213, https://doi.org/10.1080/10576100151130270.

36 Gill et al., 'Malevolent Creativity in Terrorist Organizations', 1 June 2013.

37 Gill et al.

38 Kenney, From Pablo to Osama: Trafficking and Terrorist Networks, Government Bureaucracies, and Competitive Adaptation.

39 J.-C. Spender, 'Organizational Learning and Competitive Advantage', (London: SAGE Publications Ltd, 2021), 56–73, https://doi.org/10.4135/9781446250228.

40 Amy C Edmondson et al., 'Learning How and Learning What: Effects of Tacit and Codified Knowledge on Performance Improvement Following Technology Adoption', Decision Sciences 34, no. 2 (2003): 197–224, https://doi.org/10.1111/1540-5915.02316.

41 Michael Polanyi, Personal Knowledge: Towards a Post-Critical Philosophy (London: Routledge & Kegan Paul, 1962); Edmondson et al., 'Learning How and Learning What: Effects of Tacit and Codified Knowledge on Performance Improvement Following Technology Adoption'.

42 J.-C. Spender, 'Organizational Learning and Competitive Advantage' (London: SAGE Publications Ltd, 2021), 56–73, https://doi.org/10.4135/9781446250228.

43 Kenney, From Pablo to Osama: Trafficking and Terrorist Networks, Government Bureaucracies, and Competitive Adaptation; Jacob N. Shapiro, The Terrorist's Dilemma: Managing Violent Covert Organizations (Princeton:

Princeton University Press, 2015); Thomas Hegghammer, 'Resistance Is Futile', Foreign Affairs (New York, N.Y.) 100, no. 5 (2021): 44–53.

44   J. Bowyer Bell, 'Aspects of the Dragonworld: Covert Communications and the Rebel Ecosystem', International Journal of Intelligence and CounterIntelligence 3, no. 1 (January 1989): 15–43, https://doi.org/10.1080/08850608908435089; Anne Stenersen, 'The Internet: A Virtual Training Camp?', Terrorism and Political Violence 20, no. 2 (9 April 2008): 215–33, https://doi.org/10.1080/09546550801920790; René M. Bakker, Jörg Raab, and H. Brinton Milward, 'A Preliminary Theory of Dark Network Resilience', Journal of Policy Analysis and Management 31, no. 1 (December 2012): 33–62, https://doi.org/10.1002/pam.20619.

45   Edmondson et al., 'Learning How and Learning What: Effects of Tacit and Codified Knowledge on Performance Improvement Following Technology Adoption'.

46   Dominic Johnson, 'Darwinian Selection in Asymmetric Warfare: The Natural Advantage of Insurgents And Terrorists', Journal of the Washington Academy of Sciences 95, no. 3 (2009): 89–112.

47   Dominic Johnson.

48   Milton, 'Structure of a State - Captured Documents and the Islamic State's Organizational Structure'.

49   Whiteside et al., 'The ISIS Files The Department of Soldiers'.

50   Indications of this can be found in Islamic State media content, like in a 2017 issue of the Islamic State Magazine Rumiyah, where a commander in Raqqa noted "the brothers' experiences [in Mosul] have been passed on to all the wilayat so they could benefit from them, both militarily and in terms of iman (faith)." Interviewees also mentioned seeing evidence of exchange to Algeria, Egypt, Libya, and Tunisia, but this is likely not an exhaustive list. Interview with BEE1, August 2021; Interview with BTU1; Interview with BI1, August 2021; 'It Will Be a Fire That Burns the Cross and Its People in Raqqah', Rumiyah, 2017, 34.

51   Each interview typically lasted around one hour.

52   Consent was obtained by the research assistant, who received training in research ethics and consent procedures prior to the start of the project. Participants were given the opportunity to reach out to the research assistant directly via telephone to pull out of the study or withdraw information as this was both safer and more accessible than calling internationally or emailing the author.

53   We did not use a tape recorder for the majority of interviews due to participant safety concerns. This required the research assistant to take detailed notes in Arabic. Upon completing an interview, the notes would be sent to and translated by the author, who would use the replies to inform the next

interview with the same participant type. This was an iterative process aimed at acquiring as detailed a picture as possible and to corroborate information across sources without being able to conduct follow up interviews. Around halfway through the interviews, participants who had spoken together expressed being uncomfortable with questions being updated. To avoid causing undue stress, we stopped updating questions for the second half. This was not a big issue because by this time we had been able to identify questions that gave sufficiently in-depth responses.

54 Whiteside et al., 'The ISIS Files The Department of Soldiers'; Milton, 'Structure of a State - Captured Documents and the Islamic State's Organizational Structure'.

55 The group's portrayal of its suicide bombers is an apt example. While suicide operatives and vehicles feature heavily in videos of the group's offensives, the operatives are portrayed as excited and there are no signs of coercion. An interviewee involved in dismantling old suicide vehicles, however, reported often finding metal bars intended to restrain drivers in case they tried to back out in the last minute. Moreover, Whiteside and Miranova found that suicide attack 'volunteers' could be a misnomer in some cases, as there were several endogenous group processes determining who would end up carrying out attacks. Interview with MTU1, April 2021; Whiteside and Mironova, 'Adaptation and Innovation with an Urban Twist: Changes to Suicide Tactics in the Battle for Mosul'.

56 These aspects are better explored by examining accounts by group members, like those used to inform Mironova's study of jihadi human resources, see: Mironova, From Freedom Fighters to Jihadists.

57 Huber, 'Organizational Learning: The Contributing Processes and the Literatures'.

58 Mark Easterby-Smith and Marjorie A Lyles, Handbook of Organizational Learning and Knowledge Management, 2nd ed. (Chichester, West Sussex: Wiley, 2011), 183–349; Richard Michael Cyert and James G March, A Behavioral Theory of the Firm, Prentice-Hall International Series in Management (Englewood Cliffs: Prentice-Hall, 1963).

59 Several works address these questions in the context of Salafi Jihadi groups, among them: Moghadam, The Globalization of Martyrdom: Al Qaeda, Salafi Jihad, and the Diffusion of Suicide Attacks; Jeffrey William Lewis, The Business of Martyrdom: A History of Suicide Bombing (Annapolis: Naval Institute Press, 2012).

60 Huber, 'Organizational Learning: The Contributing Processes and the Literatures', 91.

61 Interview with MD1, April 2021; Interview with MD2, April 2021; Interview with MD3, May 2021.

62 Interview with MD1; Interview with MD2; Interview with MD3.

63 Interview with MD1; Interview with BD2, August 2021; Interview with BD1, August 2021.

64 ISIS Files, '16_001042' (George Washington University, n.d.), 001, accessed 20 February 2021; ISIS Files, '16_001043' (George Washington University, n.d.), accessed 20 February 2021; ISIS Files, '16_001044' (George Washington University, n.d.), 00, accessed 20 February 2021.

65 Interview with MEE1, April 2021; Interview with MTU1.

66 An anecdote by a foreign fighter interviewed by Vera Mironova captured one of the situations that followed: "Once the group had a suicide mission volunteer detonate a car filled with explosives under a bridge. But there was no enemy near the bridge, and we could have just gone there at night, quietly positioned the explosives, and detonated them remotely." Vera Mironova, From Freedom Fighters to Jihadists, Causes and Consequences of Terrorism (New York: New York: Oxford University Press, 2019), 169, https://doi.org/10.1093/oso/9780190939755.001.0001.

67 Document Islamic State in Iraq, 'Analysis of the State of ISI' (Combating Terrorism Center at West Point, 2006).

68 Charlie Winter, 'War by Suicide: A Statistical Analysis of the Islamic State's Martyrdom Industry', 15.

69 Interview with BI1.

70 Interview with MEE1.

71 Interview with MBS1, June 2021; Interview with MEE2, May 2021.

72 Interview with BI1.

73 Interview with MTU1.

74 Interview with BEE1.

75 Interview with BEE1.

76 Interview with MI1, March 2021.

77 Kaaman, Hugo, 'Through the Desert & down the Euphrates – Islamic State SVBIED Use & Innovation', Hugo Kaaman – Open Source Research on SVBIEDs (blog), 29 May 2018, https://hugokaaman.com/2020/09/21/the-unique-svbieds-used-in-the-2013-capture-of-menagh-airbase/; Kaaman, 'Car Bombs as Weapons of War: ISIS'S Development of SVBIEDS, 2014–19'.

78 Interview with BI1. Interview with MTU1; Interview with BEE2, August 2021.

79 Operation rooms could be established for particular operations and was considered an early indicator that an attack was underway. Interview with BI1.

80 Interview with BI1.

81 Interview with MTU1; Interview with BEE2.

82 Huber, 'Organizational Learning: The Contributing Processes and the Literatures', 102.

83 Interview with MI1; Interview with MEE1.

84 Aymenn al-Tamimi, 'The Evolution in Islamic State Administration: The Documentary Evidence', Perspectives on Terrorism (Lowell) 9, no. 4 (2015): 117–29.

85 According to Whiteside et al., the Al-Bara' bin Malik Brigade was a part of the Committee for Development and Manufacturing, the Brigade likely fell under the Committee's aviation unit. 'Specimen 30C', 2015, http://www.aymennjawad. org/2016/09/archive-of-islamic-state-administrative-documents-2; 'Specimen 30D', 2015, http://www.aymennjawad.org/2016/09/archive-of-islamic-state-administrative-documents-2; 'Specimen 30E', 2015, http://www.aymennjawad.org/2016/09/archive-of-islamic-state-administrative-documents-2; 'Specimen 30F', 2015, http://www.aymennjawad.org/2016/09/archive-of-islamic-state-administrative-documents-2; Whiteside et al., 'The ISIS Files The Department of Soldiers'; Don Rassler, Muhammad Al-Ubaydi, and Vera Mironova, 'The Islamic State's Drone Documents: Management, Acquisitions, and DIY Tradecraft', CTC Sentinel, 31 January 2017, https://www.ctc.usma.edu/ctc-perspectives-the-islamic-states-drone-documents-management-acquisitions-and-diy-tradecraft/.

86 Textbook examples and templates for military orders from the ISIS Files indicates how communication along the hierarchy and between the departments might have looked like. That being said, interviewees said most communication happened over social media apps, from messaging services to video games. ISIS Files, '13_000972' (George Washington University, n.d.), accessed 20 February 2021; Interview with BEE2.

87 Whiteside et al., 'The ISIS Files The Department of Soldiers'.

88 Interview with BEE2. Interview with BI1.

89 Fisher, 'ISIS Just Pulled off Its First Carbombing with a Stolen American Humvee'.

90 Charlie Winter, 'War by Suicide: A Statistical Analysis of the Islamic State's Martyrdom Industry'.

91 Interview with MI1.

92 Mironova, From Freedom Fighters to Jihadists, 256–60.

93 Mironova, From Freedom Fighters to Jihadists, 261.

94 Mironova.

95 Interview with MTU1; Interview with MEE2.

96 Interview with BI1.

97 The geographical reach of the CDM is difficult to discern. That being said, it had a physical presence in multiple cities, with interviewees mentioning Mosul, Baghdad, Kirkuk, Fallujah, Tel Afar, and the Ramadi dessert, but this should be viewed as indicative only. Interview with MEE2; 'Specimen 30H', 2015, http://www.aymennjawad.org/2016/09/archive-of-islamic-state-administrative-documents-2; 'Specimen 30I', 2015, http://www.aymennjawad.org/2016/09/archive-of-islamic-state-administrative-documents-2; 'Specimen 30K', 2015, http://www.aymennjawad.org/2016/09/archive-of-islamic-state-administrative-documents-2; Interview with BTU1; Interview with BEE2; Conflict Armament Research, 'Standardisation and Quality Control in Islamic State's Military Production' (London: Conflict Armament Research, December 2016), 6, https://www.conflictarm.com/dispatches/standardisation-and-quality-control-in-islamic-states-military-production/.

98 Interview with MEE1.

99 Interview with MEE2; Interview with BEE2; Interview with MTU1.

100 Interview with MEE2; Interview with BEE2; Avi Asher-Schapiro, 'The US-Led Coalition Bombed the University of Mosul for Being an Islamic State Headquarters', Vice, 22 March 2016, https://www.vice.com/en/article/mbnkba/the-us-led-coalition-bombed-the-university-of-mosul-for-being-an-islamic-state-headquarters; Interview with MTU1.

101 AFP, 'ISIS Using Hobby Drones to Bomb Forces in Mosul', Al Arabiya News, 12 January 2017, https://english.alarabiya.net/News/middle-east/2017/01/12/ISIS-using-hobby-drones-to-bomb-Iraqi-forces-in-Mosul; Interview with MEE2; Interview with MEE1.

102 Hugo Kaaman, 'The Myth of the Remote Controlled Car Bomb' (European Eye on Radicatization, 15 September 2019), 7.

103 'Aleppo_RCVBIED_outcomes' (Aleppo Province of the Islamic State, n.d.), Document obtained by author; Kaaman, 'The Myth of the Remote Controlled Car Bomb'.

104 Interview with MBS1; Interview with BEE2; Interview with BTU1; Interview with BI1.

105 Interview with BEE1.

106 Interview with MD3; Interview with MI1; Christopher Woody, 'Watch a US-Led Airstrike Level an ISIS Bomb Factory Days before the Assault on Mosul', Business Insider, 18 October 2016, https://www.businessinsider.com/us-coalition-airstrike-isis-bomb-factory-mosul-2016-10?r=US&IR=T; Asher-Schapiro, 'The US-Led Coalition Bombed the University of Mosul for Being an Islamic State Headquarters'.

107 Interview with MEE2; Interview with MBS1. Statements in the interviews resonate with the observations by CAR, whose researchers in Mosul noted, "Although production facilities employ a range of non-standard materials and chemical explosive precursors, the degree of organisation, quality control, and inventory management, indicates a complex, centrally controlled industrial production system" Conflict Armament Research, 'Standardisation and Quality Control in Islamic State's Military Production', 4.

108 Interview with BEE1; Interview with MEE2; Interview with BEE2.

109 Interview with MEE2; Interview with MTU1.

110 'Specimen 17F', 2015, http://www.aymennjawad.org/2016/01/archive-of-islamic-state-administrative-documents-1; 'Specimen 39U', 2015, 39, http://www.aymennjawad.org/2016/09/archive-of-islamic-state-administrative-documents-3; 'Specimen 33W', 2015, http://www.aymennjawad.org/2016/09/archive-of-islamic-state-administrative-documents-2; Interview with BTU1; Interview with BI1.

111 Interview with MBS1.

112 'Specimen 17F'; 'Specimen 33W'; Interview with BTU1; Interview with BI1.

113 Interview with MEE1; Interview with MEE2; Interview with BTU1.

114 Interview with MEE1.

115 Interview with MEE1.

116 Interview with MEE2; Interview with BEE1; Interview with MEE1.

117 Interview with MD1; Interview with MD2; Interview with BD1; Interview with BD2.

118 Interview with MEE2.

119 Islamic State documents showing the connection to Turkey, most importantly Specimen 21Z, titled "Report on fertilizer entering from Turkey through Tel Abyad", was made public by the People's Defense Units and the Syrian Democratic Forces (YPG and SDF) in 2015. According to Tamimi, this was part of an effort on the part of the YPG "to push the line of active Turkish state support for the Islamic State that can be traced to the highest levels of government." What the document really shows, he argues, "is bribery and corruption above all at the local administrative level." Aymenn Jawad Al Tamimi, 'Archive of Islamic State Administrative Documents (Cont.)', Aymenn Jawad al Tamimi (blog), 11 January 2016, http://www.aymennjawad.org/2016/01/archive-of-islamic-state-administrative-documents-1; Conflict Armament Research, 'Standardisation and Quality Control in Islamic State's Military Production'; Conflict Armament Research, 'Weapons of the Islamic State' (London: Conflict Armament Research, December 2017), https://www.conflictarm.com/dispatches/standardisation-and-quality-control-in-islamic-states-military-production/. Interview with MI1.

120 Interview with MEE2; Interview with MEE1; Interview with BTU1.

121 The interviewee did not mention where the foreign experts were from, but in their examination of drone manufacturing documents Rassler et.al. Found a prevalence of fighters from Bangladesh. Interview with MEE2; Rassler, Al-Ubaydi, and Mironova, 'The Islamic State's Drone Documents: Management, Acquisitions, and DIY Tradecraft'.

122 Craig Whiteside, 'A Pedigree of Terror', Perspectives on Terrorism 11, no. 3 (2017): 2–18.

123 Interview with BEE1; Interview with MI1.

124 Interview with MEE2; Interview with BEE1; Interview with BEE2.

125 Interview with BTU1.

126 Interview with BEE2.

127 Interview with BI1; Interview with BEE2; Interview with MI1.

128 Conflict Armament Research, 'Standardisation and Quality Control in Islamic State's Military Production', 6.

129 Interview with MEE1; Interview with BEE1. Interview with MTU1; Interview with BI1.

130 Interview with MI1; Interview with BI1; Interview with BEE2.

131 Interview with BEE2; Interview with BEE1.

132 Interview with BEE2.

133 John Mueller and Mark G Stewart, 'The Terrorism Delusion: America's Overwrought Response to September 11', International Security 37, no. 1 (2012): 81–110, https://doi.org/10.1162/ ISEC_a_00089; Bloom, 'Constructing Expertise: Terrorist Recruitment and "Talent Spotting" in the PIRA, Al Qaeda, and ISIS'.

134 Interview with BI1; Interview with MEE2; Interview with BEE1.

135 Interview with BEE1. Interview with MEE2.

136 Interview with MEE2; Interview with MTU1.

137 Interview with MD3.

138 Huber, 'Organizational Learning: The Contributing Processes and the Literatures', 90.

139 Conflict Armament Research, 'Standardisation and Quality Control in Islamic State's Military Production', 32.

140 Conflict Armament Research, 31.

141 Interview with BEE1; Interview with MEE1.

142 Kaaman, 'The History and Adaptability of the Islamic State Car Bomb'.

143 Interview with BEE2; Interview with BI1; Interview with BEE1.

144 Interview with MBS1.

145 Interview with BI1.

146 Hugo Kaaman, 'Islamic State of Iraq – A Snapshot of SVBIED Design & Use (2007-2012)', Hugo Kaaman - Open Source Research on SVBIEDs (blog), 11 January 2019, https://hugokaaman.com/2019/01/11/islamic-state-of-iraq-a-snapshot-of-svbied-design-use-2007-2012/.

147 Interview with MEE1; Interview with MD3.

148 Huber, 'Organizational Learning: The Contributing Processes and the Literatures', 105.

149 Kaaman, Hugo, 'Through the Desert & down the Euphrates – Islamic State SVBIED Use & Innovation'.

150 Eli Berman and David D. Laitin, 'Religion, Terrorism and Public Goods: Testing the Club Model', Journal of Public Economics 92, no. 10–11 (October 2008): 1942–67, https://doi.org/10.1016/j.jpubeco.2008.03.007.

151 The advantage is captured by comparing the Martyrdom Battalion to the beginning of the Kamikaze Corps in Japan. Despite a longstanding culture of heroic sacrifice in Japan, none of the professional Japanese soldiers volunteered when the corps was instituted, and leaders had to order officers of the military academies to fill these roles. One of the officers who received this order, Captain Seki Yukio, expressed that, "There is no more hope for Japan, if it has to kill such a skillful pilot like myself. I can hit an aircraft carrier with a 1,102 lb. bomb and return alive, without having to make a suicidal plunge." Ivan Morris, The Nobility of Failure : Tragic Heroes in the History of Japan (London: Secker & Warburg, 1975); Emiko Ohnuki-Tierney, Kamikaze, Cherry Blossoms, and Nationalisms : The Militarization of Aesthetics in Japanese History (Chicago, Ill.: University of Chicago Press, 2002), 166.

152 Assaf Moghadam, 'Motives for Martyrdom: Al-Qaida, Salafi Jihad, and the Spread of Suicide Attacks', International Security 33, no. 3 (1 January 2009): 46–78, https://doi.org/ 10.1162/isec.2009.33.3.46.

153 Assaf Moghadam, 'Palestinian Suicide Terrorism in the Second Intifada: Motivations and Organizational Aspects', Studies in Conflict and Terrorism 26, no. 2 (2003): 65–92, https://doi.org/10.1080/10576100390145215.

154 The importance of territory is also evident in long-term innovative work conducted by other territorial groups, such as the FARC in Columbia. Michelle Jacome Jaramillo, 'The Revolutionary Armed Forces of Colombia (FARC) and the Development of Narco-Submarines', Journal of Strategic Security 9, no. 1 (2016): 49–69, https://doi.org/10.5038/1944-0472.9.1.1509.

155 Jackson et al., Aptitude for Destruction, Volume 2.

156 A possible exception here is the Provisional Irish Republican Army, which managed to continue mortar innovation despite increasing levels of government repression. However, technological advances in state capabilities in the last twenty years have arguably made activities of that ilk unfeasible. Hegghammer, 'Resistance Is Futile'; Bloom, 'Constructing Expertise: Terrorist Recruitment and "Talent Spotting" in the PIRA, Al Qaeda, and ISIS'; Tony Geraghty, The Irish War - The Military History of a Domestic Conflict (London: Harper Collins Publishers, 2000).

157 Hegghammer, 'Resistance Is Futile'.

Chapter 9: Armed Governance: The Case of the CIA-Supported Afghan Militias. Antonio De Lauri and Astri Suhrke

1. Barfield, Afghanistan: A Political History. Rulers of weak states commonly pursue 'medidated stateness' through alliances with localized military forces. A classic formulation of the concept in its contemporary form is Ken Menkhaus, "Governance without Government."

2. For a conceptual and empirical exploration of "multilayered governance" involving armed groups, see Kasfir, Nelson, G. Frerks, N. Terpstra, "Introduction: Armed Groups and Multilayered Governance."

3. The contemporary phenomenon of warlords (jang salar in Dari) in Afghanistan is inextricably linked to insurrections that took place in the late 1980 s. The term "warlord" generally refers to a figure who is recognized by a militia, not by a state power. In reality, there are many more nuances to the role of warlords, which suggests that the term exhibits a certain malleability. For instance, so-called warlords in Afghanistan have taken part in the post-2001 processes of "democratization," others sit in the Parliament or have government positions, and yet others have close ties with provincial governors. Therefore, warlords should not be considered to be at war with the state; rather, they are figures who play a key role in the armed governance that dominates contemporary Afghanistan. See for example Giustozzi, Empires of Mud and Mukhopadhyay, Warlords, Strongman Governors and State Building in Afghanistan.

4. Felbab-Brown, "Hurray for Militias?".

5. Prados, "The CIA's Secret War."

6. Cogan, "Partners in Time."

7. Gasper, "Afghanistan, CIA, bin Laden."

8. De Lauri, "The Taliban and the Humanitarian Soldier."

9. Wright et al., Different Kind of War.

10. Sedra, "Security Sector Reform."

11. For a comparative perspective, see for example Mitchell and Carey, "Pro-Government Militias and Conflict," Tar, "Counter-Insurgents or Ethnic

Vanguards? Civil Militias and State Violence in Darfur Region, Western Sudan," and Peic, "Divide and Co-Opt: Private Agendas, Tribal Groups, and Militia Formation in Counterinsurgency Wars."

12. Lefèvre, "Local Defence in Afghanistan"; Goodhand and Hakimi, "Counterinsurgency, Militias, and Statebuilding."

13. Clark, "CIA-Proxy Militias."

14. Mazzetti et al., "Seal Team 6."

15. Woodward, Obama"s Wars, p. 8. The information was independently confirmed by National Public Radio in the US (see https://www.npr.org/sections/thetwo-way/2010/09/22/130041571/3-000-man-cia-army-conducts-operations-in-pakistan). At the time, their main operations appeared to be against targets across the border in Pakistan.

16. Raghavan, "CIA Runs Shadow War."

17. Gibbons-Neff et al., "C.I.A. Expands Taliban Hunt."

18. Its equivalent in the south is the Kandahar Strike Force, which appears to have been less active in recent years. Another "first-generation" unit in the CIA's Army, called "Afghan Security Guards," is based in Paktika in the northeast and seems to have folded into the Afghan Local Police. See Clark, "CIA-Proxy Militias."

19. UNAMA, Annual Report 2018, 37.

20. UNAMA, Annual Report 2018, 41, n. 158.

21. See Clark, "CIA-Proxy Militias," and Graham-Harrison, "Karzai Seeks to Curb CIA."

22. UNAMA, Annual Report 2018, 42.

23. UNAMA, Annual Report 2017, 53.

24. See note 13 above.

25. See note 16 above.

26. Mashal, "CIA's Afghan Forces."

27. Purkiss, Fielding-Smith, and Feroz, "CIA-Backed Afghan Unit."

28. The CIA reportedly pays KPF members a monthly salary equivalent to that received by an Afghan general.

29. See note 4 above.

30. UNAMA, Annual Report 2018, 36.

31. UNAMA, Annual Report 2017, 53–54; UNAMA, Annual Report 2018, 41–44.

32. UNAMA, Annual Report 2018.

33. Ibid. 2018.

34. The compilation and use of the "kill-or-capture" lists were investigated by an independent commission appointed by the Norwegian government to assess Norway"s role in the international operation. See NOU, A Good Ally, sec 5.4 pp. 79–82.

35. Alston, "CIA and Targeted Killings."

36. Ibid.

37. The NDS has a Human Rights Chief, who met repeatedly with UNAMA in 2017, but was unable to provide any information about NDS Special Forces-related incidents for investigation and accountability purposes. See UNAMA, Annual Report 2017, 53.

38. For a wide range of perspectives, see Ahram, Proxy Warriors, Sanford, "Learning to Kill by Proxy," and Jentzsch, Kalyvas, and Schubiger, "Militias in Civil Wars."

39. See note 16 above.

40. Masal, "CIA's Afghan Forces."

41. Shaw and Akhter, "Dronification of State Violence."

42. Ibid., 214.

43. Dirkx, "Unintended Consequences."

44. Ibid.

45. https://www.state.gov/wp-content/uploads/2020/02/Agreement-For-Bringing-Peace-to-Afghanistan-02.29.20.pdf.

46. See comments by General Ambassador Karl W. Eikenberry, quoted in Landler, Cooper, and Schmitt, "Taliban Talks Raise Question."

47. Gannon, "U.S. Envoy Hails Talks."

48. Barnes, Gibbons-Neff, and Schmitt, "Afghanistan War Enters New Stage as U.S. Military Prepares to Exit."

49. Some NDS Special Forces are already reported to "provide security" for particular politicians. See Bakhtiyar, "Experts Criticize NDS."

50. Mitchell, Carey, and Butler, "Impact of Pro-Government Militias."

51. Up to seventeen male villagers in Wardak province were detained at a US camp in Wardak from October 2012 to February 2013 and subsequently disappeared. Only two bodies were ever found.

52. Suhrke, "From Principle to Practice."

53. Neta Crawford has persuasively made this argument in relation to civilian casualties from air strikes. If the institutional structure of an armed unit and its methods of warfare carry a high risk of 'collateral damage' during air strikes

against enemy soldiers operating in populated areas, the unit that conducts the strikes bears a moral responsibility for any civilian casualties that result, even though the deaths and injuries were unintentional and cannot be prosecuted under existing laws allowing for 'military necessity' and related norms. See Crawford, Accountability for Killing.

Bibliography

Ahram, Ariel. Proxy Warriors. Stanford: Stanford University Press, 2011. [Crossref], [Google Scholar]

Alston, Philip. "The CIA and Targeted Killings beyond Borders." Harvard Law School National Security Journal 2, no. 2 (2012): 283–446. https://harvardnsj.org/wp-content/uploads/sites/13/2011/02/Vol.-2_Alston1.pdf. [Google Scholar]

Bakhtiyar, Shapoor. 2016. "Experts Criticize Use of NDS Special Forces as Guards for Elite." Tolo News, October 23. Program Aired on Television Series Tawde Khabare (Originally Aired February 6, 2015). https://tolonews.com/tawde-khabare/tawde-khabare-experts-criticize-use-nds-special-forces-guards-elite. [Google Scholar]

Barfield, Thomas. Afghanistan: A Cultural and Political History. Princeton, NJ: Princeton University Press, 2010. [Crossref], [Google Scholar]

Barnes, Julian E., Thomas Gibbons-Neff, and Eric Schmitt, "Afghanistan War Enters New Stage as U.S. Military Prepares to Exit." New York Times, March 1, 2020. [Google Scholar]

Clark, Kate. 2017. "CIA-Proxy Militias, CIA Drones in Afghanistan: 'Hunt and Kill' Déjà Vu." Afghanistan Analysts Network, October 26. https://www.afghanistan-analysts.org/cia-proxy-militias-cia-drones-in-afghanistan-hunt-and-kill-deja-vu/. [Google Scholar]

Cogan, Charles. "Partners in Time: The CIA and Afghanistan since 1979." World Policy Journal 10, no. 2 (1993): 73–82. http://www.jstor.org/stable/40209308. [Google Scholar]

Crawford, Neta C. Accountability for Killing: Moral Responsibility for Collateral Damage in America's Post-9/11 Wars. Oxford: Oxford University Press, 2013. [Crossref], [Google Scholar]

De Lauri, Antonio. "The Taliban and the Humanitarian Soldier. Configurations of Freedom and Humanity in Afghanistan." Anuac 8, no. 1 (2019): 31–57. http://dx.doi.org/10.7340/anuac2239-625X-3623. [Google Scholar]

Dirkx, Toon. "The Unintended Consequences of US Support on Militia Governance in Kunduz Province, Afghanistan." Civil Wars 19, no.3 (Special issue: Armed Groups and Multi-Layered Governance 2017): 377–401. doi:10.1080/13698249.2017.1416851. [Taylor & Francis Online], [Web of Science ®], [Google Scholar]

Felbab-Brown, Vanda. "Hurray for Militias? Not so Fast: Lessons from the Afghan Local Police Experience." Small Wars and Insurgencies 27, no. 1 (2016): 258–281. doi:10.1080/09592318.2015.1129169. [Taylor & Francis Online], [Google Scholar]

Gannon, Kathy. 2019. "U.S. Envoy Hails Latest Talks with Taliban as the Best Ever." Associated Press News, July 6. https://www.apnews.com/1ee321b43d54476f8868465c16e536d6. [Google Scholar]

Gasper, Phil. "Afghanistan, the CIA, Bin Laden, and the Taliban." International Socialist Review 20 (2001): 2–8. http://www.isreview.org/issues/20/CIA_bin-laden_afghan.shtml. [Google Scholar]

Gibbons-Neff, Thomas, Eric Schmitt, and Adam Goldman. 2017. "A Newly Assertive C.I.A. Expands Its Taliban Hunt in Afghanistan." New York Times, October 22. https://www.nytimes.com/2017/10/22/world/asia/cia-expanding-taliban-fight-afghanistan.html. [Google Scholar]

Giustozzi, Antonio. Empires of Mud. Wars and Warlords in Afghanistan. London: Hurst, 2009. [Google Scholar]

Goodhand, Jonathan, and Aziz Hakimi. 2013. "Counterinsurgency, Local Militias, and Statebuilding in Afghanistan." United States Institute of Peace. USIP Publications, December 18. https://www.usip.org/publications/2013/12/counterinsurgency-local-militias-and-statebuilding-afghanistan. [Google Scholar]

Graham-Harrison, Emma. 2013. "Hamid Karzai Seeks to Curb CIA Operations in Afghanistan." The Guardian, April 19. https://www.theguardian.com/world/2013/apr/19/hamid-karzai-curb-cia-afghanistan-operations. [Google Scholar]

Jentzsch, C., S. Kalyvas, and L.I. Schubiger. "Militias in Civil Wars." Journal of Conflict Resolution 59, no. 5 (2015): 755–769. doi:10.1177/0022002715576753. [Crossref], [Web of Science °], [Google Scholar]

Kasfir, Nelson, G. Frerks, N. Terpstra "Introduction: Armed Groups and Multilayered Governance." Civil Wars 19, no. 3 (2017): 257–278. doi:10.1080/13698249.2017.1419611. [Taylor & Francis Online], [Web of Science °], [Google Scholar]

Landler, Mark, Helene Cooper, and Eric Schmitt. 2019. "Taliban Talks Raise Question of What U.S. Withdrawal from Afghanistan Could Mean." New York Times, January 28. https://www.nytimes.com/2019/01/28/us/politics/us-withdrawal-afghanistan-taliban.html. [Google Scholar]

Lefèvre, Mathieu. 2010. "Local Defence in Afghanistan: A Review of Government-Backed Initiatives." Afghanistan Analysts Network, May 27. https://www.afghanistan-analysts.org/publication/aan-papers/local-defence-in-afghanistan-a-review-of-government-backed-initiatives/. [Google Scholar]

Mashal, Mujib. 2018. "CIA's Afghan Forces Leave a Trail of Abuse and Anger." New York Times, December 31. https://www.nytimes.com/2018/12/31/world/asia/cia-afghanistan-strike-force.html. [Google Scholar]

Mazzetti, Mark, Nicholas Kulish, Serge F. Christopher Drew, Sean D. Naylor Kovaleski, and John Ismay. 2015. "Seal Team 6: A Secret History of Quiet Killings and Blurred Lines." New York Times, June 6. https://www.nytimes.com/2015/06/07/world/asia/the-secret-history-of-seal-team-6.html?_r=0. [Google Scholar]

Menkhaus, Ken. "Governance without Government in Somalia. Spoilers, State Building and the Politics of Coping." International Security 31, no. 3 (2006): 74–106. doi:10.1162/isec.2007.31.3.74. [Crossref], [Web of Science ®], [Google Scholar]

Mitchell, Neil J., and Sabine C. Carey. Pro-Government Militias and Conflict. Oxford Research Encyclopedia, 2016. doi:10.1093/acrefore/9780190228637.013.33. [Crossref], [Google Scholar]

Mitchell, Neil J., Sabine C. Carey, and Christopher K. Butler. "The Impact of Pro-Government Militias on Human Rights Violations." International Interactions 40, no. 5 (2014): 812–836. doi:10.1080/03050629.2014.932783. [Taylor & Francis Online], [Web of Science ®], [Google Scholar]

Mukhopadhyay, Dipali. Warlords, Strongman Governors and State Building in Afghanistan. Cambridge: Cambridge University Press, 2014. [Crossref], [Google Scholar]

NOU. 2016. A Good Ally. Norway in Afghanistan, 2001–2014. Official Norwegian Reports, 8. https://www.regjeringen.no/contentassets/09faceca099c4b8bac85ca8495e12d2d/en-gb/pdfs/nou201620160008000engpdfs.pdf [Google Scholar]

Peic, Goran. "Divide and Co-Opt: Private Agendas, Tribal Groups, and Militia Formation in Counterinsurgency Wars." Studies in Conflict and Terrorism (2018). doi:10.1080/1057610X.2019.1620432. [Taylor & Francis Online], [Web of Science ®], [Google Scholar]

Prados, John. "Notes on the CIA's Secret War in Afghanistan." Journal of American History 89, no. 2 (2002): 466–471. doi:10.2307/3092167. [Crossref], [Web of Science ®], [Google Scholar]

Purkiss, Jessica, Abigail Fielding-Smith, and Emran Feroz. 2019. "CIA-Backed Afghan Unit Accused of Atrocities Is Able to Call in Air Strikes." Bureau of Investigative Journalism, February 8. https://www.thebureauinvestigates.com/stories/2019-02-08/cia-backed-afghan-unit-atrocities. [Google Scholar]

Raghavan, Sudarsan. 2015. "CIA Runs Shadow War With Afghan Militia Implicated In Civilian Killings." Washington Post, December 3. https://www.washingtonpost.com/world/cia-backed-afghan-militias-fight-a-shadow-war/2015/12/02/fe5a0526-913f-11e5-befa-99ceebcbb272_story.html?utm_term=.188155a8ec70. [Google Scholar]

Sanford, Victoria. "Learning to Kill by Proxy: Colombian Paramilitaries and the Legacy of Central American Death Squads, Contras and Civil Patrols." Social Justice 30, no. 3 (2011): 63–81. https://www.jstor.org/stable/29768209?seq=1#page_scan_tab_contents. [Google Scholar]

Sedra, Mark. "Security Sector Reform in Afghanistan: The Slide Towards Expediency." International Peacekeeping 13, no. 1 (2006): 94–110. doi:10.1080/13533310500424868. [Taylor & Francis Online], [Google Scholar]

Shaw, Ian, and Majed Akhter. "The Dronification of State Violence." Critical Asian Studies 46, no. 2 (2014): 211–234. doi:10.1080/14672715.2014.898452. [Taylor & Francis Online], [Web of Science ®], [Google Scholar]

Suhrke, Astri. "From Principle to Practice: US Military Strategy and Protection of Civilians in Afghanistan." International Peacekeeping 21, no. 5 (2015): 1–19. doi:10.1080/13533312.2014.993177. [Taylor & Francis Online], [Google Scholar]

Tar, Usman. "Counter-Insurgents or Ethnic Vanguards? Civil Militias and State Violence in Darfur Region, Western Sudan." In Civil Militia: Africa's Intractable Security Menace?, edited by David, J. Francis. London and New York: Routledge, 2017. [Crossref], [Google Scholar]

UNAMA (United Nations Assistance Mission in Afghanistan). Afghanistan: Protection of Civilians in Armed Conflict: Annual Report 2017. Kabul, Afghanistan: UNAMA Human Rights Service, 2018. https://unama.unmissions.org/sites/default/files/afghanistan_protection_of_civilians_annual_report_2017_final_150218.pdf. [Google Scholar]

UNAMA (United Nations Assistance Mission in Afghanistan). Afghanistan: Protection of Civilians in Armed Conflict: Annual Report 2018. Kabul, Afghanistan: UNAMA Human Rights Service, 2019. https://unama.unmissions.org/sites/default/files/afghanistan_protection_of_civilians_annual_report_2018_final_24_feb_2019_1.pdf. [Google Scholar]

Woodward, Bob. Obama's Wars: The Inside Story. New York: Simon & Schuster, 2010. [Google Scholar]

Wright, Donald P., et al. A Different Kind of War. Kansas: Combat Studies Institute Press, 2010. [Google Scholar]

Postscript

1. Professor in Department of International Development, London School of Economics and Political Science, Florian Weigand. Afghanistan's Taliban-Legitimate Jihadists or Coercive Extremists? Journal of Intervention and Statebuilding-2017

2. 13 May 2022, statement by the Foreign Ministers of G7 countries and the High Representative of the European Union

3. Human Rights watch in its report (Unlawful Killings, Enforced Disappearances, Violations of Laws of War, events of 2021

4. Edward Lemon, Vera Mironova and William Tobey. Jihadists from Ex-Soviet Central Asia: Where Are They? Why Did They Radicalize? What Next? December 07, 2018, Russia Matters and the U.S.-Russia Initiative to Prevent Nuclear Terrorism.

5. Dr. William B. Farrell. Fragmentation, Frustrated Revolt, and Off-Shore Opportunity: A Comparative Examination of Jihadi Mobilization in Central Asia and the South Caucasus-15 November 2019.

6. SpecialEurasia, a geopolitical and Intelligence analysis platform whose purpose is to inform the Italian and foreign audience on local, regional, and international dynamics in Eurasia in its report. Geographical report-November 04, 2021 Monitoring Jihadist Propaganda and Terrorism projects.

7. Mohamed Mokhtar Qandi in his paper. Challenges to Taliban Rule and Potential Impacts for the Region: Internal and external factors are weakening the Taliban, making the group's long term stability increasingly unlikely. Fikra Forum. The Washington Institute for Near East Policy-09 February 2022.

8. Riccardo Valle (Islamic State Khorasan Province threatens Uzbekistan, Central Asia, and neighbouring countries. Geopolitical Report ISSN 2785-2598 Volume 19 Issue 04. Jihadest Propaganda and Terrorism Project.

9. SpecialEurasia, a geopolitical and Intelligence analysis platform whose purpose is to inform the Italian and foreign audience on local, regional, and international dynamics in Eurasia, Dilemma of Central Asian Jihadists between IS-K and Taliban Political tensions and security threats in Tajikistan in its report (Geographical report, 18 May, 2022. Geograpolitika Evrazija projects.

10. BBC report-11 October 2021

11. Afghan newspaper, Haste Subh. ISKP's Power Exaggeration: The Islamic State in Khurasan Province operates in Afghanistan in the most mysterious way possible-May 22, 2022

12. Journalist Sakhi Khalid. Hasht Subh paper. Taliban Spreads Panic in Central Afghanistan: Arrests, Tortures and Extortions Intensify in Behsud, Maidan Wardak-May 11, 2022.

13. 16 May, 2022, Afghanistan Times

14. Javid Ahmad. The Taliban's religious roadmap for Afghanistan. Middle East Institute--January 26, 2022

Index

A

Abu Bakr al-Baghdadi 33, 92, 158

Action on Armed Violence 55, 62, 78, 169

Afghanistan Independent Human Rights Commission (AIHRC) 62, 64

Afghan National Security Forces 15, 16

Ahmad Shah Massoud 68

Al Nusra 9, 36, 48, 81, 92, 124, 162, 177

Al Qaeda v, 2, 10, 11, 18, 21, 30, 35, 36, 44, 50, 51, 60, 72, 74, 75, 83, 88, 94, 95, 101, 104, 155, 157, 166, 170, 173, 176, 177, 181, 186, 188

Armoured Suicide Vehicles 12, 152

Ashraf Ghani 14

Assadullah Omar Khel 33

B

Bagram Air Base 28, 36

Baluchistan 2, 3, 4, 6, 8, 70, 71, 110, 111

C

Chechen extremist groups 93

D

Daesh 9, 17, 18, 31, 53, 54, 60, 77, 81, 83, 87, 93, 96, 99, 102, 160, 161, 162, 171, 172

Deobandi Salafist 69

Directorate of Mine Action Coordination of Afghanistan 13

E

Eastern Sabah Security Command 48, 162

East Turkestan Islamic Movement 23, 89, 156

F

Fathemyah mosque 152

Foreign Donation 109

Forum of Islamic Law Activists 51

H

Hafiz Saeed Khan 28, 30, 49, 159

Haqqani Network v, 2, 10, 35, 39, 40, 44, 50, 73, 86, 165, 168

Hawala v, 104, 107, 173

Hayat Tahrir al-Sham 81, 161

Hazara Muslims v, 15, 38, 53, 56, 63, 64, 66, 169

Human Rights Watch 14, 15, 38, 58, 59, 63, 65, 73, 169, 170

I

Illegal Mining v, 104, 108, 171, 173

Imam-e-Zaman 63, 169

International Criminal Court 40

Inter-Services Intelligence 1, 4, 6

IS-K i, iii, v, 10, 11, 12, 15, 16, 17, 18, 19, 20, 21, 22, 23, 26, 27, 28, 29, 30, 32, 35, 36, 37, 38, 39, 44, 46, 48, 50, 51, 52, 53, 54, 56, 63, 66, 72, 76, 77, 79, 80, 83, 85, 86, 87, 88, 91, 92, 93, 95, 97, 98, 152, 154, 155, 157, 158, 159, 160, 161, 162, 163, 164, 166, 169, 172, 195

Islamic Invitation Alliance 6

Islamic Movement of Uzbekistan 8, 36, 37, 81, 95, 160

Islamic State in Afghanistan (ISKP) 46, 47

Islamic State (IS) 23, 31, 91, 96

Islamic State of Iraq and Syria 27, 99

Islamic State of Khorasan (ISKP) 17, 21, 22, 24, 26, 31, 36, 74, 89, 91, 155, 158, 170

Islamic State of Khorasan Province 22, 24, 89

Istishhad 11

J

Jaish-e-Mohammad (JeM) 37

Jaish-e-Muhammad 2, 27, 36, 70

Jamaat Al Ahrar 53

Jihad-Bil-Nikah 87, 88, 172

Jihadi-Salafism ideology 50

Joint Investigation Team 3, 5

K

Katibat al-Istishadiin 13, 78, 121, 171

Katibat Imam al-Bukhari 36, 93, 155

Khyber Pakhtunkhwa 3, 16, 70

Kunduz province 32, 33

Kurdish People's Protection Units 96

L

Lashkar-e-Jhangvi 16

Lashkar-e-Taiba v, 2, 16, 21, 27, 36, 37, 74, 93, 94, 97, 154, 170

M

Mazar-e-Sharif 23, 25, 34, 59, 65

N

Narco-Money 105

National Database and Registration Authority 3

National Resistance Front NRF) 66, 67, 68, 164, 170

North Atlantic Treaty Organization 27

Nuclear Terrorism v, 91, 99, 154, 172, 195

O

Operation Zarb-e-Azb 46

P

Persian Gulf 18

Pul-e-Charkhi 28, 36

Q

Quetta Shura 2, 53

S

Salafists 20, 159, 165

Salafi-Wahhabi 9

San Jose State University 58

Suicide terrorism 10, 11, 21, 35, 39, 44, 53, 55, 62, 99

T

Tahrik-e-Taliban Pakistan (TTP) v, 27, 28, 30, 46, 49, 53, 56, 71, 72, 73, 158, 169

Takfiri groups 92

Takfiri jihadists 2

Turkestan Islamic Movement 23, 89, 157

U

UN Assistance Mission in Afghanistan 32, 58

About the Authors/Editors

Musa Khan Jalalzai is a journalist and research scholar. He has written extensively on Afghanistan, terrorism, nuclear and biological terrorism, human trafficking, drug trafficking, and intelligence research and analysis. He was an Executive Editor of the Daily Outlook Afghanistan from 2005-2011, and a permanent contributor in Pakistan's daily *The Post*, *Daily Times*, and *The Nation*, *Weekly the Nation*, (London). However, in 2004, US Library of Congress in its report for South Asia mentioned him as the biggest and prolific writer. He received Masters in English literature, Diploma in Geospatial Intelligence, University of Maryland, Washington DC, certificate in Surveillance Law from the University of Stanford, USA, and diploma in Counter terrorism from Pennsylvania State University, California, the United States.

Dr. Sanchita Bhattacharya, is Research Fellow in New Delhi based Institute for Conflict Management. Her core area of research is Madrasa Education in Pakistan, India and Bangladesh. She works on terrorism and socio-political issues of Pakistan. She also has an avid interest in the Af-Pak region. Her articles and commentaries have been published in *East Asia Forum*, *The Kabul Times*, *The Outlook*, *Firstpost*, *The Pioneer*, *South Asia Monitor* etc. She has written research papers in national and international journals and also contributed chapters in various edited volumes.